Praise for *Loose Woman*

"I loved reading this hugely enjoyable book, page turning and honest and instructive. And it's funny! Any woman torn between motherhood and career will identify with this."
— *Dame Harriet Walter*

"How very much to admire in these pages from a writer of such ability, who recreates ordinary moments from her experience with exacting clarity, ease and grace."
— *Wayson Choy, multi-prize-winning writer, member of the Order of Canada*

"An amazing journey of the self. The writing is a joy, full of insight and humour. A beautiful, heartbreaking/heart-mending story."
— *Suzette Couture, screenwriter and producer*

"Compulsive reading with very funny moments. Highly readable, entertaining, very moving."
— *Allan Stratton, multi-prize-winning writer*

"A fascinating story, beautifully and eloquently written, with great humour."
— *Curtis Barlow, cultural diplomat*

"Some of the most interesting writing on L'Arche I have ever read. Very moving in that it rings so true."
— *Associate Professor Lynn Blin, former long-time L'Arche assistant*

"A wonderful book, deftly describing complex people and complicated relationships with a light touch."
— *Professor K. Belicki, Brock University*

"A very moving story, well worth telling."
— *Judy McFarlane, author of* Writing with Grace, A Journey Beyond Down Syndrome

Loose Woman

my odyssey from lost to found

BETH KAPLAN

IGUANA

Copyright @ 2020 Beth Kaplan
Published by Iguana Books
720 Bathurst Street, Suite 303
Toronto, ON M5S 2R4

All rights reserved. No part of this publication may be reproduced, stored in a retrieval system or transmitted, in any form or by any means, electronic, mechanical, recording or otherwise (except brief passages for purposes of review) without the prior permission of the author.

Front cover design: Meghan Behse

ISBN 978-1-77180-427-1 (paperback)
ISBN 978-1-77180-428-8 (epub)
ISBN 978-1-77180-429-5 (Kindle)

This is an original print edition of *Loose Woman*.

Though all the events in this chronicle are true, many names and some small details have been changed. The timing of a few events has been slightly modified for flow.

A term or two used here were common in the seventies but are now considered insensitive and even unacceptable. I use them to be true to the time, hoping that readers understand that what is offensive now was not so then.

Once, a long time ago, I overheard someone say, "You know, I feel like a loose woman — loose, like I'm out of place and I want to be free."

And I thought, "Me too, sister. Me too."

This book is dedicated to all the loose women, everywhere.

CONTENTS

Prologue i
Act One 1
   ONE: Stayin' alive 3
   TWO: Lessons 19
   THREE: The one that I want 39
   FOUR: A keen sense of timing 43
   FIVE: Moving right along 62
   SIX: A rare excitement 69
Act Two 87
   SEVEN: Harbours 89
   EIGHT: Concrete deeds 110
   NINE: Hands in the mess 129
   TEN: We are all broken 144
   ELEVEN: The time to think box 166
Act Three 185
   TWELVE: Rich with all you have gained 187
   THIRTEEN: Choisir, c'est renoncer 201
Postscript 229
Acknowledgements 233

PROLOGUE

The storm

What am I doing here?

I was in a small orange tent in the middle of a sheep field in the centre of France, sheltering from a violent thunderstorm and attempting to comfort the terrified handicapped man in my arms.

What the hell was I doing there? I belonged in the theatre, for God's sake. I'd been voted Best Up and Coming Actress in Vancouver! A universe was waiting for me on the other side of the Atlantic and the Rocky Mountains — not a safe universe, but at least familiar and mine: a tiny apartment with a cat, actor colleagues, a sort-of boyfriend, a career that'd been steadily building over this decade of my twenties. Up and Coming.

But I was not on stage in Vancouver; I was clutching shivering Jean-Claude as a deluge battered our tent. Lying on the hard ground, listening to the crash of thunder, sheets of water hammering our flimsy refuge, I worried the tarp would be whipped away, leaving us exposed. I pictured us running through the rain-lashed fields, me and my two wards: Emile, the sweet giant with the mind of a child, and little psychotic Jean-Claude whom I was now holding close, stroking his hair, trying to appear calm.

It was August of 1979, and I was an assistant at a L'Arche community in France, one of a growing number of these communities where people who are intellectually disabled live and work side by side with people who are not. Nothing had prepared me for this new reality, and yet, to my astonishment, I'd taken to it. Though the days were challenging and surreal, filled with struggle, discomfort, and even anguish, I was enjoying them. Living and working at L'Arche was an extraordinary experience. There was a great deal to be learned from a small group of damaged Frenchmen, my housemates.

I thought of my best friend Gail, the reason I was in this bizarre situation. "Why don't you stay awhile?" she'd asked during what was meant to be a brief visit with her and her French family, and instead of heading safely home, I'd taken the offer seriously. It was a treat, I'd found, to be back in France, my home for a year as a teenager; it gave me pleasure to hear the French language flowing from my mouth, to feel so at ease in a foreign country. Especially this foreign country, my father's favourite place on earth. What would Dad think — or Gail — to see me now, cringing as cracks of thunder shook the ground?

"*T'inquiete pas*," I whispered to Jean-Claude as he nestled closer, breathing hard. "*Ça va bientôt passer.*" Don't worry, it'll soon be over. It did me good to be brave for him. If I'd been alone, my trembling would have been as violent as his.

But it was true, the gale didn't last much longer; the rumbles grew softer and more distant as the storm diminished. My companion's rigid body loosened, and he fell asleep; with relief, I extricated my arms from around him. There would be no sleep, I was sure, for my insomniac self. *Give me my own bed*, I grumbled, burrowing deeper into the mildewed sleeping bag. *Who in her right mind would volunteer for this?*

Yet while I flailed back and forth under the soft patter of rain, listening as peace returned to the universe, a voice in the back of my head was still relishing the cosmic drama above. How incredible that I, Beth Kaplan, Vancouver actress, was right in the middle of it. Volunteering to spend a few months here might be one of the wisest decisions I, the most indecisive person alive, had ever made. I wasn't sure, but the notion was starting to come clear.

Lying beside my slumbering companions, I brought back my first, unforgettable contact with Gail's new French life. In the early seventies, after she and I graduated from Carleton University in Ottawa, I flew off to theatre school in London; Gail, profoundly moved after hearing a lecture by the deeply spiritual Jean Vanier, had flown to France. Vanier had described how, living in a small town in northern France in 1964, he'd realized that countless handicapped people were shut away in huge prison-like mental hospitals. A fervent Catholic, he made the decision to invite two such men to live with him in his own house nearby. An idea groundbreaking in its simplicity: he opened the door of his home to two people in need.

Thus he founded L'Arche — the Ark — one small house that quickly grew into a series of houses around the world, where physically and mentally challenged men and women live and work in community with assistants who are not handicapped.

Gail went to spend a year volunteering at Vanier's first L'Arche community. Also working there was handsome, stern Alain, doing his compulsory French military service as a conscientious objector. In no time, it seemed, Gail wrote breathlessly that they were getting married. Married! Almost no one I knew was married; we were too young, and anyway, marriage was stuffy and bourgeois, too conventional for us wild and crazy children of the sixties. Gail was the funniest woman I'd ever met, brightening the world with her irresistible sense of humour. How would that lightness and merriment survive the drudgery of marriage?

But Gail and Alain, only 22 and 23, were old-fashioned Catholics, so marriage it was to be, one October Saturday in 1971 in a village in the north of France.

I'd have done my best to fly across the Atlantic for this event, but luckily I was already at school in London so didn't have far to travel. The weekend was memorable. My friend had not lost her love of fun, but she did look pale and overwhelmed. It was clear Alain's parents fiercely disapproved of this match. To them, unpretentious, friendly Gail was a colonial savage who didn't understand sophisticated

French ways and centuries-old traditions, which I grew to believe was one of the very reasons Alain had fallen in love with her. At the wedding, all his haughty, disapproving upper-middle-class relatives seemed to be wearing dark blue Chanel. Gail's down-to-earth working-class family from the suburbs of Montreal included an aunt in a homemade lime-green hotpants suit.

Two other disparate groups completed the guest list: a gang of long-haired university graduate hippies in bell bottoms and miniskirts, young friends of the bride and groom, including me, and the handicapped men and women of L'Arche with, at their centre, the charismatic Jean Vanier. Vanier was tall and gangly with a long narrow face, big crooked teeth, and a blazing smile that engulfed his face and caused his warm eyes to disappear; he seemed to be beaming always, at everyone, with an open-hearted warmth that exuded kindness and acceptance.

Though wanting to be near Jean, drawn by his magnetic pull, at the same time I was deeply disturbed by the crowd clustered around him. I'd never been near handicapped people before and found this group frighteningly deformed, with twisted bodies and faces and speech. But though many of them, at random times, made startling jerky movements and embarrassing grunts and shouts, no one paid any attention.

And there, walking down the aisle, was my beloved friend in a simple long beige linen dress; there she was, standing by her man, promising in French to love and obey forever. How mature she is, I thought. How brave. How insane. Such a declaration of faith in a man and a shared future was unimaginable to me.

At the end, before leaving the ancient church, the guests were asked to speak their thoughts aloud. Several thanked God for the marriage. I stood and thanked God for the gift, the incalculable gift, of Gail's laugh.

At the reception in a stark community centre hall, Jean Vanier made the toast to the bride, speaking movingly of her generous ability to "welcome the poorest of the poor," his gratitude for the commitment of two young people who had pledged to remain at L'Arche. While Vanier spoke, his circle muttered, bellowed, and groaned their agreement. They seemed overjoyed to be there, full of affection for the young couple, who were not their caregivers but their close companions.

A wedding reception like no other.

My encounter with Jean Vanier's friends that day had been my only contact with the mentally and physically challenged. Until this summer.

Now here I was, just turned twenty-nine, an actress who'd temporarily left behind a blossoming career and a social life unhinged after a decade of bad choices — the wrong drugs, the wrong men, possibly even the wrong profession, the right booze but far too much of it. Usually to be found in a small Vancouver apartment with her cat. Now living in an ancient farmhouse in central France with six severely handicapped men. At the moment, trying to sleep beside Jean-Claude and Emile in a sodden tent in a dwindling thunderstorm in a sea of sheep.

The motto of L'Arche was "Changing the world, one heart at a time." So far, the place was working wonders with mine.

ACT ONE

We do not believe in ourselves until someone reveals that deep inside us something is valuable, worth listening to, worthy of our trust, sacred to our touch.

—*e.e cummings*

ONE

Stayin' alive

All around me, the lights and cameras, the bustle of an enormous grey concrete television studio. *This*, I thought, heart whumping in my chest, *is what it's all about.*

A local TV series was casting their next episode, and I'd arrived at the CBC building in downtown Vancouver to audition. The two stars of the series, the beloved singer and actor Brent Carver and his TV sidekick, little Mikey, were friends of mine. Mikey was a talented eighteen-year-old from Burnaby insisting he now be called by his dignified full name — Michael J. Fox. If I got the part, it would be a delight to work with them both. It would be a delight just to get a job on TV, even as a day player in a non-recurring role. Television paid far more than stage work and took far less time. It looked good on the resumé.

In my near decade as a stage actress, from my first professional show in 1970 to now, November 1978, I'd done almost no television. Something about my face wasn't right for the medium — probably, I suspected, my lack of chiselled, photogenic cheekbones. I often said that my reincarnated self, next time around, would like smaller feet, a stronger singing voice, and cheekbones.

The comic part I was trying for should have been ideal for me: Maria, the awkward daughter of an aggressive Italian mother desperate to marry off her girl. But the script, in my not-so-humble opinion, was clunky and obvious, and I hated the very premise — the clichéd loud, oblivious Italian mama towing her obedient, pathetic child.

The director, who'd gone out of his way to ask me to audition after seeing my current stage production, *The Club*, was smiling as he took me by the arm and steered me to a spot on the studio floor. Directors never beamed like that. He seemed to like me. In my shaking hands I clutched the "sides," the sheets on which my part was written, as the cameramen rolled their equipment closer, getting ready to point those threatening machines at my body and face. Inside, my mind was shouting, *You didn't study Shakespeare at a prestigious British drama school so you could do crap like this!*

And then, as the cameras began to roll, I knew in a desperate flash what to do: I'd pretend Maria had had a prefrontal lobotomy. My character didn't know what she was lacking, that the words she was saying made no sense. She was damaged and needed all the kindness and sympathy I could give her. I turned off my mind and said my lines with oblivious confidence. The director grinned. "Cut!" he yelled, and then, "Perfect, Beth, I knew you'd be just right. You've got her."

The role of Maria, the Italian girl with half a brain, was mine. I had cracked the secret to getting cast on TV.

A few days later, as we prepared the shoot, the costume people told me I wasn't chubby enough for the part, they'd have to pad my shapeless dress with fake belly and bum. Imagine, *not fat enough*! Maria was bulky, slow, stunned. And funny. It made me glow to hear the cynical tech guys snicker. But even as I figured out how to do my job under the sizzling glare of television lights, in front of those pitiless pointing lenses, part of me was wondering if a big cheque for one day's work was worth my soul.

Surely none of my actor friends had such qualms; they'd take any role offered. *Why*, I asked myself on the bus home, *do I torment myself so?* The year before, I'd been offered a part at the Playhouse, the biggest theatre company in Vancouver. But I disapproved of the project, taking a silly lightweight comedy about the sexual antics of neurotic university professors on tour to the remote logging villages of northern B.C. *This fluff isn't what theatre should be,* I'd fretted. *We should be striving to make the world a better place.* And told the impatient director I needed more time to consider his offer, which meant more time fretting. How could I accept a job I had no respect for? On the other hand, it would be mad to turn down the prestigious, well-paying Playhouse.

My cheerful comedienne friend Nicky, already cast in the other female role, couldn't believe I was hesitating. "Oh get over yourself, we'll have fun," she snapped. I ditched my scruples, took the part, and behaved badly, moaning in rehearsals about the play's absurd plot and its amusing but shallow characters. Despite my complaints, the reviews were good; a newspaper critic called me *"one of the most promising new comic talents in the city,"* and though I groused that someone who'd worked in Vancouver for years was hardly "new," I was pleased with "most promising" and "comic." The tour took the company to fascinating places; I felt a profound magic in those mysterious, threadbare northern villages with their ancient totem poles buried deep in the forest. But I knew I'd been so quarrelsome the Playhouse would never offer me anything ever again. Fine.

Except that it kept happening, the offers to do plays with scripts I didn't approve of, and now television too. What mattered most to me as an actress was the truth of the words I had to speak. What was the point of this job if the words were forced and empty?

This is not a business where you get to have principles, you idiot, I thought, climbing the stairs to my attic apartment. *You can't set your own terms. Shut up and get on with it.* Though for sure, neither shutting up nor getting on with it were my strengths.

Sinking into my one decrepit armchair with the cat squeezed in beside me, I turned my gaze to the sight that always calmed my heart. I was proud of this flat, nicknamed Cosyland, at the top of a big old house next to the Hot Jazz Club on East Broadway. This was the first time I'd lived alone in my own self-contained place, the first time I'd installed a telephone in my own name. The place cost $120 a month and was so small I could cross it in six strides. But there, through the front windows if I bent low enough, was a million-dollar view of the magnificent North Shore mountains.

***

Vancouver had been the right place for me to land. In the spring of 1974 I was twenty-three, not long out of university and then theatre school, when the Canada Council gave me a small travel grant to fly from Toronto to Victoria, to do an improvisation workshop and a school tour with a West Coast company. The following January, faced with the choice between staying out west or going back to the heartless metropolis of Toronto, after much indecision, I moved to Vancouver. I'd had the good fortune to meet a nice young man who invited me to share his basement flat in Kitsilano long enough to get my bearings. Three weeks after my arrival, I was cast in a play, and that was that; the offers came regularly and almost never stopped.

My new place of residence was a raw, ugly city of scruffy buildings and filthy streets, at least, the seedy downtown where I worked. But the surroundings were as breathtaking as any place on earth: miles of beach, dense forests of ancient cedar and fir, implacable mountains looming on the eastern horizon. All that natural splendour, the briny smell of the ocean, the screeching call of sea birds, brought me comfort. I'd grown up in Halifax, Nova Scotia, with the wild Atlantic smashing over the rocks. This other, far distant coast with its salty air felt like home.

In my four years in Vancouver, I'd done shows with almost every company in town. Mostly I worked at the Arts Club Theatre on Seymour Street, which was also the centre of my social life; the theatre was a warm space built right over the dank, shabby bar where all the city's thespians gathered to drink, make contact, and flirt. The place felt like another kind of home, and Bill, the artistic director, was our eccentric, tipsy dad. Every Christmas morning, those of us without loved ones in Vancouver went, still in our pajamas, to Bill's house, to drink orange juice laced with whatever booze was around and give each other silly gifts. Bill fostered us like family. I was grateful for that. Grateful for Vancouver.

And especially grateful most evenings that autumn of 1978 to pull open the door of the Arts Club and walk upstairs into the crowded, sweaty dressing room of our current play, *The Club*. Inside, six naked actresses were cramming their breasts into flattening breast-binders, painting on facial hair, and pulling on flat white shirts and tuxedo trousers. And then I took off my clothes and did the same. Two hours later, we were a team on stage under the lights, smoking cigars, dancing, bantering, singing barbershop harmony in our deep male-ish voices. It was heaven.

The Club was a feminist musical set in an Edwardian gentlemen's club, men in tuxedos and top hats singing pompous sexist songs about their wives and mistresses — "*For a woman is only a woman, my boys,*" went one chorus, "*but a good cigar is a smoke!*" — with a twist revealed at the end: all the club members were played by women. After seeing a production in Toronto, I was convinced the best role of Freddie, the suave philandering gynaecologist, was made for me, and during auditions I was unusually forceful in seeking the part. The director hesitated; she'd met my tiny bundle of neuroses in previous plays and knew I could be my own worst enemy, tortured by self-doubt yet loudly opinionated, adept at making my own life and work, and sometimes other people's, as arduous as possible. But finally, reluctantly, she did cast me, and in rehearsal my smooth, witty, caddish Freddie came to life.

A makeup expert, brought in to show us how to look more masculine, told us that creating a male face means thickening the eyebrows and highlighting the size of chin and nose, the opposite of feminine glamour makeup which minimizes these things. "Your prominent features, Beth, make it easy to turn you into a convincing man," she said as she worked to highlight my bushy eyebrows, enormous chin, and nose a boyfriend once affectionately compared to a lump of melted Plasticine. Though this was not much of a compliment, I was elated to look in the mirror at my manly new face.

Beth might have had huge misgivings about her looks, but even with a ridiculous moustache painted on with eyeliner, Freddie was handsome.

In rehearsals, we practiced sitting with our legs spread wide, taking up space, speaking in deep, forceful voices. One afternoon I realized why it was easy to turn myself into a good-looking man, exuding sophistication and charm; I was simply imitating my handsome, sophisticated, charming father. Like Dad, Freddie relished wine, women, and song. When I picked up a fat cigar, held it under my nose to take in its aroma, lit and puffed with pleasure, I'd become Professor J. Gordin Kaplan. How many actresses, I thought with delight, get to play their fathers?

Still, on preview night, I was petrified. How dare I imagine I could succeed in this great role? That anyone would pay to see me? *Forget it, loser*, said the voice I knew so well. *You'll never amount to anything. You're lazy, unworthy, a fraud. Give up.*

That night, though my Freddie got through, he was tentative and small, without the panache he needed. Convinced the director had been right, I could not carry a role of this magnitude, I was drinking myself into a stupor in the bar when my friend Brent sought me out. I'd been mortified to notice his kind, concerned face watching from the second row. He put his arm around me.

"You're so close, Beth," he said, "just lacking confidence, that's all. One more big push of confidence, and you're there."

Truly? A literal vote of confidence from such a fine actor? The next night, opening night, the memory of Brent's words, his support, lifted my spirits enough that something resembling self-assurance and trust flooded me. I turned off the hateful critical voice and unleashed the bravado that allowed me to open body and soul to the audience, as I had ten years before in *Interview*, my first great role.

Oh Miranda
On your veranda
I know you're lonely,
And darling if I only, only, only dare, dear,
Why I'll be there, dear.

Oh Miranda, your veranda's truly grand, I sang in my favourite moment of the play, the absurd, passionate song delivered as I gazed seductively into the eyes of a giggling female audience member, my six colleagues in their tuxedos crooning backup behind me. I actually relaxed and enjoyed myself, in full control — from the top of his lacquered head to the tip of his shiny black dress shoes — as tall, desirable, cheating Freddie. It was like gliding, soaring high, arms spread, chest exposed, the wind whistling through my wide-open heart.

The role was a breakthrough, and the show was a hit. I was a hit. My success felt right and deserved, and I basked in it. Audiences loved us; the run was extended.

Photo Credit: Glen Erikson

Bobby: Tell me, do any of you chaps believe in clubs for women?
Freddie: Yes, if every other form of persuasion fails.

All of us in the dressing room got along well, with filthy jokes and sex talk flowing as if we really were men, which made the whole experience even more enjoyable. Our queen bee, the most senior actress, was the highly accomplished, gifted, brutal Janet Wright. In our previous shows together, I'd been very much Janet's junior. In *The Club*, my reviews were as good as hers; the show raised me to another level entirely. Not her equal, never her equal, but nearer than before. I had to get used to being the star, the sparkling person audience members came to watch, to strangers greeting me on the street — "Freddie, old chap!" Of course, that's what every actor strives for — look at me, don't look at *them, look at me*! For sure, I wanted the audience to look at me. But part of me also, confusingly, didn't.

One afternoon, a woman called me at home and, with trembling voice, said she'd seen the show four times and wanted please to take me to lunch. "Thanks so much," I said, "very kind of you, too busy."

Ain't that the way? I thought, peering into the mirror at my female face with its prominent features. *Finally you're a sex symbol — as a man with a moustache.* A newspaper came to interview me for a filler article on good luck charms used by various local personalities; I had to make up something about items in the dressing room. Then I learned a local theatre magazine had used my name as a clue in one of its crosswords. Fame.

Wasn't this what I'd always wanted, since the start of my acting career twenty years before? Yes. Yes and no.

***

I was eight when my parents insisted I find an edifying hobby. Ballet and Brownies came and went; piano lessons were on and off. My folks, who were skilled amateur classical musicians, Dad on violin and Mum on piano, would have liked their daughter to, say, play the cello in a youth orchestra. But there was no youth orchestra in Halifax in 1959, and in any case, I had absolutely no interest in the cello. What interested me was drama, which was not what Mum and Dad had in mind.

I took drama lessons on Saturday mornings in Mrs. Stanbury's basement. She had a cardboard castle and a trunk full of costumes, and after fishing out crowns, cloaks, wands, and swords, we made up our own version of fairy stories. Mrs. Stanbury was a go-getter; before long her little troupe was gathered around a microphone, performing a scripted show every Sunday afternoon on Halifax's CHNS radio. When local theatre companies needed a child actor, they called Mrs. Stanbury, which is how I ended up in a university production of the Greek tragedy *Medea* as one of Medea's about-to-be-murdered sons, with one unforgettable line that I bellowed from backstage: "WHITHER ... SHALL I FLEE ... FROM MOTHER'S KNIFE?"

Deirdre Downey, also eight and a member of Mrs. Stanbury's troupe, played Medea's other son. Deirdre Downey did not have a line.

Mrs. Stanbury moved us to television, and soon we had a weekly program on local Halifax TV, improvising fairy stories: Three Little Pigs, Sleeping Beauty, Snow White. Donna McTavish with her blue eyes and long blonde curls played all the princesses and little Deirdre all the elves and fairies; I, good at cackling and baring my long sharp teeth, was the wicked witch, the troll, the wolf blowing the house down. Mrs. Stanbury stood behind the camera, sternly monitoring, when we taped. This was not playtime, it was a job, and we had to get it right. A boy recognized me on the bus once — "Hey, aren't you in that TV show?" — and I felt like Gina Lollobrigida.

The Halifax Little Theatre cast me in a British comedy, *Roar like a Dove*, as Jane, a precocious ten-year-old girl, a good part for me because that is who I was. This was the real thing — a big part with rehearsals, costume fittings, makeup. On opening night, I knew I was supposed to be nervous but was not, not in the least. Instead I relished being in two worlds at once: I was myself, Beth, whose parents were out there in the darkness, swallowed up in that mysterious rustling beast on the other side of the lights. But I was also Jane, moving in a hot, bright, sideways world of strange furniture, interacting with others wearing funny clothes and lots of orange pancake makeup and saying words someone had written for us to say. "What's the matter, don't you like naked ladies?" I taunted a squeamish visitor, dangling my undressed doll in front of his face.

When I went offstage after my big scene on closing night (which came right after opening night), there was a sound from the audience. I didn't know what it was. The stage manager whispered, "They're applauding. For you." Pleasure flowed over me, a golden warmth.

That a roomful of strangers appreciated my work on stage felt especially good because I was not happy at home. My parents had separated for a time, a miserable, frightening few months. Though at last we were all together again, my mother remained weepy and uncertain, as if she might leave again at any moment, and my father was often angry, particularly at me, for reasons I did not understand. It seemed to me my younger brother Mike could do no wrong, and I could do no right; Dad called me spoiled, selfish, and lazy so often, I heard it as one word: *spoiledselfishlazy*. When I was upset, which was frequently, he mocked me with an arm flung melodramatically across his eyes. "Poor Sarah Heartburn, the Tragic Queen!" he'd yowl. Mike was cute and easy-going and, most importantly, a boy. From the moment of his birth, he'd replaced me in my father's heart. I was sure both my parents, but especially Dad, loved him much more.

On a high wooden stage was a made-up world where Sarah Heartburn felt welcome and at ease.

At the next television rehearsal with Mrs. Stanbury, emboldened by my extensive stage experience, I raised my hand. "Please, may I play the princess next time?" I asked. *Surely*, I thought, *princesses don't always have to be sweet and blonde.* Mrs. Stanbury's eyes narrowed, but later she made an announcement: "Next week, Beth is going to play the princess."

I tried not to beam at Donna. And then we learned the title of the fairy story: *The Selfish Princess*. "This princess is very silly," said Mrs. Stanbury, with a tight smile, "but she learns her lesson and apologizes."

After doing the show I quit drama, which made my parents glad. They said it was taking too much time away from schoolwork — though schoolwork was never a problem except for Arithmetic, and most years I won the English prize. But I was tired of being a villain.

Only much later did I realize that princesses are boring. Villains are mean and dangerous and interesting to play.

During my early teens, my family was moving about, including a year in Paris, so there was no acting for me. Newly arrived for Grade 13 at a big Ottawa high school, I did props for their production of *The Diary of Anne Frank*, which mostly meant standing backstage sobbing inconsolably. Anne Frank, a writer just a few months younger than I when she died, was my hero.

Starting first-year Carleton University at seventeen, I joined only one club, the drama club, along with my new best friend Gail. All of us teenaged thespians spent many hours lounging on battered sofas in the underground Green Room, rolling skinny Drum tobacco cigarettes and arguing about Grotowski, the Method, the war in Vietnam, and other topics we knew almost nothing about. I developed a life-changing bond with Bob Handforth, a visionary director, the first of a series of talented, beautiful theatre artists with whom I shared a great love and who turned out to be gay. Though in 1967 I didn't know what being gay meant, and it's possible Bob didn't either, yet.

In the middle of my second year, Bob got the rights to a new one-act play called *Interview*, about eight unnamed New Yorkers sunk in urban alienation and despair. I was desperate for the part of the lost woman searching for Fourteenth Street. She was vulnerable and frightened; I was born to play her. He cast eight student actors, including Gail and, as the searching woman, me. From the first performance we worked together smoothly, a fluid, perfectly coordinated acting machine. The play was about automation, people losing individuality in the callous anonymity of a big city, and we were choreographed every moment except when we delivered our individual monologues. Then it was just us, straight out to the audience.

During my monologue, the others were streaming by, jostling me on the streets of Manhattan, and I was begging for help as I told those watching all about it. "Can you direct me to Fourteenth Street, I said, I seem to have lost my ..." I'd begin, eyes pleading, jerking backwards to avoid being hit by an invisible car, "and then I was nearly run down!"

I was a young woman struggling to remain brave, even sane, as the chaos of the city enveloped her, as the reality of human coldness and her own isolation broke her. By the end of the monologue, she — I — was devastated, pleading for direction from each face in the audience. At the same time, I was simply a craftswoman doing her job, aware of timing, lighting, the mood shifts of that unseen, unpredictable animal out front.

Doing the monologue tore open my chest. Everything I had to give was on display, my whole being offered to them. Nothing had ever felt so good.

Bob's brilliant production was a huge success; at the Canadian University Drama League competition for 1969, *Interview* won Best Production, Bob was Best Director, and my lost woman was judged Best Performance. It felt terrific to have won, but at the same time, I didn't know how I'd done what I'd done; there was no conscious skill, no craft. It had just come out of me that way.

As we packed up, a group of actors from two of the other participating universities came to meet us. Because their shows had been scheduled on the same night as ours, they'd missed our production and had heard so much about *Interview*, they were dismayed not to have seen it. "We'll do it for you right now," Bob said, and we did, the audience sitting on the floor of his big bare hotel room, the eight of us without lights, costumes, or set, just the words, the force field of words, our idealism and love for this artform and for each other and for our director. It was transcendent. I didn't know then that even before the official beginning of my stage career, I had in some ways just experienced its pinnacle: a committed, bonded company speaking fine words in a beautifully directed, well-cast, meaningful production. The theatrical experience, for an actor, does not get better than that. Was this what I was meant to do with my life?

Interview caught the eye of a Toronto producer, and Bob and some of his cast, including Gail and me, were hired and granted an Equity card for a four-month long professional school tour out of Toronto, driving to schools all over southern Ontario, two performances a day. My parents were aghast at my interrupting university to pursue such a precarious profession, but I ignored them, convinced the astronomical sum of $150 a week made the risk worthwhile. The following autumn, though back at my studies, I was hired by the same Toronto producer for her next tour. Without even auditioning! Obviously, with well-paid jobs falling from the sky, this was what I was destined to do. The second tour was not like the first, however; I didn't like the production much and there were few kindred spirits in the troupe, so four months on the road felt very long.

Deciding to get some proper training, I considered only one theatre school: the celebrated London Academy of Music and Dramatic Art with its unique one-year program specifically for non-British students with acting experience. Despite a competitive audition process, my Fourteenth Street piece opened the doors to LAMDA. I finished my B.A. over the summer and in August 1971, right after my twenty-first birthday, I flew to London, one of two Canadians accepted that year. The other was a self-confident actor of enormous talent named R.H. Thomson.

On my first day, the drama school's director ushered me into his office for the obligatory get-acquainted chat. He wore a bespoke suit, and I, a dress made from a purple Indian print bedspread, my face half-hidden behind a glossy curtain of hair. "So, Beth, what exactly do you hope to do in the theatre?" he asked, in his perfect rolling tones. This was, I discovered later, a practical question that someone like R.H. might answer, "I'd like to do repertory, especially Shakespeare," or, "I'm here to learn a mid-Atlantic accent and fencing."

"I believe in the theatre as a tool for social change," I replied. His eyebrows rose. I continued, glowing with earnestness, "I'd like to touch people's lives as a force for good."

"Ah," he replied. A pause. "Well," he said briskly, standing up, "I do hope you have a fruitful year. Best of luck."

Back then, I didn't understand the genetic link not just to my inborn talent, but to my socialist idealism. I knew that my great-grandfather on Dad's side, the Jewish-American side, had been a renowned Yiddish playwright nicknamed the Jewish Shakespeare. It was years before I found out that as well as writing seventy or eighty plays for the stage, Jacob Gordin had even been briefly an actor, and throughout his life was a socialist fiercely determined that his theatre, all theatre, should change the world for the better.

Eighty years after Gordin's stellar theatrical career was launched on New York's Lower East Side, a great-granddaughter who knew next to nothing about him stood in a British theatre school echoing his oft-expressed sentiments exactly. I'd already figured out one huge reason I was so keen on acting: it was an occupation in which my formidable parents had no interest or experience, a world and a skill all mine. But later, learning about my ancestor led me to wonder if in fact I did choose the theatre, or if it chose me.

In any case, my genetic link to the Jewish Shakespeare did not help me through the fraught regime of theatre school. It was a hard year, living in a chilly bedsitting room, the youngest in class, routinely being ripped apart and sewn back together. At least, that was the goal of the training process, though the sewing was not nearly as firm as the ripping. By the end of the year I still didn't have much clue what my new profession entailed, but I did learn to exercise my lips — by repeating, quickly, "Billy Bunter bought a broken buttered biscuit" — to do a courtly dance, and to parry and thrust with a sword. At Easter, outside Southwark Cathedral, my class performed a medieval morality play about the Massacre of the Innocents. As I battled the Roman soldier who wanted to tear the infant from my arms, I realized that in the fray, I'd dropped the bundle of rags representing my baby and was standing on it. Here I learned the first law of performing on the road: *Even if you're standing on your baby, keep going.*

When the year ended, I flew back to Canada and, dazed to be out of school for the first time in nearly two decades, made my way to Toronto. My first acting job was with a starry-eyed new feminist troupe in which all the actresses quickly came to despise each other. The review of our show was headlined, "*Good Night, Ladies, and Better Luck Next Time.*"

This profession, I soon discovered, was emphatically not easy or lucrative, after all. Auditioning was time-consuming and humiliating, made worse by my own profound insecurities tripping me up at every turn. On the one hand, I believed myself to be a superb actress — had not the world corroborated this? — a great talent too often wasted in flimsy productions; on the other, that I was spoiled, selfish, and lazy, unworthy of success. And then, in play after play, the reality of stage life dawned. The money for theatre work, when there was any, was terrible, and rehearsals could be brutal, sometimes with directors of limited skill and sympathy or other actors determined to make time on stage as unpleasant as possible. My experience in *Interview*, I realized to my chagrin, was not the norm, it was the very rare exception.

In 1974, during one particularly dreadful production — Greek tragedy performed in high school cafetoriums, with chunks of the script chanted in ancient Greek and the male actors costumed, to the scornful delight of our teenaged audience, in leatherette mini-skirts — I asked a seasoned actress, who'd seen the show, how to survive it.

"What devastates me most," I told her, "is that I'm afraid we're turning those poor kids in the audience off theatre forever." She considered a moment, her face grave.

"Think of this production," she replied, "as a cruel and ugly child that has been entrusted to your care."

As my career progressed in the seventies, through nine tours and a series of musicals, dramas, comedies, and new plays, this advice proved invaluable; whether the show was a success or a failure, I had to take the best care of it possible. Collective creations, where the whole company was involved in the writing and shape of the show, were by far my favourite experiences. If I was not simply pretending to be someone else, if I could speak my own words in my own voice, I felt linked to the most important part of the process, for me — the thought behind the writing, the realities, ideas, and truths a playwright was exploring through the minds and mouths of the actors. But those experiences were few.

Once I was triple cast in a new play, all stereotypical female roles: a mother, a prostitute, and a secretary. As the secretary, I had to keep typing while listening for an important cue, my fingers on remote control, unconnected to my brain. One night, I happened to read what was written, over and over, down the page.

"*Get me out of here*," I'd tapped blindly, night after night. "*Get me out of here.*"

But the reviews for my work were almost universally good, and for better or worse, I'd stayed right where I was, supporting myself for years, barely, on the meagre wages of an actor. It was my job to do everything possible to move ahead in my career.

Yet something in my gut was dragging me backward. It was a voice saying, *Maybe not.*

TWO

Lessons

My hectic days were always on the verge of whirling out of control, but during the run of *The Club* in Vancouver, things got particularly complicated. Besides singing and dancing in eight shows a week and keeping up with the many other demands of an actor's life, I was also managing to fit in a passionate affair. Later, looking back at this era of frantic excess, I wondered how I'd coped with both an exhausting show and an exhausting sex life. Adrenalin, I guessed. Desperation. Booze. And, let's not forget, youth.

    A great deal was asked of theatre professionals to augment what happened in front of the audience. Despite my busy year at drama school, I still, when I could squeeze them in and afford them, took voice and singing lessons, flute lessons, tap dancing lessons, improvisation classes. There were meetings with agents and directors, auditions, the shows of my peers to watch, and many late nights schmoozing — seeing and being seen — in the bar. Little time for activity outside the theatre.

    But what life I did have offstage had been just as draining as my profession, because of men. Complications with men. Too many; not enough. Not The One, just a stream of unsuitables, one after the other, my heart brimming with hope then shrivelling with disappointment. Where was he?

In the last few years, as the seventies drew to an end, there'd been a lot of one-night stands. It was my duty, after all, as a feminist, a dedicated women's libber, to have many sexual partners; we modern women had been freed to be as promiscuous and keen to have unattached sex as men. I was well acquainted with Erica Jong's notion of the carefree "zipless fuck."

But that fall, I experienced something different. My sort-of boyfriend Richard was on vacation in Europe, undoubtedly having affairs of his own, when Daniel, a fellow actor from Toronto and the friend of a friend, came to Vancouver to audition and called me. We met for drinks and found we had much in common, including a passion for social justice and pedal steel guitar. After drinking and talking animatedly for hours, I fell for his blonde, blue-eyed intensity and brought him back to my place. He was entertaining and attentive. He was also rough, keen on biting and smacking and other activities I had no interest in doing. Keen on parts of the body I had no interest in exploring. Though I tried to be amenable.

But Dan actually listened and thought about me. He told me honestly, as he squeezed the soft flesh of my belly and thighs, that I was badly out of shape and needed, for both my professional and private life, to exercise. I knew that but did not want to hear it. "Sex with you, cowboy, is exercise enough," I said, poking his lean stomach.

To my surprise, my new friend from Toronto offered to come with me one afternoon to a meeting of the Vancouver Artists Alliance. The year before, when a filmmaker friend and I realized that important decisions were being made affecting local artists and none of us understood how or why, we'd founded an advocacy group to do research and provide information to actors, dancers, writers, and visual artists about government grants and the inevitable cutbacks affecting us all. What a boost that day to see Daniel sitting in the front row, applauding my efforts as chairperson. Such avid support flowing my way. Someone on my side.

That night, he was in the audience of *The Club*. It was strange to have my secret lover, who'd explored every inch of my female body, watch me prance about as a man. He was there in the bar afterwards, waiting to hug and congratulate me. He enjoyed the show; he loved Freddie. After two bottles of wine, as we walked back to my place in the early morning, he asked, grinning, "Have you ever fucked in an alley?"

I had not, and we did, right out in the open where anyone might see, my back shoved up against a cold brick wall. It was scary, uncomfortable, and exciting, another tale to tell. Back at Cosyland, we wrestled, making ferocious love on the kitchen table and the floor, and when he bit me hard, I tried to bite him back. When he punched me in the face, I was sure he'd done it by mistake in the heat of the moment, but even so, the shock and pain made me cry. He held me in his arms and consoled me, and I did my best to hurt him in return, flailing away to little effect. There was fury, or at least the thrill of violence, in the attraction between us.

I remembered a late night when I was seventeen, sitting in my parents' silent kitchen after a date with James, the pompous, bearded twenty-two-year-old chairman of our university drama club who'd become my first real boyfriend and to whom I would soon surrender my virginity. He recounted an anecdote about himself, and I laughed — not with him, but at him. When he leaned across the table and slapped me across the face, I sat cowed, cheek stinging, punishment deserved because of my disrespect.

But with Daniel, I thought as he snored beside me, *the blows aren't punishment but a mutual kind of sex play.*

More or less mutual.

Early next morning, he left to go back to Toronto. "I hope one day you realize you're beautiful," he said matter-of-factly, as he walked down the stairs, "and that you learn to keep your eyes open when a man is making love to you."

Yeah, yeah — guys were always lecturing me, handing me lessons. Always some improvement required. I managed not to cry until his taxi had pulled away, and then sat eating a pile of toast at my kitchen table, feeling sorry for myself.

All I wanted was love. Great love, true happily-ever-after love, and in my twenty-eight years, I'd never come remotely close. The right man — who would that be? A combination of Paul McCartney, the best Beatle of the huge eyes, velvet voice, and haunting melodies, whom I'd adored since the age of thirteen; Pierre Trudeau, for a decade the prime minister of Canada, sexy, charismatic, arrogant in a good way, and incredibly smart; Paul Newman with his sensitive wise-cracking fast-driving manliness. And of course my dad, at least, the good side of my dad, brilliant, generous, witty, committed to changing the world for the better. All I wanted was a musical, artistic, funny, clever, decisive, idealistic, tender, handsome, strong, gentle, female-loving man. In my deepest recurring fantasy, he was for some reason an Israeli violinist, a renowned musician with deep dark eyes and curly black hair, vibrating with soul.

Instead, I fell for the completely wrong men, most of them gay, and other wrong men, even occasionally gay ones, fell for me. I almost never liked the men who liked me; instead I longed for the most improbable and inaccessible ones. Tough-minded Janet, my *Club* co-star, instructed me once that the way to get men, to spark their interest, was not to care about them, or at least to pretend not to care. But I cared far too much to pretend not to care. Yet, strangely, I seemed to do everything possible to keep a real partner at bay.

After watching me play a man so convincingly in *The Club*, my lesbian friend Helen, who in a past incarnation had been married for decades, suggested I consider switching to her team. She said making love with women was much better than with men. "An orgasm *every time!*" she boasted. But frequency of orgasms didn't matter to me; they were something I could produce perfectly well on my own. What interested me was tenderness and concern. Warmth. Constancy. Trust. Someone right there when needed and out of the way when not.

Helen had met my parents. "You're the boy in your family," she told me. "You're gregarious, flamboyant, highly intelligent, like your dad."

I didn't want to be a boy. I wanted to be a girl, and loved. Just as, on stage, I wanted to be loved. We all wanted to be loved. That's why we were there.

The evening after Daniel left, as I got into costume for the show, I had to slather on flesh-coloured makeup to cover the bruises on Freddie's body and face. My close friend Lani noticed the marks and was furious at my lover, but I was nonchalant and even gratified. Daniel liked to tell Catholic jokes, including one about a nun who died a virgin and whose tombstone read "RETURNED UNOPENED."

At least that would not be me.

"Richard," I wrote next day in my diary, "*is like a heavy coat over my shoulders, warm but weighing me down. Daniel is like a kite, distant and blithe, pulling me up.*"

I considered trying to have a frank breakup talk with Richard when he returned but just couldn't face it. Impossible to talk to someone who wouldn't talk back; easier to drift.

"*The main thing these days is the strange absence of my perennial FEAR,*" I sat writing as my cat tried to swat the pen:

> *the gnawing at my soul that tells me how inadequate and shallow and unworthy I am, and this all is useless anyhow, why bother? It's not there today. It must be there somewhere, but this lovely creamy voice is on top, saying You're okay and you've got talent and you know what you're doing and you're a nice person and everything's okay.*
>
> *I hope I'm passing out of a long fog, the years of worry and eating and searching.*

There was always hope.

"*No fretting from now on!*" I wrote.

As if.

***

On New Year's Eve of 1979, I dressed and made up with particular care; my musician friend Nancy had asked me to be her guest at a big wrap party for a TV variety show. I loved parties where I might encounter Mr. Right or, more importantly, a director or producer who'd take me under his wing, so I made clear to Richard, my kind-of boyfriend, that this was an important professional event for me, and he should celebrate with his own friends.

Nancy and I teetered in our high heels into a hotel room full of impressive television personnel, with snazzy uniformed waiters floating about carrying trays of free stuff — all kinds of liquor, platters of fancy French cheeses, dishes of sweets. For a moment, I contemplated trying to reign myself in, to exert some self-control, and then, with no struggle at all, I folded, and the gates to propriety went down. It was New Year's Eve, and I was going to imbibe as many of those free drinks as possible and have a very good time.

As I jabbered and clowned in the elegant white room, one friendly waiter after another kept taking away my empty glass, while I reached for whatever was full on his tray: wine, beer, rum and Coke. At midnight, I was talking to a dignified producer about his work and mine, trying to sound witty and worldly. But as my voice grew louder, my mind was growing fuzzy, and then came the vodka and orange juice. Or maybe several. The last thing I remembered was sliding to my knees and flinging my arms around the calves of my new dear friend. I was laughing. He was too. I think.

I woke up in bright sunlight, my head a giant throbbing puffball, eyes hot needles of pain. How did I get home, into my own bed? And what was that smell? Groaning, I dragged myself into the kitchen. The window was open, and the flat roof outside was shining black. Tar. Through my brain haze, I remembered the landlord telling me a workman would be coming soon to tar that roof. What a day for him to choose.

For some reason my big cloth purse, strangely bulgy, was lying in the bathtub. Lifting it out and prying it open, I discovered a wooden cheese tray and an array of French cheeses, melting in a smelly heap. What in God's name —?

But there was another smell. I traced it to the broom closet in the kitchen, where I was disgusted to find — yes, it was true — vomit on the floor. Who would do such a thing? In a flash, I knew: the man who'd tarred the roof. He must've climbed in through the kitchen window to vomit in my broom closet! The landlord would hear from me.

The phone rang, a very loud, unpleasant noise. It was Nancy, chuckling. Last night, when I became incoherent, she told me, she decided to put me in a cab. As she was guiding me to the door, I'd lurched back to the food table. "They won't be needing this!" I cried, and stuffed the entire cheese tray into my purse.

Christ. I'd made a spectacle of myself in front of important television people, then come home and thrown up, for some incomprehensible reason, in the closet. *Well*, I thought, sipping a second strong coffee, *at least it wasn't cocaine. At least some random TV guy didn't accompany me home.* But it was beyond alarming that someone with my face and body had done stupid things without my conscious mind knowing anything about it.

When I went out, there was Brie all over the keyhole of my front door.

I headed straight to the ocean. Going to the shore was like prayer for my atheist self, a time of reflection and silence in a place of worship. As often as possible, I'd go to Kits Beach or the seawall to listen to the heartbeat of waves washing in and out, to breathe in the sharp wet tang of the sea, the smell of home.

I sat on a log, wrapped in a thick sweater, smoking a cigarette, listening to the water and the seabirds and thinking about what this brand-new year would bring. 1979. I'd turn twenty-nine in August, frighteningly close to thirty. Would I still, God help me, drink so much? Would there at last be real love? Would I have done what was necessary to climb higher in my career? I thought of Mikey Fox, who'd confided in us that he wanted to try his luck in Hollywood.

Janet had laughed. "Mikey, I hate to tell you this," she'd said fondly. "You're a damn good actor, but you're just way too short."

Mikey said he'd go anyway. He was determined to let nothing get in his way. It took that kind of stubborn guts to make it. Was I capable of believing in myself like that?

But then, was climbing higher in my career actually what I wanted for the future? The confusion tormented me. Surviving as an actor was struggle enough; ambivalence about my career made it harder.

The rhythmic swoosh of ocean washing over stones eased my soul, if not my aching head. After inspecting a hundred pebbles to pick a few of the prettiest for my collection, I looked up and there they were, my impassive stone friends in the distance. Impossible to take yourself too seriously in Vancouver because the mountains were always there, towering against the sky, to remind you how infinitesimal you and your concerns really were.

My friend Charles, an actor from L.A., told me once that Vancouver was for "wood-shedding."

"If you need to get away and figure things out," he explained, "you go out behind the woodshed and think fo' awhile."

Charles was one wood-shedder, and I was another.

Brushing the sand off my jeans and shoes, I climbed up the hill to the Kitsilano house Richard shared with two housemates; he'd told me to come over for a late lunch today. At least I wouldn't have to conceal my fogged-up misery from him, since he undoubtedly had a hangover too. "Happy New Year, Miss Beth!" he cried, opening the door, enveloping me in his arms. It was a treat to be hugged by a handsome man wearing cashmere, though I wished, especially today, that he did not use quite so much cologne.

We'd been sort of together a year. Richard was such a flirt and so unreliable, nothing about him was sure. In fact, it was easy to list what I didn't like about him: that he was hypercritical and hung-up, for example, especially about his vanishing hair; he'd been told hot water would stimulate the follicles, so he showered twice a day. Every Friday, this thirty-two-year-old drove across town to his parents' house to drop off his dirty laundry and pick up a basket of clean clothes, washed and folded by his mother. She was a lovely woman, gentle and giving, and I knew she wanted me to commit to a life with her son.

But Richard had hurt me plenty, criticizing me in front of my friends and his, abandoning me at parties to go off and chat up someone else. When a friend complained about a similarly capricious boyfriend, I told her we were founding members of the We Deserve Better Club. Yet we both concluded that an unsatisfactory steady guy was better than none.

After lunch, as we drank coffee, Richard said casually, "I have something to tell you." I braced myself. What now?

"It's funny, actually," he said, lighting his cigarette and mine. "Ward Bingley was at the party last night. We had a long talk and now I have a huge crush on him."

What was he talking about? Ward was a local arts critic, lively, young, married.

"You should know, Miss Beth — I guess I'm bisexual," Richard said casually, gazing out the window. "I love you, of course, I love women and always have, but sometimes I get infatuations on men."

Through the haze of smoke, he looked wary, as if expecting me to be shocked or angry. But though his announcement was a surprise, I had dealt with this kind of surprise before. *Of course you're bisexual*, I thought. *That's my pattern*. Falling in love with good-looking, interesting, artistic men who turned out to be gay was something I did.

"Well, Richard, thanks for telling me," I said, spearing another big piece of pie. "Should I challenge Ward Bingley to a duel?"

He didn't laugh; sense of humour wasn't his strong point. Not for the first time and not, I was sure, for the last, I wondered why we stayed together. But I did like him a lot. Richard was well read, well-travelled, smart. He was attractive and cuddly with a big round head like a panda, a calm, undemanding lover who felt safe in the darkness. Among other jobs, he was an agent for writers, which intrigued me because I'd always dreamed one day of becoming a writer. He loved the theatre and actors and coming to the bar to gossip and complain along with everyone else. And I loved having someone in my life, however unpredictable, who just might be by my side when needed. When I was strong and successful at work, Richard was very much in evidence. When I was lost, he was on the other side of the room.

Sometimes I turned elsewhere for companionship. And so, obviously, did he.

***

I'd been asked to audition for the next play at the Arts Club, *The Shadow Box*, the story of three families dealing with terminal cancer in a hospice, and was excited to be cast as plain, unhappy Agnes, along with some of the best actors in Vancouver including Janet and my young TV friend, Mikey Fox, as her son. Here was a chance to show off my range — playing a charming roué in *The Club*, which would close on a Saturday, and, opening five days later, the same actress, me, as a homely depressed middle-aged woman who has spent years looking after her angry, dying mother. I imagined rave reviews. My career would explode into the stratosphere.

While I swaggered and crooned at night as Freddie, during the day we began rehearsals for *The Shadow Box*. It was my task to bring to life a submissive, repressed daughter, abjectly devoted to the selfish parent who demeaned her — no music or satire, no handsome, no fun. Some of her lines were heartrending. "It all went wrong," I said in rehearsal, trying to feel the words in my core, as Belle, the actress playing my mother, pretended to sleep in her wheelchair. "What happened, Mama? There must have been a time when I loved you."

At the play's denouement, Agnes is forced to realize that her efforts to make her mother happy are instead prolonging the old woman's agony by keeping her alive. She has to process painful information and disintegrate, downstage centre. A spectacular breakdown scene for an actress. One, that is, who knew what she was doing.

This time, success in the part was not hampered by lack of confidence; I simply had no idea how to play someone so weighed down, so hopelessly devoted to a hurtful parent. There was no point of connection between us, no way to open my soul to let her in.

I watched Janet, a terrifyingly powerful actress, work steadily to make her portrayal of a woman furious at losing her husband to cancer grow deeper and richer. She too had a breakdown scene, only hers she managed perfectly, building to a climax with real tears, even in rehearsal, a remarkable feat. In theatre school, I'd learned that if you needed to cry on stage, you could turn away from the audience and pull out one of your nose hairs; the stinging pain produced tears. But Janet was not pulling out nose hairs; she just cried. I knew actors did not like to divulge professional secrets, but one night at the bar I ventured to corner her. "Janet, your breakdown is so good. How do you produce tears on demand like that?"

Even though she was slightly shorter than I, she always seemed to be looking down at me. "It's easy, Beth," she said, taking a swig of her drink and a thoughtful drag of her cigarette, exhaling over my head. "I imagine my children dying." She walked away.

No! I thought. *I could not in a million years do that to myself.*

Then I remembered two years before, while I was doing a show that required me to cry, my mother had had a mastectomy, and in the scene, I'd imagined her anguish in order to generate tears. That's what was required.

But nothing worked with Agnes. When a role comes to life, the words resonate through an actor's whole being, or she has technique enough to fake it effectively. Otherwise, the audience senses emotion that's shallow, a lie. As I struggled in rehearsal, the lines coming out flat and forced, Bill the director had no idea how to help me. Late one night, sitting in a corner of the bar with another gin and tonic, he called me over for a pep talk. "A good actor, darling, pulls the zipper down," he said urgently, in his high-pitched nasal voice. "You need to reveal your insides, be vulnerable. What makes a performance moving and memorable but the truth of the soul shining through it?"

Wise words, more useful than "Do it fast," which was often what he gave as direction. I was desperate to follow them, but something was blocking me. The zipper for Agnes, a woman who loved her mother too much, was closed, and I knew no tricks to force it open.

Nothing to do but go back to the bar and drink. In my diary, I wrote

> *Maybe NOW is a good time for your nervous breakdown.*
>
> *What it gets down to is that I dislike almost everything about myself. The way I relate to people, the world around me, myself. I think my work stinks. How long can you go on through the days going: WRONG. NO, STUPID. STUPID. JEEZ YOU'RE DUMB. SHALLOW!!!*
>
> *But that happens because I judge myself on everything, and my scale gets out of control. I've lost perspective.*

I often lost perspective. The fact that this time I'd lose it in front of an audience was terrifying. But what made me feel better, always, was going over experiences and feelings in my diary. I felt like the writer whose quote I'd copied at the beginning of the notebook.

"*The last and good resort is the white page and the faceless strangers who may or may not hear,*" wrote American author and journalist Martha Gellhorn, once briefly married to Ernest Hemingway. "*I will talk to myself, on paper; I've been talking to myself in my brain, silently, all my life.*"

Talking to herself on paper — like Anne Frank, here was another kindred spirit.

In case I didn't have quite enough on my plate, my actual mother Sylvia was flying in from Ottawa to see the closing of *The Club* and the opening of *The Shadow Box*. Despite my great love for my mother, she was the last person I wanted to see during this stressful week, and I wrote to ask if maybe she could come later, at a better time? Much as I wanted her to see Freddie, I did not, absolutely did not, want her to meet Agnes. But of course she came anyway.

There in the audience of the last *Club*, as we danced and sang in our top hats, was my fluttery British mum. That night, instead of singing to a blushing stranger, Freddie sang his melodramatic song straight to Mrs. Sylvia Kaplan: *Oh Miranda, on your veranda...* What a privilege, I thought during the curtain call, watching her applaud, to stand on stage and sing a love song to my dazzling mother, who could do no wrong and whom I adored.

In my gut was the bitter knowledge that this applause meant nothing because Agnes was coming right up. There must, I reflected once again, be a less shockingly insecure way to make a living.

The following Tuesday night, Mum came to the first *Shadow Box* preview and sat patiently in my tiny apartment afterwards, sipping that day's 46th cup of tea, as I wailed about my failure in rehearsals. Trying to be helpful, as she always did, she told me what I should do as Agnes. "You're rushing through the scenes," she said. "Take your time, my love. Slow down and savour the delivery of the lines."

But that was the exact opposite of what the director — "Do it fast!" — wanted. I grew more confused and frightened.

Though for an actor the only voice that matters must be the director's, it didn't occur to me not to ask Mum for advice. I hadn't lived at home for a decade, but my mother still loved to give me expert counsel; I always listened and even sometimes obeyed. Five years before, landing in Toronto after theatre school, I'd found a day job as an arts conference coordinator, and Mum came to see me there. "When I worked in an office, *ma chère*," she said, shifting my telephone to the other side and rearranging my papers, "I had my In and Out boxes within reach, like this. And lots of file folders — can you get more? There. Isn't that better?"

It wasn't, particularly; my mother hadn't worked in an office since 1950, when she was pregnant with me, but I left it her way. Mum loved me more than she loved anyone on earth, except my father and Mike. We spoke often by phone; she'd let me know if there was anything she needed, and I'd drop everything to get it for her. What she needed most, though, was my time and undivided attention, which were easy to deliver.

If there was one thing I knew for sure, it was that this enchanting woman had my best interests at heart. I could not have been more devoted to her. In fact, she and my ferocious, spectacular dad were why I'd moved to the other side of the country — to get far away from two people who had such total command of my heart.

As I walked into the theatre before *The Shadow Box* opening night, my stomach convulsed. In the dressing room, there were no flowers for me. Everyone else had flowers and cards, as actors should on opening night. Mum didn't know about this vital theatrical tradition, which provided support and comfort for nervous actors. But Richard, my sort of boyfriend, did, and still nothing came. Janet's place in the dressing room was almost impassable through the jungle of blooms.

When, sick with fear, I walked onstage that night in the small, hot Arts Club Theatre, squashed, devoted Agnes with her bun, glasses, and shapeless grey sweater, I couldn't help but register that out front, the two people who mattered most, my mother and the director, were sitting side by side. She, my greatest love, who felt I should delve thoughtfully into the words, and my boss, who insisted I pick up the pace and drive the scenes fast and hard. I felt like a machine with dials being twisted in two different directions. Dizzy with fright and torn in half.

Agnes's crisis of truth came, and as I'd dreaded, her big moment was hollow, my gut unattached to the words in my mouth; all I felt hurtling my way from the audience was judgment. During the curtain call, dazed by my plunge within a few days from sexy triumph to the pit of defeat, I wanted to disappear. The voice inside told me to leave the theatre and never come back.

At the opening night party downstairs in the bar, I did my best to smile while polite people congratulated me on what for sure was a dismal failure. My mother, pleading fatigue, had gone home. Richard let me know he was disappointed in me by keeping to the other side of the room, hanging out with his own non-theatre crowd. When he finally came over, his Italian designer clothes impeccable as always, a cigarette dangling from his fingers, he kissed me on the cheek and said, "Oh well, there'll be another show."

After a desultory exchange about the play itself, which he'd found over-emotional and clichéd, I dared to ask him, "Why didn't you send me opening night flowers?" Annoyance flickered across his face.

"I gave you flowers last time," he said, and turned back to his friends.

For the rest of her visit, Mum happily organized my apartment while advising me on my life and career. As she tidied Cosyland's kitchen cupboards and dissected my current circumstances, Mum sought guidance, as she always did, about her own considerable list of problems; most of all, what did I think she should do about Dad? She was always going on about his travels, the possibility of affairs, what she felt was his mismanagement of money. And what should she do about the house, her ever-fragile health, her gaggle of admirers, her complex life in general? I did my best to listen carefully and give her, if not solutions, at least a range of ways to tackle what was bothering her, though I knew from experience that nothing I said mattered. Mum loved to beg everyone she met for guidance, a pursuit I called "Seek the Expert," but despite her earnest solicitations she rarely followed what she was told.

It was a treat to have my very best friend there with me in the tight confines of Cosyland. It was a pleasure to reclaim my solitude when she left.

After she'd returned to Ottawa, a brown paper parcel came in the mail. "*Saw this, thought it might inspire,*" said the card. My sweet mother, so considerate and generous. Inside was a book entitled *Acting: The First Six Lessons*.

Acting: The First Six Lessons. I'd attended one of the best theatre schools in the world and been a member of Actors' Equity for nine years.

Really, Mum? I thought, my chest burning. I slid it into the bottom row of my bookshelf and never touched it again.

Over the weeks of the run, especially after Bill took the time to work with me one-on-one, Agnes did improve. "You think too much, Beth," he said. "You're too busy looking at yourself as the character, too aware of the audience." Gradually, as I relaxed and figured out how moments could work, I felt Agnes expanding until she filled the whole stage, not just a timid bit of it, and was glad to be pulling my weight. Still, I took little pleasure in the show and was relieved when it closed.

My next jobs were lined up to open not long after, with two different companies: an imaginative, humorous version of a classic Molière comedy with country-Western songs we'd write ourselves, followed by a brief run playing a lonely Louisiana single mother who spoke lyrical lines in a southern drawl while prowling the stage in a "teddy," a lacy pink undergarment. In the first, we were all involved in dreaming up character and music, and the other was a new one-act by a draft-dodger poet I liked, whose writing I'd do my best to help flower.

Work I could do justice to.

***

In late March of 1979, it was time to leave Vancouver for a rare out-of-town gig; I'd been hired for a spring show at the big Anglophone theatre in Montreal and would be back east for eleven weeks. Cosyland was sublet to a director who'd look after my cat, and I'd had a goodbye meal with Richard and his housemates. "Miss Beth," he cried at the dinner table, tasting a vinaigrette he'd asked me to make for the salad, "this dressing is terrible!" We exchanged hugs and promises to write.

The night before flying off, I went to the bar to say a boozy goodbye to foghorn-voiced, mullet-haired Lani, my best actress friend, and all the others. Lingering at the door a moment, I took in the insane swirling mass, spotting Lani, Janet, and other colleagues, great actresses all: Susan, Lally, Nora, Goldie. There were a few guys I was interested in and others I'd had dalliances with and was anxious to avoid, various directors I should talk to but was shy to approach and seem too forward, a playwright or two, some regular hangers-on who had nothing to do with the theatre, just liked the incestuous buzz of it all. A usual night. The room, and after a bit all of us in it, stank of beer, smoke, and sweat.

I plunged in. Drinking talking laughing drinking smoking chatting reminiscing gossiping singing along with the music joking drinking talking.

As I lined up to buy another drink, Jim, one of the theatre technicians, a burly moustachioed man who'd worked on several shows I'd been in, came over holding a fresh beer that he offered to me. Surprised, I thanked him and turned away to join another group; he followed. As the evening whirled by, he stayed stuck to my side. I had no interest in him; he was not unattractive but not at all my type. Yet there he was, and there he remained. Even though I said no thanks, he bought me another beer, and I drank it. Every time I turned around, Jim was nearby, smiling protectively.

After a few hours and many beers, my throat was raw from shouting above the music. "Stayin' Alive." "Y.M.C.A." "You're the One that I Want." Louise, one of the Arts Club stage managers, waded through the crowd to ask with a smirk if I wanted to go to the back room. This was code, a special invitation; back there you could partake of illicit drugs, whatever was around that day — cocaine, Thai stick, poppers. Though I didn't want to offend her, I declined this time, again. I didn't go back there much after an uncomfortably close encounter, a few years before, with coke. Now I preferred the simple high of beer, a great deal of beer.

Though as drunk as I got, in comparison with some, my intake was pathetic. Four years before, newly arrived in Vancouver, I spent my first tentative evenings in the bar watching the great actresses of the Vancouver stage at play. Their consumption of booze and drugs was astounding. Super-human. *I will never be that good an actress*, I'd thought in despair. *I cannot drink that much.*

God knows, I'd tried. In awe I watched my colleagues knock it back with an almost desperate ferocity and still entertain everyone in the bar, knowing they had to get up to rehearse in the morning. They might have looked and sounded rough next day, but they were always there, ready to go. *That's what a real pro is*, I'd thought. *Hungover and game.*

At last the club started to close down, and the stoned revellers careened out the door. Limp and unsteady after hours of non-stop booze and talk, I headed out to find a taxi. But somehow I found myself being steered, Jim's hand on my back, a smile on his face, toward his truck. I went, knowing what was happening, too flattened to stop what came next.

I wanted to go home. But instead, I was with Jim, in Jim's truck, and then in his apartment, and then he was all over me. My clothes and his were on the floor and I was in his bed, which was a mattress on the ground covered with a grubby sheet.

I did not say no. Though I turned my head away so he could not kiss me, I did not fight him off, did not resist. Numb, passive, I was subjected to something I did not remotely want. He was a big man smelling of rye and cigarettes, and what he did to my body felt like violation. It felt like rape.

As he lay on top of me, I took my mind somewhere else and turned to stone. There was a woman in this situation, but she was not me.

It didn't last long and then he fell asleep. In the morning, as I dressed quickly to get away, I saw gloating in his face.

At home I lay for an hour, immersed to the neck in a tub of hot lavender bubbles, scrubbing my skin with a facecloth, replaying scenes of other bad, sad experiences with men. I decided to do what

I'd done all my life with unpleasant memories, which was to push them as far away as possible. I would put the night in a box, close the lid, and never open it again. Janet had a saying in rehearsals, when forward momentum got bogged down. "Moving right along," she'd scowl. It had become my mantra.

Anyway, I thought, as I sat, limp and exhausted, wrapped in a towel and contemplating the beloved mountains, *I'm about to fly off somewhere brand new.*

Moving right along.

Later, when rage and disgust consumed me and I couldn't help but bring the scene back, I asked myself how it had happened, how I could have been so docile, so submissive, and could find no answer. I had permitted it. It just happened.

Men could do what they wanted with women; that's the way it was, the way it had been since forever. My mother told me that after the war, when she was working in Eastern Europe for the United Nations, her boss had made clear that he was attracted to her Lauren Bacall smoulder. If she'd sleep with him, she'd live in luxury; if she didn't, he'd send her to a remote, primitive location. Mum intimated that she'd said no but had managed to escape exile. In my one experience as a waitress during the summer I turned eighteen, the sleazy maître d' used to fondle some of the younger girls in the back room; they had to put up with his groping hands and worse if they wanted to keep their jobs. He left me alone, I suspected, because I was not poor and sweet and blonde. Also because his boss, the manager, was my uncle.

Men ruled the world. At least they did until feminism came along, for me only six years ago in 1973, to change everything. *Surely it won't be long*, I thought, *before Western society changes so much that women will never have to put up with that shit ever again.* But revolutions took time.

The theatre hadn't produced issues of sexual coercion for me, no casting couch; many directors were gay. Though it was different for actress colleagues who were hired for their good looks, I'd not had to use my body or my sexuality to get a part. I considered myself one of the strong ones. And yet I'd just let myself be used as if I were helpless, as if I could not shout no, stop, leave me alone.

My profession required me to have a clear, agreeable, animated voice, and I did; producers were increasingly hiring me for radio work and voiceover. But when I needed most to speak out and defend myself, that excellent voice was mute.

THREE

The one that I want

The night after the ordeal with Jim, as I flopped about with my usual insomnia, one scene sat with crushing weight on my chest — not what had just transpired, but another experience. Of all the miseries I'd endured, there was one that still pierced my heart.

At the age of twenty-three, I moved from Toronto to Victoria to perform in a play that would go on an extensive school tour. Answering an ad in the newspaper, I rented a small bedroom in an airy apartment, the whole second floor of an old house.

My new landlady, Ann, did freelance work for CBC radio. She was an exotic, fragile-looking, pretty woman older than I and also single, and we began killing a bottle of wine together in the evenings. I confided in her all about my desperate crush on Tony, a talented, blindingly handsome actor in the same show. My passion for him had tortured me from the first day of rehearsals, when I'd fallen down a well of hopeless longing. Tony paid no attention; it was clear that though he liked me as a friend and enjoyed our time together, he was not interested in me romantically. "Why not?" was my anguished cry to Ann. "How can I change his mind?"

But I was sure I knew the answer. He was not attracted to me because I was plain and unfeminine. Too big. Too smart. Too loud.

When our tour landed in Calgary, to my joy, he and I were assigned a two-bedroom motel cabin. I prayed that our nightly proximity would launch our romance, but it did not. One evening he brought a girl, an old school friend, he said, back to his room. As I lay in my bed listening to them talk and laugh in his bed, every molecule of my body ached with misery. I wanted to pull the pillow over my face and suffocate. But my passion did not diminish.

Tony was also new to Victoria and lonely, so I invited him to join Ann and me sometimes at her apartment in the evenings. As the three of us sat and drank, I'd tell funny stories about my life to make them laugh. If Tony enjoyed my humour and my hospitality, perhaps he'd grow to love me back. In the meantime, I could at least take care of him, make sure he had pleasant company and lots of laughs and good things to eat and drink. That setup was fine with him, too.

One morning, as Ann and I drank coffee, she said, "Beth, you're such a great raconteur, so eloquent and articulate, and your stories are important for women to hear. I should tape you and see if someone is interested."

Really? Tape me? "Women would benefit greatly by hearing your stories," she said. I was flattered.

That evening, she had ready several bottles of Cinzano, our drink of choice, and a tape recorder. She poured me a nice full glass and then another, we chatted as we usually did, and then at some point, she turned on the machine and started asking questions — about my childhood, my parents and adolescence, my life now. The stories rolled out. Well into our session, I told her how, at eighteen, I was in the middle of losing my virginity when the phone beside my bed rang, and I automatically reached out a hand to answer. The call was for my roommate. "I'm sorry, she's not here right now," I said, while my boyfriend continued to do what he was doing. "Can I take a message?"

Ann and I laughed and laughed.

I rambled on in a warm drunken glow; Ann was so interested, listening so hard, and not only she but other women would benefit from hearing my stories. The same thing happened the following evening — a great deal of wine and the same avid, intent listening and questioning, as I told stories even more personal, family secrets about my parents' marriage, their affairs, my own secrets.

Deep inside, a sharp voice wondered if I should be revealing myself and my family like this. But I was a child of the sixties and wanted to be daring and free, to make a difference. Sock it to me. Let it all hang out.

One morning a few weeks later, my father phoned. "A colleague just told me to turn on the radio," he said, "because my daughter is on the Peter Gzowski show. Are you out of your goddamn mind?"

Here was the part I hadn't thought about: Ann had sold the tapes of my life to "Morningside," Gzowski's immensely popular show on CBC. Two mornings in a row, I was featured on national radio, narrating the most intimate details of my life and my family's. Ann had changed my name, as she'd promised she would. But everyone who knew me recognized my voice, and someone told my father, who listened, with the entire country, to his daughter tell about losing her virginity and other amusing tales, including ones about him.

I'd fantasized for years about being on the Gzowski show and had often interviewed myself in the mirror. "Beth, thanks for coming on the show. Tell me about your new smash hit play and your meteoric career."

"Great to be here, Peter. Well, hardly meteoric, my career started slowly, but I stuck with it, and at last…"

Now I had actually been on the show, in the most humiliating way.

I moved out of Ann's apartment the following month, partly because of the broadcasts, and also because while I was away one weekend, she slept with the man I loved who did not love me, and on my return she couldn't wait to tell me all about it. "Tony and I are wild about each other," she said. "But on our first night together, we simply couldn't have sex until the morning, because we both felt so guilty about you. He cares a lot about you, Beth, and so do I."

She left the apartment to go to him. My legs buckled and, unable to move, I sank to the floor. What a valuable moment. Forever after in my acting career, when I was called on to portray desolation, I simply brought back the minutes I spent face down, leaving damp patches on Ann's living room rug.

In the years that followed, I ran into Tony a few times, as good-looking and charismatic as ever with a successful career in theatre and films, playing heartthrobs. My heart throbbed still when we chatted. His affair with Ann lasted a few years, after which many more women went on to love him, followed by many broken hearts.

For ages, a mutual friend informed me, Tony had been living happily with his very plain partner, whose name was Maurice.

Ann and I also ran into each other occasionally; I noted that she'd continued to latch onto interesting women to give her fresh material and a professional boost. My insides heaved whenever I saw her face. But though I would always dislike and avoid her, I didn't blame her anymore. Sleeping with a friend's beloved and sharing the details were not choices I'd have made. But as for the taping, the fact was that I knew the tape recorder was running. I knew Ann was a professional journalist doing her job, prying out juicy tales in order to sell them. My need to tell stories, my burning need to be heard was greater than my good sense.

It was hard to acknowledge that I'd once been so gullible and defenseless, so eager to please. But there it was. Forever, presumably, in the archives of the CBC.

FOUR

A keen sense of timing

Here she is, I joked to myself as the plane landed, *the sophisticated in-demand Vancouver actress being flown across the country for a show!* My career was moving up a notch. Through an actor friend, I'd sublet a sunny furnished apartment in an old house downtown, with sloping wooden floors and a kitchen table painted bright yellow. I bought daffodils and peanut butter and made myself at home.

Montreal, I already knew but rediscovered quickly, was a dynamic city — cosmopolitan and European yet inexpensive, full of unconventional artists. People were out on the streets at all hours, making even Vancouver look boring and bland. Thanks to the year I'd lived with my family in Paris, my French was fluent, and I delighted in the twang of the Quebecois accent and the confluence of Frenchness and Jewishness in downtown Montreal, the deli bagels and fat salty smoked meat on rye next to chic boutiques and *boîtes de nuit* — nightclubs.

Unfortunately, though I tried to convince myself otherwise, the new play I was there to do, about an Anglo-Irish woman dealing with two suitors, the first Irish and the other Quebecois, was weak and unconvincing; once more, characters with no depth floundered in a plot that gave no insight into being alive in the world today. I was aware the political situation in Quebec was tumultuous. "Separatism" was the word of the day; hangdog chain-smoking René Lévesque, leader of the separatist Parti Québécois, was determined to take his province out of the Canadian federation and, mad as the idea sounded, turn Quebec into an independent country. My French-Canadian colleagues were deeply unhappy with Canada and even with the English language they were often forced to speak, so any play dealing with French-English relations had to tread carefully. We were concerned about backlash after our playwright did an interview with an Anglo newspaper in which she expressed concern about the violent separatist FLQ. But luckily, her play wasn't interesting enough to cause trouble.

As we rehearsed, I once more had to suppress the urge to rewrite the script.

In my mailbox one March morning was a welcome treat: a fat envelope from my best friend Gail, whose once-a-year Christmas letter always arrived months late from France. When we met, I was just seventeen and she, I never let her forget, thirteen and a half months older; two years later, we'd become professional actresses in *Interview* together. But after university and drama school I'd made a solo life in the theatre, whereas Gail ended up married to a Frenchman and the mother of three French children. Three, for God's sake. Almost none of my friends had one child, let alone three. *Catholics!* I thought.

Her missive told of the funny things her kids had said, her husband Alain's interesting work with the handicapped, her own demanding days. I tried to imagine my hilarious, stylish former flatmate buried alive in snotty noses and diapers, dealing with her French spouse. We'd been so close back then; I loved her as much as I loved anyone except my parents, Paul McCartney, and whatever hopeless guy I had a crush on at that moment. But she'd spent the seventies being a housewife, while I was living my exciting life of parties and openings and lovers. "I envy you your freedom," she wrote. Though, she told me, she did very much appreciate her life in fabled Provence.

Immediately, I sat at the yellow table to begin a reply, scribbling on about Montreal, the latest shows, the latest men, movies, and music, and about my parents, whom of course she knew. Though she was a private person who rarely confided in me, or in anyone except perhaps Alain, I always told her exactly what was going on in my heart — this time, my panicked sense that with my twenties nearly over, I didn't know why someone doing so well should feel so dislocated. As I wrote, I felt calmer. Nothing better than getting out a pad of paper and writing, page after page flowing by — though I wished my friend and I could sit with a beer, as we used to, and laugh till the tears ran.

A few days later, my best Vancouver friend, who'd been away when I left town, also got in touch. Shayla was a petite socialist firebrand with frizzly black hair who worked for a co-op radio station. As we got caught up by telephone, she told me she'd just booked a flight. She was heading to Greece for a few weeks in late spring, all by herself.

"Great idea," I said. "Wow. When are you leaving?"

"End of May," she said. "I'm going to land in Athens and decide from there. I need to get away — away from work and men and have some 'me time'."

"You have to go all the way to Greece to get 'me time'?" We both chuckled.

An idea began to stir. My Montreal show closed May 20. Compared to Vancouver, Montreal was practically halfway to Greece, wasn't it? Didn't I need some me time too? For years I'd wanted to go to Greece; Greek Day in Vancouver, with its generous quantities of food, wine, and music, had convinced me of that.

I never made major decisions quickly, preferring to inspect all angles with care, make lists of pros and cons, and consult everyone I knew. But this time I did not hesitate. "Shay, do you want company on the trip?"

She did, and we began to make ecstatic plans. I'd fly from Montreal at the end of May to meet her in Athens, we'd sail to the islands, she'd sunbathe, I'd visit ruins — and then, tanned and relaxed, we'd fly home, I to look for an acting job, and she to resume her work of changing the world, one radio documentary at a time.

It was completely irresponsible to consider charging off to Europe instead of flying home to hunt for work. And yet it felt like a window opening, light and air coming in. A change. I hadn't travelled abroad in years. Being in the theatre meant that when I wasn't working, I had time but no money, and when I was working, I had money but no time. Not much money, mind you. A few years before, my taxable income as a self-employed actor had been $203.

But this year, there'd be just enough of both time and money to get me to Greece. I'd already been hired for a show, Chekhov's *Three Sisters*, at the end of far-away November, but I'd have to look for summer and fall work when we got back in June.

Ah well — I'll cross that bridge, I thought, and went to a travel agent. The cheapest fare to Athens went through Amsterdam, so I'd stay there a couple of days. And since I was already travelling that huge distance, I made an unusually brave decision: I'd extend the end of the trip a bit, and after almost three weeks in Greece with Shay, I'd go on without her to the south of France and spend a week with Gail and her family. A treat to look forward to: June of 1979 swanning around southern Europe, with a few days at the end in the home of my long-lost pal.

I hoped no tempting job offers would come along for the early summer to interfere with my trip. Bill, the Arts Club artistic director, had mentioned hiring me not to act in but to direct a show in the fall, an interesting if scary possibility. "You think like a director," he said, which was news to me. I remembered something he'd told me another night in the bar. "You're not self-centred enough to be an actress," he said over his glass of gin, "and you ask the wrong questions. Actors ask, 'Is it working?' You ask, 'What am I doing right or wrong?'"

I didn't have the slightest idea what he was talking about. But maybe, I thought now, he meant I should try a different branch of this profession.

During rehearsals, as often happened, my co-star — the lanky actor who played my Irish boyfriend — and I developed an intense attraction to each other. Keeping the play going was hard enough without a complicated romance, so it was just as well our affair was only a drunken one-night stand. "*What is it,*" I wrote in my diary, "*about being in a strange town that makes you want so much to sleep with someone?*" But once was enough. In any case, he turned out to be uncircumcised which was a complete turn-off. I'd become acquainted with a number of penises but never one shaped like that.

Despite the diffidence I felt about the play, the reviews were all right, mostly slamming the playwright but liking the production; one said, "*The pivot of the story is a woman played with a keen sense of timing and much vigour by Beth Kaplan.*" Hardly a rave, but I'll take vigour and timing, I thought, and settled into the run. I developed a special friendship with Seamus, the sixty-year-old Irish alcoholic who played my Irish alcoholic father. A tough veteran of decades on the stage, Seamus was often drunk during performances, even the matinees. The rest of us got him through. That, too, was our job.

A director I admired a lot, a big hairy man who specialized in new Canadian plays, came to see the show. I was desperate to impress him, hoping he'd invite me to work with his company. He didn't like the play, though — "Badly conceived and carried off" — and worse, he didn't like my performance. "The character wasn't anywhere near manipulative enough," he said, "and your attempts to be unsophisticated were laughable. Even those ridiculous loafers you wore were far too chic." Humiliated, I didn't tell him the understaffed costume department had had trouble finding shoes for my size ten-and-a-half feet, and those ridiculous loafers were actually mine.

"Anyway, Beth," he said, lifting a fresh beer to his lips, his other hand buried in the thick auburn hair of his girlfriend, a documentary filmmaker, "you're too intelligent to be an actress."

What? What did that mean? Was Glenda Jackson not intelligent? Vanessa Redgrave? That new young American actress with the weird name, Streep, I'd just watched in *The Deer Hunter*? What a silly thing to say. And yet, I thought, perhaps in a way he's correct. Not manipulative enough, the wrong shoes — because I'd spent rehearsals trying to be pleasant and not asking the right questions. Is it working?

"*I admit it,*" I wrote late that night. "*I'm not a very good actress. There is something about me that people like, and I've made it work for me, but I'm over-sensitive, unfocussed and afraid on stage.*"

How else to make a living? How else to make a mark?

***

Three weeks after opening, I received a call from Shayla. Her plans had changed: she'd been offered a terrific media job that was to start right away, and she'd cancelled her ticket to Greece. She was really sorry, but our journey together was off.

I'd paid for the trip, was happily planning where to go and what to bring, Gail had written to say she couldn't wait for my visit to Provence — and now this adventure was to be sacrificed because selfish Shayla had a great new job? Incensed, I raged about this betrayal in a phone call to my mother. She interrupted my tirade.

"Why don't you go anyway?" she said.

"To Greece? Alone? Are you mad?" I replied. This solution had not even occurred to me. I'd travelled by myself a bit, but just to visit people — going from my home to someone else's. The thought of flying on my own to a country where I couldn't even read the alphabet, and then navigating my way around for weeks, was terrifying. How strange that my always-fearful mother, who saw murderous boogeymen and life-threatening diseases around every corner, was proposing something so daring.

"Why not? Travel is good for the soul," she said. "You need a change. Go on — it'd be marvellous for you to get away."

No! No no no. I was simply not made for solitary adventure and would never manage alone. A litany of potential disasters assailed me: I'd get lost, be attacked and robbed, or simply lose my money and wander homeless, helpless, hungry, thousands of miles from home. It made me furious that Mum was always pushing me, that now she wanted to put me at risk that way. Easy for her to say "Go on"; she'd be in her sunny kitchen pruning her houseplants while I was struggling to make myself understood on the other side of the planet.

I had a frightening dream that night, probably triggered, I realized afterward, by the horrific events that had taken over the newspapers a few months before: over nine hundred followers of some madman had committed suicide by drinking poisoned purple Kool-Aid. In my dream, sensible people the world over were committing suicide because the atmosphere had been poisoned with plutonium, and a lingering death was imminent for all. Some of our family friends were already dead, and my father was in his room writing a suicide note. I had to write a suicide note too, and yet I did not want to die. In the dream I sobbed as I contemplated saying goodbye to life, and when I awoke, my cheeks were wet.

How much time I wasted while I was alive! had been my thought in the dream and was my thought again when I woke up. *All those years of anxiety and self-doubt.*

Stop now, Beth, I said to myself. *Live your fine life and stop dragging yourself down. Get on with it!*

I often said or wrote encouraging things to myself. The hard part was following through.

Since my dreams rarely stayed with me, it felt significant that this one had, and in such detail. As I pondered what it meant, the thought dawned that perhaps I should reconsider my refusal to travel alone. The trip was paid for, after all; a shame to waste all that money. And this time my mother was right, I could certainly use some time away. Greece was not Vietnam or Rhodesia, it was a more-or-less Western country, and once I got to France I'd be safely stowed with friends. Couldn't I cope till then?

After much mulling and indecision, long lists of pros and cons in my diary, I took a deep breath and decided. I'd show Shayla. I'd show myself. Get on with it.

So I prepared for my solo expedition. One afternoon at the Army-Navy discount store I bought a cheap suitcase, a cheap rain jacket, and a pair of very cheap corduroy shoes. Into the new suitcase I threw a sundress, some T-shirts, shorts and underwear, a bathing suit, a pair of pink jeans, a camera, and a packet of traveller's cheques fresh from the bank. Ready to go.

***

When you set out for Ithaka
ask that your way be long,
full of adventure, full of instruction...

Have Ithaka always in your mind.
Your arrival there is what you are destined for.
But don't in the least hurry the journey.

Better it last for years,
so that when you reach the island you are old,
rich with all you have gained on the way...

During the run of the play, a series of Montrealers came to the show and to my dressing room afterwards, including Carol, a classmate from Halifax I hadn't seen since Grade Six nearly twenty years before. "How do you remember all those lines?" the visitors all asked, as if that mundane task was the hard part. Even when the show wasn't that good, audience members were awestruck about the life of an actor.

Hearing about my upcoming trip to Greece, Carol thoughtfully sent me "Ithaka," a beautiful poem by C.P. Cavafy, a

Greek poet of the early twentieth century. It referred to the hero Odysseus, who took ten years to make the odyssey from the wars to his home, the Greek island of Ithaka. I put it in my suitcase to reread on the road. The poem, I gathered, was about not rushing to arrive but relishing the voyage. And that, for the length of my own odyssey, I'd resolved to do.

"*I need a place to get away from everything,*" I wrote, "*an unpressured situation — essentially a place to go into hiding. To learn to cook and sew and how to remember people's names. To read all those books I've always wanted to read whose titles I can't remember. <u>To listen more and talk less</u>.*"

A group of hippie actors I once worked with produced a satirical game show. Whenever contestants didn't know an answer, they could escape the action, while the clock ticked, to stand in the Time to Think Box.

What I needed right now was a Time to Think Box.

***

Before departing for Europe, I took the train to Ottawa to spend a few days with my parents. It was always a relief to go home to the tall Victorian house downtown that Mum, long before everyone was doing such a thing, had gutted and renovated. It felt good to walk in the hundred-year-old front door knowing that here, for a while, I was safe and would be looked after.

Yet after only a few hours, though I idolized these people and their home, I felt restless, enclosed, and stifled, as if I were once again a powerless child. My main consolation was the free food. I stuffed myself like a starving creature.

My mother and father were everything to me, still the most powerful people in the world. Since childhood, I'd been ambivalent about them both, adoring, hating, needing, shoving away; as an adult, I'd tell people, laughing, that my mum and dad were fabulous human beings but not, repeat not, the best parents. At the same time, though for years hot or ice cold about Dad, I worshipped Mum.

And with good reason. Sylvia Mary Leadbeater, born in a thatched cottage in an English village, was a six-foot-tall blue-eyed blonde who'd been compared to Greta Garbo or Ingrid Bergman. She sewed and knitted, was a skilled gardener, played the piano and all sizes of recorder, took cello, painting, and pottery lessons, made her own brown bread and tart Damson plum jam, and campaigned for peace with the Voice of Women. Vivacious and open, with an intense blue gaze and a soft British voice, she set out to seduce everyone and everything she met — men, women, animals, plants.

But sometimes, secretly, I imagined her as a spider, a pretty spider ensnaring us all in her comfortable web, immobilizing us with the sticky strands of her phenomenal charm.

People said my handsome, charismatic father, with his thick dark hair, youthful grin, and unstoppable charm and energy, looked like John F. Kennedy or Leonard Bernstein. J. G. Kaplan, known as Gordin, was a research scientist and Dean of Biology at the University of Ottawa, recently chair of several international scientific conferences, a fundraiser for survivors of polio — he was one himself — and an activist campaigning first for nuclear disarmament and then for an end to the Vietnam War. In 1958 he wanted my brother to get the good education he felt was unavailable for boys in the public schools of Halifax, so he founded the Halifax Grammar School, a superb private boys' school that soon turned co-ed and flourished. Dad was a fluently bilingual gourmet, aficionado of the wines of Burgundy and of all things French, a larger-than-life *bon vivant* who in his spare time played the violin and viola in a string quartet made up primarily of other Jewish scientists. He was idealistic, gregarious, urbane.

He was also a volcano, simmering, ready to explode.

So yes, my parents were rare and exceptional; friends during my teen years were jealous. Your folks are incredibly hip and youthful, they said, lefty and artsy and aware.

But my growing up had been fraught with battles — my father's rage, my mother's recriminations, guilt trips, and weeping. Very early, after my parents' temporary separation when I was six, I took on as my task the struggle to hold our family together and felt I was barely succeeding. For many years, ours was not a happy home, and yet, strangely, it was a home I was reluctant to leave; inertia ruled until, as I was preparing to start second-year university, Mum decided it was time to move me out. I didn't realize until later that her urgent need for me to go away was at least partly because she had a young lover, a married Frenchman much nearer my age than hers, whom she wanted to be able to see without worrying I'd turn up. She just said, "Let's go look," and drove me around Ottawa until we rented a three-bedroom apartment. I found two roommates, and just after my eighteenth birthday I moved out, never to return.

And yet, more than ten years later, Sylvia and Gordin Kaplan remained my frame of reference. Everyone I met, including the psychiatrist I consulted during a despondent time of unemployment when I was twenty-two, had in short order to hear a great deal about them. During our second session, the shrink interrupted me to bark, "Beth, why do you talk about your parents all the time?"

I paused, taken aback. What a foolish question.

"Because they're so much more interesting than I am," I replied.

"Well, there's your problem, right there," he said, closing his notebook.

At twenty-three I moved west, as far away from Ontario as I could get while still remaining in Canada. Though I didn't know at the time why I'd transported myself to the other side of the country, the unconscious impetus was clear: if I didn't get out of the orbit of my parents, I'd live in their shadow forever.

Sometimes life encourages us to be smarter than we know we are.

On my first morning home, as I ate breakfast, Mum informed me once more that she thought I should get out of the theatre, something I'd pondered too, I told her, but for very different reasons. I had a higher goal in life, to make a positive difference to our small rotating planet, and didn't know if that could be fulfilled as an actress. Whereas, "How will you ever find a husband? It's impossible to meet eligible men in the theatre," Mum said, as she slid two perfectly poached eggs onto my toast.

I snorted. The last thing a loud, proud feminist like me needed. A great boyfriend and lover, yes, absolutely; a great role with rave reviews and a fat paycheque, yes. But a husband? What would I do with such a thing? How like Mum to see my life only through the prism of her own. "Your father," she'd told me, "is my investment." Not remotely what I wanted for myself — an investment.

Anyway, she was ignoring the fact that I already had a boyfriend, sort of. Who was not in the theatre and definitely not an investment. But she was right that if I were seriously looking for a life partner, the theatre would not have been a good place to start. Almost all my male colleagues were gay or irretrievably neurotic — and often both.

That afternoon, Mum took me to visit Martha, a young scientist colleague of Dad's I'd befriended on my visits to Ottawa. After the recent birth of a baby, Martha had decided to give up her research and stay home. Dad was sorry she'd abandoned a promising scientific career, but he didn't judge. My mother disapproved of working mothers, saying they were selfishly putting their own needs ahead of their families. Martha, she said, was doing absolutely the right thing.

The whole setup repulsed me; a once interesting woman sat in stained sweatpants with a squealing toddler throwing toys at her feet. Martha wanted to talk about feeding problems. Little Mark was a fussy eater, she said, so she'd devised a way to make him eat. After the plate of food was set down on her son's highchair, Martha would flip herself upside down and do a handstand and make funny faces. "He giggles," she told us with pride, "and while his mouth's open, some of the food gets in. It really works. I wonder if other mothers have thought of this."

I didn't know whether to laugh or scream.

"Martha's a bit too focused, yes," Mum said, as we drove away. "It'd be good for them to have another child. And incidentally, my love," she said, patting me on the knee, "if you ever decide to have a child on your own, your father and I won't leave you in the lurch."

"Why bring that up, Mum?" I snapped. "Still worried I'll never hook an investment?"

Many times my mother had managed, in her inviting, intent way, to draw out my secrets. Now I found myself confessing the one thing I'd managed to keep from her — the abortion I'd had two years before. "It was one of the worst periods of my life," I said, knowing she of all people would understand, "and a pregnancy would have been a disaster."

It happened during the most frenetic, out-of-control epoch of my life. After moving to Vancouver with no money and all my possessions shoved into two suitcases, I'd rented furnished rooms in a series of communal houses. Several moves later, I was happy to find a room in a clean, pretty house shared with three housemates, two of whom, I soon learned, were cocaine dealers. Large bags of inviting white powder sat on the dining-room table, and I couldn't help but discover just how potent this drug was, how scintillating, how expensive. Coke made me feel clever, sparkly, vivacious, like a human mirror ball. At 5 a.m., after hours bobbing up and down with a fifty dollar bill up my nose and lots of alcohol and tobacco for added intensity, I'd feel the fizz start to ebb from my bloodstream and be desperate for more.

I started sleeping with the dealer whose bedroom was across the hall, a good-looking, volatile, black-haired carpenter impressed by my acting credentials. He said he was a member of a West Coast Indian band, and it was only through the bagpipe records he put on as we sat speeding and glazed in the pre-dawn darkness that I discovered his parents were Scottish.

After a few months of spangled nights, I was depleted and broke. A director I'd auditioned for telephoned one morning, wanting me to come in that afternoon and read again, a much-desired callback for a much-coveted role. I said, no, sorry, not feeling well, can't make it. I'd been up all night, so stoned I couldn't move, and could barely wrap my tongue around the words I was attempting to speak.

When my friend Lani heard I'd turned down a callback, she was livid. "You can't handle blow," she snapped at me over her sixth beer. "If you don't move out of that house as soon as possible, I'll come and fucking drag you out myself." The next day, as I did my laundry at Pinky's Laundromat on Main Street, I saw a hand-printed notice, "*Small bachelor apartment to rent, with view*," went home to call and then right out again to take the place on the spot.

One of life's invaluable lessons: just how easily a life-sucking addiction begins. My lover in the cocaine house gave me a farewell gift: two psychedelic peyote buttons in a buckskin bag he had sewn and beaded himself. They eventually shriveled into hard beige beans, and I threw them out.

But just before I left that house for good, in the chaos, I realized my period was late. No, surely, not possible. A visit to the doctor confirmed my worst fear: the recently installed IUD had failed to do its job. I'd taken the pill for a few years, disliked the notion of such powerful chemicals controlling my hormones, and opted instead for a small failsafe device bouncing around in my uterus. Now I deeply regretted that decision.

For a few days, feeling my breasts swell and with a sudden hunger for ice cream, I fantasized about becoming a single mother, like Morag Gunn in Margaret Laurence's latest novel *The Diviners*, a feisty, unapologetic woman raising her baby without a father. I felt wise and maternal; the two of us, my perfect child and I, would make our way bravely into the future together. At last, someone to have and to hold, someone to love and need me, always.

But the lunacy of that notion kicked in. On top of my unpredictable and penniless lifestyle, I wanted nothing more to do with the man across the hall, and I had absolutely not one iota of knowledge about or interest in children. In the end, after some anguished pondering of this very grown-up decision, I felt I had no choice, and my sympathetic doctor immediately booked an abortion. I convinced myself that the IUD still careening inside my womb, and more importantly all the booze, smoke, and blow that had flooded my system for five solid months, had obviously damaged the embryo. That made it all easier.

The dealer, bemused, told me the other woman he was sleeping with was going through the same process and might even be at Vancouver General at the same time. This was, shall we say, a low point. After sitting in the waiting room with four other women — one I chatted to, haggard, Serbo-Croatian, "Ve hef fife cheeldren already, thees one ve cannot hef," she murmured, looking at the floor — I was whisked through the hospital procedure with a woman anaesthetist, a woman surgeon, and kind, efficient nurses. I woke up unharmed and unpregnant, profoundly grateful to live in a country that had made this operation safe and legal. And profoundly grateful I remained. My abortion was an experience I did not take lightly and about which I had not one single moment of regret.

It was a painful relief to pour this distressing story out to Mum. Her response was a shock.

"How could you have done something so dreadful?" she cried, tears in her eyes, her face reproachful. "Your father and I would have helped you. I'd have raised your baby myself!"

I was thinking of a lifetime link to the cocaine dealer and a just-launched career that entailed rehearsing by day and performing at night for almost no money — how exactly would a baby have fitted into that scenario? Whereas all she could think of, it seemed, was the grandchild she might never have. Her vehement judgment stabbed me to the core.

Since it came from her, I figured I must deserve it, and yet I knew I didn't. How in the name of God did she think I'd care for a baby when I could barely look after myself? Mum liked to tell people about the revelation that came to her when she held my newborn self in her arms for the first time. "Looking at her," she'd say, brimming with tender emotion, "I knew at last why I'd been put on this earth."

Why she'd been put on this earth? Sweet words intended, surely, to let me know how much my arrival mattered to her. I appreciated that. But in August 1950 my mother, one year married, was a gorgeous twenty-seven-year old with many interests, gifts, and skills. How troubling that all this exceptional young woman needed to validate her existence was a baby. Even if that baby was me.

Her words felt like a caress but also a weight I had to carry. Another responsibility to fulfill.

**

Dad was as always preoccupied with his work at the university and his causes, but we found a bit of time one evening, when Mum was busy, to talk. "How's my little Pupikina?" he asked, the affectionate Yiddish nickname he always used for me, and I told him funny stories about the plays I'd done recently and my nutty friends. He and Mum were going soon to Florida, he told me, to visit his father Pop, and they were considering a trip to France, which made him happy; he was crazy about France. My brother the twenty-five-year old pothead, who'd been busted twice in his teens for growing marijuana and once for theft, hadn't been arrested recently, so that was good. Dad wasn't a huge hockey fan and neither was I, but we both rejoiced that the Montreal Canadiens, the Habs, had just won the 1979 Stanley Cup against New York.

As we talked, Dad was stroking Tippy, my mother's sappy, lovable beagle, and I was surprised at how gentle he was with the dog. Mum had had many pet cats and dogs throughout her village childhood in Britain: Scamp, Bob, Fluff, Blackie. My father grew up in a constantly changing series of Manhattan apartments, bigger or smaller, midtown or suburban as the fortunes of Pop's dress manufacturing business fluctuated; he wasn't even allowed to own a goldfish. Though my own childhood harboured a never-ending series of cats, we'd had only one dog, a dachshund given to us by German friends when I was ten. We were all crazy about the little low-slung beast.

But when she had an accident, when she peed on the carpet or worse, Dad pushed her muzzle into the mess and beat her with a rolled-up newspaper. Someone had told him that's how you trained dogs. But it seemed very wrong to me, not just inflicting pain on a tiny creature, but the logic of the punishment: sometimes she'd made the mess hours before, how could beating her now make sense to her dog brain? Dad was the same with my brother; Mike could get away with mayhem one day and be spanked for the exact same behaviour the next. It made me sick with rage, the inconsistency and injustice of it, the bullying and cruelty. The way Dad used to swat me, casually lifting his hand and whacking the side of my head. I hated him when he hit the dog, or Mike, or me.

Punishment was what fathers did, what they were expected to do, what Pop, I knew, had done to him. But that did not make it easier to excuse. Back then I called Dad "Generalissimo," though not to his face. I'd spent my childhood trying to dodge his critical slings and arrows as well as his smacks, and had realized recently that even now, when someone near me raised a hand in greeting, I ducked.

But these days things were different: I was an adult, and at fifty-six, he'd mellowed. His power over me had faded as I grew old enough to defend myself, and even better, after I left home; we'd begun to appreciate each other as human beings, and our bond was growing steadily stronger. This man in earlier times had been an infuriating parent, but he was also, then and now, a magnificent citizen of the world. Dr. J. Gordin Kaplan, with his campaigns for nuclear disarmament and against war, was working to save our planet from annihilation. How many people could say that about their fathers?

For the first lap of my journey, Dad had arranged for me to stay at the apartment of a former student of his: Kate, who lived and worked in Amsterdam but was doing research temporarily in Turin. He gave me the key and instructions about how to get to her place. This arrangement would save me a lot of hassle and money. "Kate's a great girl, big-hearted," he said.

My mother, in several long weepy talks, gave me another view of Kate, who'd worked in Dad's lab for several years as part of his inner team. During that time, Mum told me, secretive Kate had had a baby she'd given up for adoption. No one knew who the father was; she'd told no one and was always alone. My mother was sure the baby was Dad's.

"Oh for God's sake, don't be ridiculous," I said, cramming a third piece of peanut-butter toast into my mouth.

"They were always together," she said. "Kate set sights on your father the minute she saw him, I know it."

I was used to Mum's belief that every sentient woman within a radius of a hundred miles was desperate to bed my father.

"I want you to keep your eyes peeled in Kate's flat," Mum said.

As I did my final packing for Europe, listening to the exquisite Mozart sonata pouring out from the living room and reluctantly removing the heavy pot of peanut butter I'd bought to bring with me, I remembered the psychiatrist who thought I talked too much about my parents. How could I not? Who else had parents like these?

And I recalled something Richard had brought up after meeting my folks, whom he'd of course adored. "I don't know how you manage to combine the arrogance of your father," he'd said, shaking his head, "with the insecurity of your mother. But you do."

I didn't know how I did it either. There were two of me, it seemed: a little one like the anxious side of Mum, quivering with fear and self-doubt, and the other like Dad, large and loud, impatiently trumpeting opinions. I felt like Alice in Wonderland, shrinking and ballooning, either too big or too small.

Somewhere in the middle, fitting neatly into my own body and mind, was where I longed to be.

FIVE

Moving right along

Feeling already like a seasoned traveller, I chatted excitedly with my airplane neighbours over Eastern Canada and the Atlantic, all the way to Holland, telling my tale and asking theirs. Made my way through the tidy cobblestone streets of Amsterdam, noting with amazement that almost everyone in this Dutch city spoke English, whereas in Montreal, many French-Canadians refused to do so.

Walking into Kate's meticulous, cramped apartment in a modern low-rise at the centre of Amsterdam, I dropped my suitcase and started searching for love tokens from my dad — photos, letters, mementos. Nothing. If there were any, she'd hidden them. I wondered briefly if Mum would want me to rummage in Kate's drawers.

But there were lots of cold Heinekens in the fridge, so I opened one and then a few more, to toast the fact that here I was. Here I actually was, for two and a half days in Amsterdam and then on to Athens, all by myself, far from home and my Canadian self. I felt exhilarated. This was living, and I vowed to take full advantage.

Next morning, after consulting my list of the most important things to do in Amsterdam, I made my way through the drizzle to the Rijksmuseum — one of the great art museums of the world, I'd heard — and stood for a respectable amount of time in front of Rembrandt's massive "Night Watch." Such a famous national treasure, and I'd never heard of it. The painting of lots of men with interesting faces was indeed impressive, lace and gold, the detail of the clothing, the beautiful eyes. Who was the woman at the back with the chicken on her belt?

Rounding a corner, I was delighted to see the work of an artist whose name I knew well — Vermeer. We had studied "The Milkmaid" in Mrs. Ryan's Grade Eight Art Appreciation class, discussed the play of light, the strength in her arms, the folds of her skirt, the green of her sleeves. Even at the age of twelve, I'd loved the maid's solemn absorption, the meticulous details of cloth, jug, bread.

I stood looking at the familiar image, the serving girl concentrating, her lips slightly parted, all curves and health in the silence of her kitchen. The next canvas, a woman in blue reading a letter, her absorption and funny hairdo — and was she pregnant? The third, a woman holding a lute, being handed a small letter by a smiling servant — from whom? Vermeer capturing intimate moments in the lives of ordinary women, and we the voyeurs from the future staring at them, invading their privacy.

And then I looked at "The Little Street."

Two women working in the town of Delft — one in the doorway of her home, the other in a passageway. Two children, backs to us, playing on the ground in front. A purple vine enveloping the house to the left. All those windows and chimneys and doors. The quiet routine of daily life, even the children still, the sky grey yet bright, the street paved with golden stones, everything as it should be. The brick. The brick — like nothing I'd ever seen on canvas, so real I could feel its roughness. I was there with those women and their tiny lives, inside their tranquil brick world. I wanted to sit on a stoop near them and watch the river.

As I looked, something inside me lifted. How clear and dear and beautiful — not just this painting but humanity, all of us alive on the planet. Over 300 years ago, an artist had worked to translate what he saw and felt onto a piece of stretched cloth. And here, centuries later, was a viewer from the other side of the world moved to the point of exquisite pain. My chest hurt, my eyes stung with tears, my nose ran.

Never before had I felt this bewildering sense of being torn open by a work of art, of seeing not just with new eyes but with a new heart. I stood and looked and felt my insides grow bigger, and wept.

On the first full day of my European sojourn, I'd been given the gift of Johannes Vermeer.

Impossible to look at other paintings, not after that feast of peace and light. There was only one thing to do after such an experience — go to a café and drink some Heineken, which to my delight was not an expensive import, like at home, but on tap everywhere. I sat drinking, feeling envious of painters, whose work would endure for centuries. Nothing remained of my artistic endeavours, except for the chubby Italian daughter I'd played on television, a few parts on radio, and, I hoped, some faint memories of my theatre roles in the minds of the audience. And in my own.

To balance high culture with the opposite, and having heard there'd be free samples, I decided to spend the afternoon touring the actual Heineken factory. But I'd missed the tour, so I went back to Kate's to sleep off art shock instead.

A friend who'd heard about my trip insisted I visit a happening place called Melkweg, and posters on lampposts told me Melkweg, that very evening, would be hosting an event called Rock Against Racism. A good cause, so despite a great deal of trepidation, I sought it out, a large industrial building packed with young people, with loud rock bands on several floors. Nothing like this in Vancouver or even Montreal: hippies and yippies of every shape and size, punks with shaved heads or stiff straight up hair, big army boots, chains and dog collars, painted faces, torn clothes held together with safety pins.

Inside, many kinds of smoke made the air impenetrable, and, I guessed, every kind of pill, mushroom, and chemical was being ingested. Leaning against a wall, feeling square and invisible, I noticed a poster for the hit musical now playing locally: *De Club*. I wanted to point to it and tell someone, I played Freddie the gynaecologist in that.

O Canada. A blinding hit of homesickness. *Girl*, I said to myself, as a surly man walked by bristling with safety pins that stuck out of his cheeks and eyebrows, *you're not at the Arts Club bar anymore.*

Around midnight, I left with relief to walk home through the sleeping city. As I headed down one of central Amsterdam's deserted pedestrian streets lined with blank closed shops, footsteps echoed behind me, and someone spoke. I turned; it was a young black man saying something to me in Dutch. Before I could move, he swung his right arm around my neck; in that hand was a knife, held under my chin. "Gif me you money or I kill you," he said. I was pinned to him as he struggled with his left hand to grab my handbag.

No way would I give up my bag. This was not happening. It was a scene in a movie.

"I don't have any money!" I cried, choking.

"I don belief you."

"Help! Help me please!" I screamed at the top of my trained actress lungs. "POLICE!"

He snarled, grabbed the wallet out of my bag, and released me. Turning to run as I continued to shout, he twirled back and slashed at me in fury; the knife blade missed my arm by an inch. And he was gone.

How could you do this to me? I wanted to yell after him. I was just at Rock Against Racism!

Trembling in the middle of the still-deserted street, I walked as fast as possible to the safety of Kate's flat, double-locked the door behind me and lay shivering in bed, drinking one last beer. Just what I'd been afraid of — and on the very first day! Very bad start to my Grand Tour.

But as my heart rate slowed, I realized it could have been much worse. There was little money in the wallet, maybe ten guilders; my traveller's cheques and passport were safely in my suitcase. He did have my driver's license and my Equity, ACTRA, and International Theatre Institute membership cards — lucky guy, those would be so useful to a Dutch drug addict. But he also had my Chargex card, which was a drag. Tipping a last beer down my throat with a steady hand, I calculated that there were enough traveller's cheques — barely — to survive a month on the road and get to Gail's in France, where I could borrow money to get home or ask my parents to wire more. I'd be fine.

How closely his knife had missed. But it had missed.

After a fruitless visit to the police station next morning — "A young Negro man in jeans?" said the smiling policeman in perfect English. "Oh, we'll have no trouble tracking him down" — and a call to the Canadian embassy, I summoned up Janet's favourite expression, which was now mine: moving right along.

I'd been dreading it because it would hurt so much, but this was my last chance to go to the most important place in Amsterdam, for me: Anne Frank's house, the famous House Behind, where she, her family, and the others had hidden from the Nazis until in 1944 they were betrayed and sent away to die.

When I was nine, someone gave me the first of many five-year and one-year diaries, sweet little books with tiny locks and keys. A girl who loved writing, I started each one, determined to keep going, and then petered out after a few months.

At thirteen, I read Anne's diary, which felt like a dear friend exactly the same age speaking directly to me. I took to heart every word she wrote — her sharp insights and sense of humour, her self-deprecation and fear, her passions and desperate hopes for the future. At the end of the book, I was so overwhelmed with sorrow that I could hardly breathe. It was impossible such a vital, clever, generous young spirit had been obliterated, and that she had been one among many, so very many. How to understand something incomprehensibly cruel and unjust? How could there be a god to allow it? I felt I might never be happy again.

At the back of my mind was the knowledge that if we'd been living in Europe only twenty years before, I too and all my family, my Jewish father, Protestant mother, and half-Jewish brother and self, would have been rounded up, like the Franks, to be murdered. Thinking about it, I was shocked to realize that though we Kaplans were safe from annihilation in the WASP enclave of Halifax, still, vicious prejudice festered there. On the surface, the worst anti-Semitism my family had encountered, at least overtly, was being denied membership in the Waegwoltic Club almost all my schoolmates belonged to — no Jews or even half-Jews allowed. I didn't understand. What was wrong with us? Dad said people had always hated and excluded Jews. But why? Wasn't my family just as nice as Gillian's and Kathy's and Linda's? My summers were spent not learning to swim, sail, and play tennis with my friends at "The Waeg," but reading.

We suspected that my father's difficulties at the university, where he'd been denied a promotion that should have been his, were due to anti-Semitism. Though there was a small tennis club right on our street, my mother drove across town to play; the club down the block was restricted. And seared into my heart was the time I'd left a lunch gathering with a school friend and her family and immediately turned back to get a forgotten sweater. As I walked into the room, my friend and her sister were snickering; their father was saying with derision, "… just another mouthy Jew." When they saw me at the door, they all froze.

Surely, I thought, incredulous, *they can't have been talking about me*. They'd been so friendly a moment before. I wasn't even officially Jewish, since my mother was not. So though I wasn't anything else, I was not really Jewish. But that would not have mattered to the Nazis. Anne Frank was my sister.

Anne's red plaid notebook gave me an idea that changed my life. No wonder I didn't enjoy writing in restricted little five-year diaries, with their rigid allotment for each day. What I needed, like her, was an ordinary notebook. At the corner drugstore, I spent ages choosing exactly the right one — a plain black spiral-bound scribbler with wide lines. Thus began a routine of writing in notebooks, limitless space for each day, keeping myself company with words, struggling to comprehend people, circumstances, and myself by pouring it all out, page after page. There were stacks of notebooks now, my whole inner world from the age of thirteen on paper, thanks to Anne.

Seeing the actual House Behind, a museum sacred but haunted, was unbearably moving. Standing in Anne's bedroom, her cut out pictures still stuck to the wallpaper, I thanked her for all of us, the countless readers who'd been transformed by her words, and for me in particular, for what she had given to me. Anne had shown that a teenaged writer had the power to change the world. If only she could know the enormity of what she'd accomplished.

And then, eyes swollen, I walked out into the rain, to shop for a new notebook to chronicle my journey.

SIX

A rare excitement

The plane swooped low over the islands, real Greek islands in a sea of blinding turquoise, the ground brown and grey, the houses white and pink. There was a lump in my throat when we finally landed: I'd made it! Crowds, noise, fumes, bedlam in the airport, an ornate Greek stamp in my passport, and out into the soft burn of the Mediterranean sun.

The contrast from Amsterdam to Athens could not have been more extreme — from flat, calm, and antiseptically clean to chaotic, crowded, smelly, and filthy. I loved it.

I found the little hotel a Greek friend in Vancouver had recommended, with a friendly young desk clerk. My only definite plan for three weeks in Greece was to end up on the island of Crete, in a seaside village the same friend had told me about: "Agia Galini is charming, inexpensive, perfect for you," he'd said. As Athens screeched and belched smoke and foul exhaust fumes around me, I decided to head to the island sooner rather than later.

During a busy two days, I made many new tourist friends, including a honeymooning couple from Belgium and a self-righteous Canadian boy who insisted that $18.50 a night for my hotel room was far too expensive, even with its cute desk clerk as an added benefit. As I wandered streets heaving with tourists, a harmless man desperate to sell me a watch followed me for hours. To shake him, I charged through the Acropolis and lingered in the overwhelmingly full Archaeological Museum, where a six-foot-tall *pithos*, a decorated storage pot 2500 years old, enchanted me.

Then hours sitting in the Plaka drinking beer and eating a lifetime's supply of moussaka, yogurt, spanakopita, feta, and olives. On my first night, when I got back late to the hotel, the desk clerk was just getting off work and invited me to a *taverna* for coffee. Giani and I sat outside talking about Canadians, at least, the ones he'd met at the hotel. "Ninety-nine percent of all Canadians are boring," he said, "and they talk like it's still 1930. They're sheep." And we talked about Greeks, whom I couldn't make sarcastic remarks about as I'd only met him. "In Greece," he told me, chuckling, "all the women are married, and all the men are single."

Giani and I talked till 1 a.m. and ended the night locked in a fiery embrace on the floor of my room. He was uninhibited and energetic, telling me he could only make love if he talked a lot first and if his feet were warm; and he certainly had, and I guessed they were. He didn't seem to find this particular Canadian boring. "I want to be the best for you," he kept saying, which was considerate of him, though I didn't give a damn about his performance, it was just fun to have some company.

I wasted the whole morning of the next day sleeping and didn't see Giani when I got back that night. Exhausted, I didn't want to. He had been amorous and effusive during our tryst but was distant as I checked out. *What's your problem, you silly little man?* I wanted to say but didn't. *We young Western feminists can do whatever we want, and that includes you.*

Time to escape the stink of Athens for fresh sea winds. Here I was, navigating strange foreign lands with surprising ease. Why hadn't I unleashed this adventurous, independent, unfettered Beth before?

Ignoring the shaggy Cretan who wanted to buy me a coffee and would not leave me alone, I stood on the overnight ferry with the breeze in my hair and my nose pointing due south.

***

Agia Galini on the southern coast of Crete was a tiny paradise, a poor village on the Aegean where the industry for men was fishing and for women was cooking and cleaning for tourists, mostly in their own homes. The narrow dirt and stone streets rang with the sounds of English, Swedish, and German, as travellers young and old drank, ate, and shopped. I found a room in a small house turned into a hotel — Hotel Moderna, though nothing was modern there — where the family slept in the kitchen so foreigners could inhabit the rest of the house.

Right away I became attached to a merry drunken group from London's East End, especially Steve, a Cockney cab driver, and his Dutch hairdresser girlfriend. They told me about the beach just beyond the village where tourists could sunbathe nude, a magnet for Germans and Scandinavians, who were all nudists. It immediately became a magnet for me too; I found I liked sunbathing without a suit, offering my whole body to the sun. I was starting to like her, my despised body with its soft round curves where they shouldn't be. There were so many shapes and sizes brazenly on display here, my own was relatively normal.

Every day, though, as I had for a decade, I wrestled with my appetite, trying to cut down, berating myself for eating too much, jotting calorie lists at the back of my new notebook.

Bread: 100.
Beer: 100.
Salad: 250?

On the road, eating less was a hopeless cause. I should have been furious with myself and my appetite, as I had been since the age of eighteen when a friend made me horribly aware that my body was not like Twiggy's. Yet here in Greece, the easy-going way of life, not to mention the loose flowing sundress I wore every day, took away the pressure to starve.

As a solo woman, I was surprised how easy it was to meet friendly souls, fellow travellers from around the world. When an attractive, dark-eyed medical student from Geneva sat beside me on a local bus, we struck up a conversation and decided to hang around together. On a broiling day when the temperature, we were told, had climbed to 40 degrees Celsius, Frank and I went for a long hike along the wild rocky Mediterranean coast — deserted except for twelve naked Germans camping in a clump — and made love on the damp dirt floor of a cave that smelled of the sea.

That night we drank *retsina* at a *taverna* on the beach, watching the men steam in on brightly coloured fishing boats and anchor right in front of us. A giant ivory moon floated full and low, painting a shivery silver path across the water straight to us, and I was comforted to know this same magnificent moon was shining around the world on all my family and friends.

"I really like you, Frank," I said, raising my glass in a toast.

"You are sympathetic to me also," he replied, blushing.

Frank was sensitive, shy, and very, very clean. We enjoyed each other's company, and then he moved on.

After three fine days swimming, eating, walking, exploring, and swimming some more, I was sitting at a raucous dinner with the English group when they began to talk about an organized tour they were taking the next day. A bus was leaving the village at 6.30 a.m., they said, to take them and others to the top of the Samariá Gorge, the longest ravine in Europe, and drop them off. They'd hike eleven miles downhill through a deep cut in the earth's surface and emerge, five to seven hours later, at a seaside village where they'd board a ferry to the bus back.

This European trip was the limit of wild adventure for me. Others were toting backpacks and crashing at youth hostels or even camping on the beach, while my ungroovy self carried a suitcase and slept in safe if cheap hotels. I'd never liked physical challenges. At theatre school, there'd been a stage fighting class in which our teacher, the charismatic B. H. Barry, tried to teach us body awareness, strength, and courage. "The purpose of life is to release," he'd urged us all during our first class. "Open up. Release. You're beautiful!"

And then he divided the class, half of us gathered around the front of the piano and the other half lined up behind it. He instructed the first in the line behind to climb up on top of the piano and to fling himself off into the waiting arms of his classmates.

He wanted me to do it too. Never. No way. Even tobogganing down a small slope, even staggering around an ice rink scared me, and now I was supposed to jump off a bloody piano? But B. H. forced me, and finally I did, I climbed the piano and leapt off, rigid with panic. And though he had guaranteed I'd be safe, my body was so stiff that my limbs were hard to grasp, my classmates nearly dropped me, and I got hurt. Instead of learning trust and courage in stage fighting class, I got hurt over and over again, because I was so afraid I'd get hurt.

My body possessed no strength or courage; I had a brain that never stopped buzzing, perched above a vehicle with arms and legs that transported its heavy, anxious head around. My only body awareness concerned how many excess pounds were packed around my belly. I hated to move, hated exercise. I liked to sit in a comfortable chair and read and write.

So hiking for seven hours down a steep gorge, especially treacherous this year, they said, because heavy rains had caused parts of it to flood, and I with only a pair of flimsy corduroy shoes? Not in a million years.

I signed up.

If I'd had to do it alone, I would never have gone. But the jolly Brits, including Steve's gang, were on board. There was a guide — one guide, yes, for thirty stumbling tourists, but still, a guide. So for once, the word that came out of my mouth was yes. At 6:20 the next sharp, clear morning, bread and cheese in my bag, corduroy shoes on my feet, I was waiting and ready to go.

We were let off at the entrance, given brief instructions, and that was it. Our job was to make our way, in any manner we could, down this giant gully to the sea. One look at it, desolate miles of rock, trees, and water, cliffs on either side stretching to the sky, and I wanted to rush back to the nice safe bus.

We started to hike, at first a steep descent straight downhill. For an hour, I stuck with my British friends, who as usual were telling jokes about their hangovers. We lurched along the path following the river, stepping or climbing over rocks, ducking overhanging tree branches, pushing through prickly shrubs. But then I needed to get away from them, to relish the silence of this primordial place, the scent of wild thyme and oregano. I didn't want to listen to human chatter. Forging on by myself, I left my companions behind.

The route led eventually to the river and vanished; this must, I reasoned, be one of the places the swollen river had submerged either the path or the steppingstones usually there to allow safe passage across. The only way to continue, except to swim, was to find a foothold along the rock face and inch along sideways, clinging to stone and bush. I realized that my habitual crippling anxiety would make this tricky feat even more dangerous. But if I doubted myself, I'd never be able to advance.

So I put fear aside. Finding a foothold, I edged out along the rocks above the river and moved forward. I felt the machine beneath my shoulders doing its job — strong legs, strong hands, heart pumping. When I found the track again, I was still alone, not sure who was ahead and who behind, but it didn't matter. The others were nearby, and the path was clear.

Hours of risk, fright, and pleasure under the relentless sun, hiking through bracken and brambles, teetering across rocks in the river or even, pants rolled up, carrying my shoes, splashing through thigh-high water, climbing, descending, moving onward past crags and crevices to the sound of Greek cicadas and birds, water careening over stone, my own breath. Sitting in the shade, propped against a monumental chunk of striated yellow rock, I ate my bread and cheese, drank some water, hiked on.

I remembered how much I'd hated gym class, how weak and bored and clumsy I felt, all of us girls in the gymsuit uniform, a ridiculous blue one-piece with puffy bloomers. Only once, playing basketball, I'd come to life, running, passing, throwing, feeling my lungs expand, a lithe body churning beneath me. The gym teacher was astounded. "What an encouraging change, Elizabeth," she said. "Good work."

But my enthusiasm didn't last. In my mind, athletic girls were tough and mannish, greasy with sweat. I was already concerned about being flat-chested and sucky, derided for getting good marks; the last thing I needed was another way to make myself unattractive to boys. Besides, my dad, with his polio-damaged legs, couldn't move fast. Why should I?

Yet here was my minuscule self, slogging through a vast stone channel.

Five, six hours later — I didn't know the time, my watch had hit a rock and cracked — I saw turquoise glittering in the distance. Nearly there. I was careful not to slip down the last bit that wound through a pine forest. I'd been afraid of twisting or spraining my ankle, falling and breaking an arm — how far away were the others? What would I do?

But those things did not happen. I jogged the last kilometre through a herd of grazing goats, ran onto the beach, flung off my sweaty t-shirt and burr-covered jeans and plunged in my underwear into the warm, brilliant blue water. Joy flooded me. Here was a revelation: I had a body, and it knew how to accept a challenge and work hard.

How much is possible, I thought, diving beneath the waves, *when I relax. When the voice in my head says "You can do it" rather than "You can't."*

I finally understood the words of B. H. Barry, the man who'd worked to attach my body to my brain so I could travel with them both, in all their splendour, through the valley and into the dazzling sea.

If only you could see your most cowardly pupil now, B.H., I told him as I emerged, dripping, onto the sand. *I've released. I'm open. I'm beautiful.*

***

Before my departure, my parents and I had chosen a date — June 8, my brother's birthday — for me to call home; that day had come. I'd been sending postcards or letters every few days but needed to hear their voices and they, I was sure, to hear mine. I got a bus north to the city of Rethymnon where the telephone office was open all day, and after lining up in debilitating heat for my turn, I thrilled to dial — collect — that familiar 613 number. There they were, waiting, Mum anxious and excited, Dad, listening on the extension, funny and reassuring. I told them about life on the road, seeing art and antiquities, meeting fascinating people from many countries, about the suffocating heat. Every day, I told them, I wore my one lightweight sundress that I washed at night, and in minutes, it was dry. They exclaimed at my tales, their bohemian daughter on the road; they were as proud of me as I was of myself. I was doing the right thing.

They told me all was well at home except that Pierre Trudeau and his Liberals, who'd been in power throughout the seventies, had been ousted by the Conservatives, led by a bumbling young man whose nickname was Joe Who. My poor country. My country. Canada.

After hanging up, I sat in the shade, tears in my eyes, feeling solitary and forlorn. A very old, bent Greek with a theatrical grey moustache, wearing traditional high leather boots even in the extreme heat, edged closer and began to chat, and we managed a conversation in rudimentary German. When he pointed to me and said, *"Du ... mich ... zusammen?"* — you, me, together? — I laughed out loud. Even at ninety, they never gave up.

"Greek women," I wrote to Mum next morning, as nearby my landlady Elpira pegged up yet another load of laundry, *"have it hard; they marry young, have many children, work constantly, are old at forty."* My freedom as a young single woman, I thought, must be unimaginable to Elpira. Though she was not necessarily jealous. The Greeks, both male and female, seemed to heartily disapprove of the footloose young tourists they were required to cater to. I wondered when feminism would make its way to Greece; how an acceptance of women's equal rights could infiltrate such a macho society.

Is it possible to be a staunch feminist who really likes men? I wondered in my diary as I dove into my last breakfast on Crete, the same I'd had every day: a bowl of thick yogurt with honey and slabs of bread. We women's libbers liked to quip, with Gloria Steinem, that a woman needs a man like a fish needs a bicycle. It was fun to pretend that men were useless and unnecessary, but it wasn't true. Women couldn't move pianos or squash enormous spiders; we couldn't have children on our own. We needed men, just as men needed us. *Why*, I thought, able to see my world more clearly from a distance, *does Women's Lib seem to be increasingly about condemning and excluding men and not about making life for both sexes freer and better?*

"I am strong," the feminist Helen Reddy had sung years earlier, "I am invincible, I am woman."

Well, I might have conquered the Samariá Gorge, but even so, I was really only one, or sometimes two, of those things.

As I stood on the ferry watching Crete fade into the horizon, a young woman in a yellow sunhat tapped me on the shoulder.

"Excuse me, are you from Vancouver?" she asked.

"God, someone from home," I replied, "here of all places!"

"I recognized you right away," she said. "You were in that musical with the women dressed as men. You were fantastic."

What were the odds of meeting a fan of Freddie's thousands of miles from home? It felt like true fame, if fleeting.

With a variety of temporary tourist friends both male and female, including two Cockney air-conditioning engineers and a Stanford mathematician heavily into Greek dancing in those silly bobble-topped shoes, I explored the crowded tourist meccas Santorini and Mykonos. In between, with an American lady painter, I enjoyed a few days on quiet unfashionable Naxos, reassuringly peopled with actual Greeks. Magical islands scorched by the sun, fields of silvery olive trees, sunflowers, gladioli, and wildflowers, festoons of hibiscus, morning glory, oleander, honeysuckle. Whitewashed houses, marble stairs, ruins, beaches, donkeys, boats. White and blue, blue and white and gold. The silence at midday, when in the breathless heat everyone slept, including all the cats, flopped together, dozing in the shade.

I liked this country so much, I imagined myself staying to become a tour guide, living in a little house in a mountain village, pots of scarlet geraniums on the windowsill, chickens clucking in the yard, my body nimble and brown as I milked the goats. Many before me, I learned, had also had this fantasy; there were lots of young Anglophone women asking to become guides. And my Greek was non-existent.

Maybe next year.

With the flute seller, Crete.

From Naxos one morning, I took a boat tour to the holy island of Delos, one of the most priceless archaeological sites in all of Greece, said to be the birthplace of the great gods Apollo and Artemis and thus, the guidebook said, "the birthplace of light." That, to someone addicted to light, sounded like the right place to go, though all I expected to find was the usual ancient Greek rubble with a temple or two. On the boat, the guide explained that at the top of the uninhabited island was an amphitheatre dating from 300 BC, and as soon as we'd docked, while the others wandered off to other sites, I bolted straight uphill. I wanted time alone in a theatre.

It had stirred me throughout my stay to see how much Greek culture valued the theatre; there were amphitheatres all over the country, surviving from pre-Christian days, some still in use. This one was a battered but magnificent ruin, a huge semi-circle of crumbling marble seats intercut with steep staircases, almost surrounding a large oval stage of packed earth — the arena where millennia ago, the men and women of my profession, my fellow actors, my brothers and sisters, had earned a living declaiming Sophocles, Aeschylus, Euripides. Angling — like this — out to the audience, to be better seen and heard by the bobbing heads out there, all those eyes and ears waiting for a glimpse of truth to move and enthrall them.

Striding to centre stage, I planted my feet and stood looking up and out, imagining the lights — did the ancient Greeks have lights? Flaming torches, maybe? — the rustles and murmurs out there among the watchers, the camaraderie and bravado here, amongst the performers. Our fear of making mistakes, forgetting lines, destroying the illusion. Our joy when we got it right and spirited audience members to a whole imaginary world created just for their edification and pleasure. What an astounding workplace.

I'm here too, an actor in 1979, I said to the ghostly throngs looking back. *I too, though on the other side of the world, am a mouthpiece, a sacred vessel, a transmitter of cathartic emotion so all those people out there can feel and learn and go home maybe a little changed. But I wonder if I want to do it anymore.*

I waited for a reaction but there was none. They weren't judging, just watching. Row upon row of broken grey seats, crowded with silent Greek ghosts.

Clambering up one of the staircases, I sat down. *Row E Seat 9, it would have said on my ticket two thousand years ago*, I thought. *E9 is watching you*, I called silently to the stage. Now I was sitting surrounded by faceless others, waiting for those thespians down there to reveal something wise and rich and new. I stared at the performance space. *Show me.*

How did I end up in such a gruelling profession? I asked myself. *Why should I stay?*

Sitting on the hard stone seat at Delos, I acknowledged once more that even after years of more success than setbacks, I still didn't know where I belonged: on that wide platform, exposed in front of hundreds of eyes, doing the job I was good at and might have been born to do. Or sitting here in the audience, anonymous in the dark, a passive — or, to put it a different way — a stress-free onlooker, committed to another job, whatever that might be. On stage, or in the house?

The answer to my anguished question came as clearly as if spoken by a voice, mine or someone else's: *Here*, the voice said. *You want to be right here.*

Sitting in E9.

Really? I couldn't believe it. Surely not. I walked down to the stage again, looking out, up, and around, aware of myself as a small figure in a huge empty space. Did I really want to abandon all the years of study, auditioning, performing, the friendship and romance in the Arts Club bar, the possibility of larger roles, maybe even, someday, actual stardom?

I brought back one moment from my career, a farce called *El Grande de Coca Cola*, the saga of a Latin American family doing an absurd circus act. On opening night, my petite friend Lani and I made our entrance wearing multi-coloured dresses covered with ruffles and giant fruity headdresses like Carmen Miranda, I in platform heels so

I towered above her. At the sight of us, the audience went mad. We stood grinning as they howled and applauded, and I knew I could stretch it, milk it, if I pretended in character to be surprised and humble. So I did, Lani did too, and the laughter went on, wave after wave rolling in. We'd stopped the show. Our skill and power as actresses was generating that magical noise, giving that much pleasure. A profoundly fulfilling moment.

Yet there was so much else, the opposite of fulfilling, that went into making that moment.

Maybe there was something else for me to do. Maybe…

Voices — the crowd from the tour boat. My solitude here was over.

Turning to go back down the hill, I picked up a shard of red clay from the ground and, though pillaging was forbidden, quickly stashed it in my pocket. Probably, I told myself, the piece of pottery was just a bit of modern flowerpot. Perhaps, though, it was a very old remnant of an actor's broken makeup container. I'd keep my own bit of *pithos* to remind me of what happened here, the new kind of light flickering in my heart.

That evening, in a sweltering taverna, I sat opposite my most recent temporary travel companion, an artist I'd encountered on the ferry; Denise and I, both travelling solo, had decided to spend a few days on Naxos and cut costs by sharing a room. Exotic, confident Denise was the first woman I'd met to deliberately let dark roots show through her bleached blonde hair; I thought it looked cheap, but she said it was all the rage in New York. Now, as we discussed our careers over cigarettes and wine, she told me proudly she'd recently had a piece shown at the Whitney Museum of American Art. I was impressed, though the image on the postcard she handed me, a green fan-type thingie with scrawls around it, left me baffled. "Mmm, wow. Cool. What an interesting concept," I said with enthusiasm, not wanting to give my confusion away, and then jumped in to tell her about my revelation that afternoon at Delos. E9.

"So weird," Denise said, shaking her head and pouring me more harsh retsina. "I'd never give up painting, especially now, after the Whitney." She frowned, looking intently at me. "You're good, right? A good actress?"

"Well … yeah," I said; Canadian self-deprecation came more naturally than American boastfulness. Denise kept stealing glances at her green fan postcard as if she couldn't believe how gorgeous it was; I was certainly not going to divulge to her some of my more notable professional failures. "Most of the time, yeah, I'm good."

"Then why would you quit?"

I drank some more. Good question.

***

Waiting at Patras for the ferry to Ancona, Italy, I already missed Greece and yet was glad to be travelling on. The second last phase of my Grand Tour, a brief jaunt from Greece through Italy to France was about to begin. On the dock, Greeks milled about in a chaotic pile, noisy, friendly, badly dressed, in huge contrast to the Italians who were urbane, polite, and restrained, small tidy people in exquisitely tasteful clothes.

A man came over and introduced himself — Horst, a beefy blonde German in his late thirties who was on his way back from a German nudist colony on one of the islands. When he heard I was heading to Florence by train, he offered me a ride there in his Volkswagen van. Anxious to save every penny, I accepted, and looking at his map and noting that the longer route into the mountains went by the town of Assisi, which a well-travelled friend had said was a must-see, I persuaded him to make a detour. It was heaven to putter along in a van listening to a Cat Stevens tape, instead of in a noisy train. There was a stack of Krishnamurti tapes too. Horst told me he was soon to inherit millions from his family's wheat starch business; in the meantime, because he was unhappy, he had tried many kinds of self-help and healing interventions and was about to do birth therapy, whatever that was.

The Italian countryside, shrouded in mist, looked organized and friendly, so green and neat after Greece, and the tranquil mountain town of Assisi was indeed stunning, with medieval cobbles and arches and especially St. Francis's basilica with its exquisite frescoes by Giotto. Horst and I wandered and sightsaw. I was discovering I didn't like him much — he exuded the condescension and aggressive sense of entitlement I assumed were the domain of the very rich — but was grateful for the company and ride. He even treated me to lunch in a small *trattoria* — chicken in a sauce of olives and red peppers, with wine mixed with water in the Italian way. After the meal, as we drank bitter black espresso, he leaned his big red face toward me with a smile.

"It is goot you are not pretty, yes? Alzo these physical things do not get in the way."

I couldn't speak and left the table to cry in the bathroom.

Someone had once told me, "Your face is not beautiful but it's real. You have a Communist face." I hoped that meant forceful, honest, and strong, like poster images of noble Soviet workers. Instead, I feared it might mean hefty and coarse, without cheekbones. But my German acquaintance had taken insulting frankness to a new level. When I got back to the table, he apologized by saying he should have made clear I was not pretty to him, though others might find me pretty. When he saw I was still upset, he said, "What iz wrong? Has no one efer zaid that to you before?"

I was subdued on the way to Florence. We arrived in the evening, and after another quick meal and then finding three cheap hotels full, Horst proposed that he push down the back seat of the van so we could both sleep there. The penny-pincher in me agreed, though making insistently clear, once again, that there would be absolutely no intimacies.

But when we were parked on a side street on the edge of the city, lying side by side in the dark of the stifling van, he pushed himself over and started to climb on top of me. It was revolting.

"I told you I wouldn't do this!" I cried, struggling to push off his bruising weight.

"I didn't sink you meant it. You can't zeriously expect me to lie next to you and not haf sex?"

"Yes, I do expect it."

"Lots of girls zay that but zey don't mean it."

He was a big man and a bully. I struggled but could not fight him off. What had I brought on myself now? Hadn't I been here before?

He sat up.

"I drife you," he snapped, "to a fucking hotel."

In silence, at midnight, we drove from one hotel to another, trying at the height of the tourist season to find a more or less affordable room, I, praying he wouldn't simply dump me on the street. Finally, I found one. He handed me my suitcase and drove off without a word. In the closet-sized room, as I sank, weak with exhaustion and relief, onto the bed, there was a knock at the door. The smarmy young desk clerk was leaning on the doorframe, leering at me.

"You musta need sometheeng, yes? I geev to you."

"No!" I cried, slamming the door in his face. "Go away!"

The reality of what had just happened hit: Horst could easily have raped me. And yet he had not. The two sides of being a young woman on the road, alone: meeting nice people was great. Meeting creeps was not. *You've been fortunate so far, you careless idiot*, I chided myself. *Don't push your luck.*

> *Hope the voyage is a long one.*
> *May there be many a summer morning when,*
> *with what pleasure, what joy,*
> *you come into harbours seen for the first time;*
> *may you stop at Phoenician trading stations*
> *to buy fine things,*
> *mother of pearl and coral, amber and ebony,*
> *sensual perfume of every kind –*
> *as many sensual perfumes as you can;*

and may you visit many Egyptian cities
to gather stores of knowledge from their scholars.

The voyage, so far, had been far more valuable than I'd anticipated. But already, after the coming week with Gail and her family in Provence, I'd be flying back to Vancouver. I'd carry with me many fine things: the swell of emotion provoked by Vermeer, my triumphant plunge into the Aegean after the Samariá hike, the startling voice on Delos that said, "You want to be here. Sitting in E9."

I looked out at the dark velvet of the Italian sky. Time was pressing. In a year and a month, in August 1980, I'd turn thirty. Thirty! Thirty meant the end of everything.

This is your Time to Think Box, I whispered, as stars glittered like tiny marquee lights in the black dome above. *Make good use of it.*

ACT TWO

I am never alone. Always in good company. My own. And that's enough.

—Louise Weiss

SEVEN

Harbours

Despite a nearly sleepless night, I awoke excited to be in Florence. Leaving my suitcase at the hotel, I spent an energetic day, marching through the Uffizi — lots by the great master Botticelli but sadly, no Vermeer — and shopping on the Ponte Vecchio, where I bought and immediately put on a shapely black dress with multi-coloured polka-dots that, despite the extra pounds from so much Greek yogurt and honey, I thought suited me well. After stopping for a beer at a *trattoria*, I ended up at the home of Jimmy and Marco, two young Italian Americans who leaned over to chat and eventually invited me to join them for a meal with their extended family, a crowd of genuine Italian aunts, uncles, and cousins. At one point, Jimmy asked, "Beth, are you by any chance an actress?" When I nodded, he said, "I knew it. The stature, the presence, the voice."

    I blushed, and not from my overflowing glass of Chianti. Jimmy was cute. Too bad I had to rush to the station to get the overnight train to Nice and then on to Avignon.

As the train chugged through the night, I lay on the top bunk in my new Florentine dress, smiling, thinking about my best friend. How good it would be to have a real catch up with Gail, at last. Despite the thousands of miles and the difference in our lifestyles, we'd stayed in touch, although, except for a few rare visits or expensive phone calls through the seventies, we'd had to make do with the mail. I'd never stopped missing her and the spectacular laugh that emanated from her core, shook her body, and exploded into the room.

Alain, as slight, serious, and good-looking as ever, was at the Avignon train station to meet me, and we drove in their little Renault through fields and towns uphill to Gordes, which he told me was one of the most famously picturesque villages in all of France. Rounding one corner, we stopped at the lookout to take in the breathtaking vista on the other side of the valley, the town's medieval houses of dusty ivory stone clinging to the side of a mountain, a chateau rising in the middle. Alain drove along steep winding streets and braked in front of a small shabby house on the main road out of town, which I later learned was a short walk down the hill from his work.

It was my dear Gail's house all right, no mistaking that. Her room in our shared Ottawa apartment had been chaos, and so was this place — a minefield of clothes, toys, breadcrumbs everywhere. And there she was, my dearest friend, laughing. "Kaplanski!" she cried, as we hugged. "Where have you been all my life?" Both of us cackling. Oh, it was good, after weeks of anonymity on the road, to be with someone who knew me, had known me for more than a decade. Good to be with such a joyous person, her good humour spilling out through that generous body. She'd told me once that her two role models in life were Jean Vanier and Lucille Ball, and that defined who she was — a spiritual comedienne. Now also, amazingly, a very good cook who'd made a delicious *daube provençale* and strawberry pie for our reunion dinner. But also, I immediately saw, an irritated, disorganized mother.

Gail and I had clicked from the moment we met in a Modern French Literature class. We were the only ones who spoke fluent French, I from my year in Paris, she from growing up near Montreal with a Francophone mother. The class was a joke; the professor was a timid Italian who droned on about Sartre, Camus, and *l'existentialisme* and was terrified of his students. During one discussion, in an unforgettable moment, a bored young man who had never opened his mouth put up his hand. As Gail and I breathlessly awaited his input, he asked, "How do you spell SART?" That was the only time he spoke all year.

In that class, I made one of the great friends of my life, and through the years that friend and I would periodically turn to each other and say, "How do you spell SART?" It didn't take much for us to fall about.

The Gail of the sixties was solidly built with long bleached blonde hair, wore slightly too-tight dresses from trendy Montreal boutiques, and was famous in our circle for two endowments: her breasts and her laugh. Both were enormous, ridiculously outsized. Her guffaw was a volcanic eruption, spraying from her gut and shaking her entire being. It was one of our jokes, eventually, that I was small breasted and funny and she was hugely buxom and funnier, just bigger in every way. But there was never a hint of competitiveness between us, just mutual support and merriment.

In our first stage appearance as Gertrude's ladies-in-waiting in *Hamlet*, I had a bigger part: I had a line. But Gail looked better in her Elizabethan gown: she had cleavage. And, during one performance, a trendy purple wristwatch she'd forgotten to take off.

At the start of second year we opted to become roommates and rented a conveniently located two-bedroom apartment we couldn't afford; two guys eventually shared the place and the rent with us, sleeping in the dining room, and one of them, occasionally, with me. Gail didn't sleep with anyone; she remained a virgin, a good Catholic girl who didn't even consume much by way of alcohol or drugs. At one party, she did drink a lot and then vanished into the only bathroom; the door remained locked while people outside pounded in vain. Eventually, beside herself with embarrassment, she let me in; she'd thrown up everywhere. I cleaned up the room and my friend and took her home. This was an event she'd have preferred to forget, but I enjoyed reminding her of it every so often. What are friends for?

The family of five had only recently moved from northern France to Gordes, where Alain had founded and was the director of a brand new L'Arche community called *Le Moulin de L'Auro* — the Mill of the North Wind. I knew few details about my friend's life as a French housewife, except how unimaginably different her days were from mine. To me, children were irrational, tiresome, noisy producers of unpleasant bodily substances, leaking out at both ends. How would I manage a few days in a houseful, even if it was the house of my best friend?

Gail had moved her son Charles, the oldest, into the bigger bedroom where the two girls slept, so his minuscule bedroom, with its minuscule child's bed, was for me. At least I could retreat periodically from the chaos to my own space. Watching Charles and his sisters at dinner that night, I ascertained that Gail's son, at seven, was already an ultra-French know-it-all, his father's miniature twin. Four-year-old Rachel, gangly with brown hair and freckles like her brother and dad, was cheeky, bright, and obstreperous; she and Charles fought incessantly. Miriam was chubby and blonde, very cute at two, so stubborn she was virtually immovable.

I knew there were people who were "good with children," interested in them, but I couldn't imagine it myself. Why bother? With their scuttling legs and unpredictable movements, children were like spiders; they scared me. And they were so honest and unpretentious, staring into my face with their bright little eyes, I suspected they could see right through me, see my fakery and fear. I'd never been one of the little girls who mooned over babies. Yes to cuddling motionless plastic creatures, like my doll Betsy Wetsy who, when you stuck a bottle into her mouth, soaked her diaper through a hole in her bottom and had to be changed. No to babysitting the bothersome, boring real thing, even though that was almost the only way a girl could make her own money. As an adult, I didn't have to deal with children because I didn't know any.

I did my best to be good with Gail's, reading them picture books in English and French and holding a sticky hand on walks and shopping trips, if necessary, as we meandered slowly, oh ... so ... bloody ... slowly ... along. But otherwise, I waited impatiently for them to go to sleep so Gail and I could talk. And talk and talk and talk — about our friends and families, about my career in Vancouver and her hopes for a future career maybe teaching English, about feminism in our respective countries and women's place in the world today. The recent shocking election in Canada; the convoluted politics of France. Our weight, hair, clothes, shoes. Our music.

Gail wanted to know what was going on in the world of pop, and I was ashamed to say that because I was mostly rehearsing and performing at one theatre or another, I'd missed much of the music of the seventies. In the sixties, while I remained a faithful Beatlemaniac and devotee of Led Zeppelin, the Who, the Stones, and the other great English groups, Gail had been a fan of Motown. I told her the little I knew about the new musical movements, like punk, where angry musicians in torn clothes held together with safety pins screamed foul words; disco, where the singers wore glittery bellbottoms and swayed in unison; and New Wave, where everyone was so cool and hip, you had no idea what they were singing about. Gail was my only friend who loved to dance as much as I did. When the kids and Alain weren't there, we tried to find good stuff on French radio so we could boogie around the living room, just like the olden days.

We gossiped and reminisced endlessly about our friends from Carleton, including our talented buddy Danny Aykroyd, another member of the drama club, who'd gone to New York where he was now one of several Canadian stars of an improvisational comedy TV show called *Saturday Night Live*. I reminded Gail that once, when I was alone in our apartment, there'd been a knock on the door; it was Dan. "Got a match?" he asked, grinning at me and opening his hand to reveal about forty joints. But though a really nice guy, Danny was manic and overwhelming; I did not want to vanish into a tunnel of dope with him and gently turned him away. Later I wondered what would have happened if I'd let him in.

Would I now be in Manhattan, taking care of a rising star and a tribe of little Aykroyds? Extremely unlikely.

Gail had lots of stories she was anxious to tell, particularly complaints about the difficulties of living in France. Like the time, not long ago, she'd been looking for an address and went up to a man on the street. "*Pardon, monsieur,*" she said and then asked him in her grammatically perfect, slightly English-accented French for a street name.

"STREET BY FOUN … TAIN," he bellowed in exaggerated English, over-enunciating as if to a small deaf child and pointing the way. "Wa-ter. WA-TER!"

"They can always tell you're not French," Gail said, frustration in her voice, as we did the usual towering pile of after-dinner dishes. "You're not one of them, even if for your entire adult life, you've made this place your home. It takes three generations to make a friend in France!"

That sounded like the definition of hell to me. But she loved her adopted country, or maybe just her Frenchman and the three small dual Canadian and French citizens they had created. The youngest of whom, she was chagrined to discover when she went to check on them, had just "*fait caca*" in her parents' bed.

The one thing we did not discuss, ever, was Gail's marriage. I never hesitated to reveal almost every detail of my romantic adversities, and my few other married friends liked the chance to let off steam and vent frustration with their spouses. But not closed-mouthed Gail, though it was clear her marriage had its problems. Obstinate, contradictory Alain had an authoritative code of ethics and was not a man who'd ever praise others or accept an iota of praise for himself. He never noticed if the house had been cleaned or if Gail looked pretty or had made delicious food, and he put his wife down witheringly for things she'd done or not done, sometimes with complete justification, I thought, and sometimes not. She snapped back, and they argued often, their bickering tedious and unpleasant. I saw no physical interaction between them, no tender gestures or hugs or even the obligatory French kiss kiss kiss on both cheeks. Just nagging, chiding, resenting, in both their official languages.

Yet there was also, clearly, a robust link, incomprehensible and undeniable. There they were, solidly entwined, presumably forever. It must be their Catholic faith that gave them such force, I thought. God was on their side. Even their profession — assisting the handicapped — conferred a blessing, though it helped that Alain came from a wealthy family. He, Gail, and the kids lived like paupers in the battered rented house, but there was a ton of money in the background; Alain had just bought a big piece of land nearby and was designing their own home, and the family diamond on Gail's finger was huge. Talk about having it all, I thought peevishly — both a humungous diamond and a heavenly reward for poverty and good deeds.

But I didn't envy Gail's life one little bit. The kids were always there, squabbling and shrieking, and so, every evening and every weekend, was the husband. The thought of yoking myself to some guy for the rest of my natural days was as unthinkable as wanting to become someone's mama. My first long-term boyfriend James had offered to marry me one day if we could live in separate apartments in the same apartment building. Though I was not interested, at nineteen, in cohabiting with a partner, that kind of bloodless unromantic arrangement held no appeal either, and we eventually broke up. But later I thought his proposal sounded pretty good, providing the best of marriage, companionship and sex on demand, without the worst — surveillance, negotiation, and constant, constant compromise.

My model for marriage was my parents': my mother talented, manipulative, and dependent, my father successful, heedless, and domineering; Mum nagging and weeping, Dad shouting, and I siding with neither, judging them both wrong and ridiculous. Their *marriage* was wrong and ridiculous. The only thing worse than my parents' marriage through my childhood was the thought of them divorced, unleashing two crazy single people upon the world.

Very early, my parents had divided us up, my brother belonging to my father, I to Mum. She still doted on Mike, but I was harshly cut off from Dad. It had taken me years to grasp how immature and selfish my parents were to channel their anger at each other and the world through their children. In fact, I was grasping it still. And yet they'd surprised me. After Mike and I left home, my parents began to enjoy each other's company again, beginning, it was obvious, to fall back in love, deeply in love, with the person they'd first met in 1944. It was a treat to watch this embattled couple aging into a serene kind of happiness.

So being chained to someone was completely out of the question, unless you wanted children and could survive the stress of them for twenty years or more until at last they went away and left the two of you in peace so you could discover each other again.

That didn't sound like such a good deal to me.

And yet, said a small voice, *do you really want to spend the rest of your life alone?*

Could I find a way to love without losing myself? A man who would not consume my soul?

***

Now that I would be living for a few days in the maelstrom of Gail's family life, I tried to make myself useful. I did dishes, swept floors, and watched her cook, taking note of her best recipes, though I never, ever expected to make *boeuf en daube* or *île flottante* myself. Most of the family groceries were bought during weekly expeditions to a cavernous supermarket in a nearby town, but if Gail needed something from the local shop, I'd offer to walk the ten minutes downhill to the village to buy fresh baguettes or leeks or a bottle of good red wine cheaper than Coca Cola, at small shops where everyone knew and greeted everyone else, all the shoppers carrying their own baskets or string bags. The direct route meant following the busy main road, but I preferred the footpath along the cliffs with a spectacular view of the whole dusty green and grey Luberon Valley, bathed in the soft, clear, intense light of Provence.

Sometimes I stopped to sit with my feet dangling over the edge, gazing to the horizon, absorbing the deafening screech of cicadas, the low murmur of bees, the hot air pungent with lavender, rosemary, basil, oleander, wild thyme, and in the distance, the growing grapes in scores of vineyards. I'd pick slender stalks of dried flowers, so delicate, pale yellow, grey, and green, to fill the empty vases at Gail's. As my eyes, ears, and nose relished this sensory banquet, my stomach growled in anticipation of an even better kind of banquet: the meal to come. Every morsel of it, but especially the cheese.

The cheese! I adored cheese, and here it was served at room temperature after both lunch and dinner on its wooden cutting board: *chèvre* and *banon* — local goat and sheep's cheese — Camembert, Cantal, and Brie, with an endlessly replenished basket of the bread famous for its chewy golden crusts and flavourful spongy centre. Sometimes I couldn't stop myself from making embarrassing moaning noises as I ate. "*The* pain *is so good*," I wrote to my mother. "*As in bread.*"

But there were rules to be learned about the French table, and Alain was the man to teach me. After my first fumbling encounter with their cheese tray, he gave me an uncompromising lesson in how to slice cheese: the polite way with a triangular cheese like Brie is never to cut horizontally across the tip, which is selfish, taking the best end piece for yourself, but to slice lengthwise along the side, so everyone shares the soft tip and the harder crust further up. He taught me that the proper way to pass a salad bowl is with the serving implements always pointing toward the person reaching for the bowl, that you never use a side plate for your crust of *baguette* but just put it on the tablecloth, and other rigorous laws of French life. I felt like the Wild Woman of Borneo blundering into civilization.

One day I found out how Alain came by his *noblesse oblige*, when Gail and I joined him at a bistro lunch with his visiting father, whose bald head and forbidding craggy face I remembered from their wedding. I ordered *potage* — the soup, which sounded delicious. Alain's father shook his head.

"*Mademoiselle*," he said disapprovingly, "*on ne mange jamais le potage à midi.*" One should never eat soup at midday.

Oh for God's sake.

I liked and admired Alain, yet he intimidated me. Trained as an aeronautical engineer before devoting his life to L'Arche, he was highly educated and intelligent yet deeply religious, two states of being I found impossible to reconcile. How could you be really smart and well-educated and still believe in God? And even more incomprehensible, in the conservative Polish Pope John Paul II and his behemoth of a Catholic Church, with its abhorrent lack of concern for social justice and its medieval bans on homosexuality and birth control? A birth control ban obviously being obeyed by this fecund Catholic couple.

Alain was always working, admirably dedicated to his good cause, yet also self-righteous and judgmental as only a Frenchman can be. He and I immediately discovered that we enjoyed provoking each other into argument. Gail joked that a marriage between Alain and me would last ten minutes, and she was right; I'd never have tolerated his rigid officiousness and critical French snobbery, and he, I assumed, my sloppy North American self-indulgence. Though I also appreciated that he was so assuredly in charge, efficient, capable, decisive. The boss. The man.

At one meal, Alain and I launched into a noisy fight about circumcision — I completely in favour, Alain heatedly against. "Mutilation!" he cried.

"Beautification!" I retorted, before realizing that Alain must be uncircumcised himself. Well, not his fault. And since Gail had never seen a circumcised man, poor soul, she didn't know the difference, and I was not about to enlighten her.

I explained that my father spent the last year of the war in an American army MASH unit, in which one of the most common jobs of the medical team was to circumcise soldiers who were infected and in agony. "Much cleaner and healthier," I said, "to get rid of it at the start."

"Barbaric," said Alain.

"But of course," I continued, "besides the all-important aesthetic and health elements, there's a Jewish instinct there too. I may only be fifty per cent Jewish, but it would be unthinkable to have an uncircumcised son."

This was what the French did for amusement — sit around the table with another glass of wine, an array of sublime cheeses, and a basket of bread, arguing about anything and everything, just arguing, because discussion and disagreement were as essential as breath. Alain and I began a new squabble about the vital topic of toilet paper; he thought the soft North American stuff was an extravagant, unnecessary indulgence, and I that the useless waxed substance the French used on their bums was a self-punishing waste of time and paper. Gail and Alain bickered about the best place to buy onions, about the man in the market who'd sold Gail a basket of overripe strawberries — should he have warned his customers? Why didn't Gail notice, and should she have taken them back?

"But Alain," I protested to defend her, scooping them up, "Gail was right to buy them. Mmmm, delicious!"

I could do this.

Something in me felt at home in France. Though I hadn't spoken French for years, my accent, I noted, was better than Gail's. Maybe I almost sounded — and, with my dark hair and small breasts, maybe I almost looked — authentically French. I'd absorbed a lot when living here as a teen, not just a new language but a whole new culture, another way of being. Now, thanks to Alain, I even knew the correct way to slice Brie.

We talked at one meal about "callings" — that each of us should discover what he or she is called to do. "*Gail*," I wrote that night, "*is called to produce delicious food for us all to eat, and I to diddling about commenting on it.*"

It made me laugh to remember one Sunday when Gail and I were flatmates in Ottawa and friends came for brunch. Gail's job was to make a stack of pancakes, only she got impatient pouring small puddles of batter into the frying pan and instead, to save time, poured all the batter in at once to make one nice big pancake. The bloated brown slab was raw inside and burnt outside, causing general hilarity. That was Gail's level of culinary expertise before she started cooking for a French family.

***

My friend arranged that for one whole blessed day, the children would go to stay with Alain's parents, and we three adults drove to a coastal area called the Camargue, to swim and picnic on a bizarre nudist beach, huge stretches of sand with nothing but wind and sea and occasionally, a naked man in a cowboy hat, a naked woman on a moped. In such an open environment, we were not shy with each other, Gail's white watermelon breasts, mine like oranges but a nice pale brown, Alain — well, I tried not to look, but yes, definitely uncircumcised. As we ate our picnic, his hair kept blowing into his mouth, so he borrowed my barrette to pin it back. An unconventional man indeed.

We drove on to the picturesque town of Nîmes to sightsee and watch the movie *Hair* playing there in English with French subtitles. I told my friends that Dad, visiting Toronto while I was living there, had taken me to see the musical, and during the show, when the audience was invited to climb onstage and groove with the actors, he was eager to get up and dance, and I wouldn't. It wasn't that I didn't want to groove with my dad; I just had no desire to get up in front of all those people and have them watch me show off and make a fool of myself. An odd feeling for someone who'd just trained to be an actress.

But I'd loved *Hair*, its raucous beat and celebration of youth, freedom, and sensuality, and I enjoyed the movie. Gail and Alain did not; it was just too American, too casual and flashy for their French tastes. On the way back, the two of them argued about whether bread got stale in the car, and I, in the back seat like a child, looked out the window at the lush glories of summertime Provence.

The following evening, we all went up the hill to dinner at the Moulin, Alain's L'Arche community. The mill dating from the twelfth century that gave the place its name had been transformed, he showed me proudly, into a serene round chapel. The community lived in a converted building nearby, with a modern workshop behind. In the old, low-ceilinged manor house was a big kitchen, a dining-room with a long wooden table and benches, a threadbare communal living room, and upstairs, austere bedrooms for the five male and female assistants and the ten retarded boys who lived and worked there.

The first thing I learned was that they were not ever, ever, called retarded but handicapped, and the second, they were definitely not boys, they were men. When Alain introduced them, though I thought I'd been prepared by my encounters at the wedding, I was horrified at how malformed, even grotesque some of them looked to me: Maxime with a huge distended head, his face covered like a prize-fighter's with bumps, cuts, and bruises from his many falls during epileptic fits, some of his teeth broken and one eye swollen nearly closed; Gérard the opposite, his head too small for his angular jerky body, his narrow white face in a permanent scowl; the placid giant Emile with a vacant gaze and the mind of a nine-year old. There were others less frightening to look at and communicate with: Jean-Joseph, the least handicapped, who, despite a mouthful of jagged teeth, had a cool rocker vibe with long hair and jean jacket; Antoine, almost handsome with a wide cherubic face and a dark thatch of hair, though prone, Alain told me, to psychotic rages; and best of all Jean-Claude, as compact as a child, sunny, affectionate, hyperactive, and also, apparently, psychotic.

The dinner was surreal: everyone including, to my amazement, Gail and Alain's young children behaved as if this was normal, a dining table surrounded by terribly damaged, in a few cases barely functional men. It looked to me as if being with these handicapped adults was like being with children — the infinite care and patience required, the selfless putting aside of one's own needs to tend to someone who couldn't help but be demanding. The young assistants who worked there were cheerful and patient, helping some to eat, defusing the confrontations that arose like summer storms and just as suddenly abated. Everyone, regardless of ability, had the chance to speak and be heard; giggles, chatter, and weird noises filled the room. We all helped with the clean-up; I dried the dishes with the epileptic Maxime, trying not to look too closely at his mashed-in face or notice that he could barely hold a dish in his thick clumsy hands.

Through the course of that extraordinary evening, when the shock of first seeing those faces and bodies had passed, I realized that with time, perhaps I too could treat this situation as ordinary. Because, off-putting as were their looks and manners, the men were not monsters but human beings with needs just like mine. As Alain said, "If your foot is injured, you don't cut it off, you look after it. We have as much to learn from these men," he told me, "as they to gain from us."

Until then, I'd had no extended contact with anyone handicapped except Muriel, a girl in my junior high school class. Muriel was what we called simple-minded. We were told she'd fallen out of a car onto her head when she was small, and her brain had been damaged. She was very slow and odd-looking, always pushing her glasses up her wide flat nose, and I didn't know how to talk to her, so I kept away. She made me uncomfortable.

Muriel, I thought, was a genius next to these guys.

As we left, Jean-Claude and Emile gave me a warm hug, and I was moved to have been accepted so quickly into this very strange group, which was not nearly as frightening as I'd imagined.

In the morning I came downstairs to find Gail reading *Elle* magazine in an armchair in the living room; we both chuckled when I pointed out that she was sitting on a heap of the children's wet bathing suits. As she changed into a dry skirt, she said she had a favour to ask. "I'm desperate for a haircut," she said, "but that means driving twenty minutes to Cavaillon, and I'd rather not drag the kids along. Will you stay with them so I can go?"

Stay with them? Stay alone with three young children?

I really did not want to but had no choice — what decent person would deny such a simple request? Especially from a dear friend who was my entry into the daily life of France and who, twice a day, was cooking a delicious meal followed by superb cheeses. "Okay," I said, dread in my heart.

And then she said, "There's a chicken in the fridge for you to cook for dinner."

Cook a chicken? I'd never done such a thing. How was that done? Did you have to pluck it first? Gail blinked at me behind her thick glasses; she hadn't put in her contacts yet.

"You've never cooked a chicken?" she asked.

I resented her incredulous tone. "When would I? I never use the oven in my apartment," I said. "I'm at the theatre or tired or out. I don't cook."

That was not exactly true — I cooked poached eggs, and I made toast, lots of toast. For much of my life, I'd lived on toast, covered either with peanut butter, the divine foodstuff I was managing to survive without on this long sojourn in Europe, or melted cheese. Or my culinary *pièce de resistance*, melted cheese on toast with a poached egg on top, followed by peanut-butter toast for dessert. And delicious it was too.

Gail got the chicken ready in the roasting pan, showed me how to turn on the oven and about how long it should cook, how to tell if it was done. She kissed the kids, told them to be good, grabbed her car keys and purse — was that relief or gleeful triumph on her face? — and was gone.

I turned and there they were, three little French fiends. No television to keep them quiet and make my job easier. Just their old toys and books, the dusty yard, and me. The hours stretched ahead.

"Story?" I asked, reaching for a book.

We read all the stories; that took fifteen minutes. Oh God, I thought, now I have to get on the floor and pretend. I hate this. How could Gail have done this to me?

We did puzzles and built things with blocks, and Rachel wanted me to tickle her. I could hear my voice feigning sweetness and fun. After a bit they began — thank the good lord — to play by themselves, and I was able to put in the chicken, all the while rushing back to make sure they were still alive. How did their mother do this all day, look after irrational self-destructive creatures and cook at the same time? For that matter, how had my mother coped all those years ago?

Mind you, Mum only had two, me and Mike, and let's face it, I thought, I was no problem; I was terrified of my parents and tried never to displease them. The first time I'd had the courage to really challenge them and go my own way was when I fell in love with the Beatles of whom they fiercely disapproved. I was thirteen-years old, for God's sake, before I dared stand up for myself! Gail's kids were way ahead of the game.

Shrieks from the living room — Charles and Rachel were battling over a book, he teasing and she yelling. I ran in to separate them. "You stop that right now!" I shouted at Charles. "Give that back to her."

They stopped to look at me, assessing my angry face, and turned again to play. The oven was on, the chicken safely inside, perhaps I could actually do some reading. What I wanted most in life, always, was to sink down and plunge into words on a page. I'd read anything — the backs of cereal boxes, bits of paper stuck to trees. I picked up Gail's *Elle*, a guilty pleasure she and I shared, but my few minutes of peace were interrupted by more fighting. I parted the siblings again and, thinking longingly of my quiet little apartment and my quiet little cat, sat down to open the delicious magazine.

The third time, Charles was goading his sister so mercilessly that in fury, I raised my hand and smacked him on the side of his head, just like my father used to smack me, though not as hard. The boy didn't cry, but that sound, the crack of my skin against his, was shocking. This was not my child! And I'd hated my father when he slapped me. How could I turn into the same kind of bully?

I didn't apologize, noting that the slap had encouraged my young charge to leave his sister alone and move to the table to draw. He made some colourful, imaginative pictures for me, so I gathered all was forgiven. A few days before, when the kids were squabbling and I was exasperated, Gail had said wearily, "Remember they're only little, Beth, we can't ask them to behave like adults." I kept her words in mind and was careful not to lose my temper again. Miriam fell at one point and howled, and I picked her up and comforted her. This was better; I liked the image we presented, adorable crying child becoming quiet in a pair of sympathetic arms, and wished a grown-up were there to witness our sweet tableau.

The chicken was pink and runny, but the children ate it without complaint, with some cold cooked rice I found in the fridge and a tomato Gail had told me to slice. These kids ate raw tomatoes; I hadn't touched a tomato until I was at least twenty-four. When my friend returned, refreshed with a splendid haircut, we were all more-or-less fed, and her children had not murdered each other. A job well done. Heartened, I offered to organize her untidy kitchen and asked her to teach me to cook.

As we drank our bowls of *café au lait* next morning, she said she had an idea. "You don't have any definite plans after you leave here," she said. "Want to stay a while longer?"

The thought had occurred to me too, but I hadn't wanted to look at it too closely. I was enjoying being far from my life in Vancouver and rediscovering France. My friend and I got along so well, it was a marvel we still had so much in common after all our time apart. Why go back home to unemployment? But what would I do here, besides be an *au pair* and delivery girl for Gail? Thanking her, I said I was grateful for the kind offer but would have to think about it. And I thought that the answer was no.

There were things about my current situation I found awkward — being a hapless guest in Gail's topsy-turvy house, trying to cope with the relentless noise and demands of children, the very Frenchness of life here which though pleasurable was also challenging. I was worrying, as always, about my weight — trying again to quit smoking and so eating even more than usual, and the food was so very, very delectable. Several times, I'd stolen to the village *boulangerie* to buy secret treats — flaky *croissants* or *pains au chocolat*, even just a half-loaf of divine crusty *baguette* — and shove them down my gullet. When I'd sneezed recently, the waistband button had popped off my skirt.

There was a feeling so small and strange it was hard to acknowledge. Seeing my best friend married with children, behaving in many ways just like my mother, made me feel that, since I was not married with children myself, I must still be a child. Or else a spinster, like the solitary career women my family had befriended during my childhood, who came over regularly to warm themselves at the fire of Kaplan family life. Gail's friends kept arriving to visit with their kids, their many, many kids, droning on about schools and toilet training and where to buy cheap shoes, and I thought I must be the only unencumbered woman in the whole of Provence.

And sometimes, though it was fun living with Gail, I disliked living with her marriage. When we got together with her other friends, she tore into her husband. "Suffer, suffer, flagellate," she said. "That's what Alain does to relax. He gets a migraine." She complained to his face, as well as to her friends, about his relentless, nit-picking sense of duty. I knew what she meant; sometimes I too found his sanctimony hard to take. At one supper, I'd offered him the last bit of a ratatouille Gail had made, avoiding the burnt chunks stuck to the bottom of the pot. "But there's lots left!" he cried, seizing the spoon and scraping onto his plate a sodden mass of carbon. "You come from a throwaway society. Here we do not waste."

Alain had been profoundly affected by a lengthy visit to India; waste of any kind infuriated him. He complained incessantly about his wife's careless ways. "The light is on!" he'd grumble as we approached the house. "You left the light on as usual."

I thought their lives together must be wretched. But they didn't seem to think so. Maybe the fact that he liked to find flaws and she had no problem providing them made them both happy.

At dinner that night, as we devoured Gail's delicious *courgettes farcies* — stuffed zucchini — Alain and I began an argument about the fate and value of marriage. I brought up recent statistics showing that more than half of modern marriages end in divorce. Alain replied vehemently that this was a great tragedy of our times; that couples who marry should, if possible, no matter what, work to stay together.

"You're so behind the times, Alain. We live much longer than we used to, and marriages don't have to last a lifetime anymore," I said, pouring myself another glass of wine, enjoying that welcome blur in my brain, "only till children are no longer dependent. Why should people who can't bear each other stay together?" This was a pointed question. I really wanted an answer.

"Tell me this, Beth," he replied. "Are they any happier alone?"

He'd stumped me, for once. I didn't know what to reply — how would I know? — and the discussion ended.

But then my host surprised me with a proposal. "We have a big problem at the Moulin," he said. "In August, the community is scheduled to leave Gordes and go away on vacation, like everyone else in France. But the assistant who was supposed to drive the minivan has a family crisis …" Alain had a bit of a lisp in English, so he said "hath a crithith," – "…and is going home. We need someone to drive. What about you?"

I didn't understand.

"You'd live at the Moulin until August and then drive some of the community to a village called Le Theil in the centre of France. The family of one of the assistants has an empty house they're giving us for the month."

Cancel my return ticket, just like that, and stay for the whole summer? An interesting thought — but to work in the community? So much to digest. My head reeled. First, most importantly, L'Arche was a Catholic institution, and Alain thought enough of a half-Jewish atheist, an actress who had no experience with the handicapped, to make this offer. Okay, he was desperate, but still.

I found out just how desperate: if he didn't find someone, he'd have to drive the group himself, and he and Gail had planned to spend August camping with the children in Corsica. Gail was livid when she heard they might not be able to go. "We never see you, Alain!" she said. "Enough is enough. We have to spend August as a family. It's out of the question to spend it with the community."

If I agreed to stay, I'd be helping my friends. That would be good. But — living with those disturbing men? I could never be as understanding and patient as the assistants I'd observed, never. And then driving them all to some place in the middle of nowhere that would probably be horrible, with no escape route, for a *month*?

Forget it, said my sensible voice. *You're no saint, you'd never hack that way of life. You can't afford to throw your time away being a do-gooder. Anyway, too many unknowns, it's all too risky. Go home and find work like a responsible adult. Grow up!*

You have a job in November, my adventurous voice said, *and almost enough saved to get by till then. This would be a valuable experience for the summer, and it'd pay for itself — you get free room and board and a salary for your work.*

An extremely small salary.

There were a host of issues to sort out, I told my friends, before I could give a definitive answer. Calling my mother collect, I told her the situation — "What a marvellous opportunity!" she enthused — and asked her to get in touch with the man subletting my apartment in Vancouver and looking after my cat, to ask if he'd continue. And could she see about getting me a temporary driver's license, since mine had been lost? I did not tell her how. Plus I had to find out if I could change my return flight.

My tenant said yes, and the new driver's license would soon be on its way. But Air Canada did not allow change or cancellation on its lowest fares, so my return ticket would be forfeited. Tossing hard-earned cash down the drain. Accepting Alain's invitation would be a self-indulgent waste of time and money, a terrible mistake.

Everything in me — my natural trepidation and reluctance, my automatic "no" — urged me to turn the offer down and go home.

Packing up my little room at Gail's, I moved up the hill to live and work at L'Arche.

EIGHT

Concrete deeds

The first blow of my new situation was that I'd have to share a bedroom. I'd had acute insomnia all my life and to even think about sleep, I needed absolute silence and darkness at night, not to mention privacy and space. Here, a stark white-walled room with two single beds, two dressers, and a chair. Immediately I thought, *This will not work.*

But the south-facing window looked out over the fields and woods around the Moulin, with the purple humps of the Luberon mountains in the distance. And my roommate was Mireille, whom I liked instantly. A fine-boned sparrow of a woman — brown hair, brown eyes, brown clothes — she was, it seemed to me, the ideal person for L'Arche, sweet-natured and empathetic, yet strong. Egoless. The opposite of me. And also, I found out, from a wealthy family like Alain, only her background was actually aristocratic, with a regal "*de*" in her name. And yet no one could have been more unassuming and badly dressed than Mireille.

I wondered if perhaps it was easier to take the risky path of dedicating your life to "the poorest of the poor," as Jean Vanier often said, if you'd come from security and comfort. Even if you rejected the family wealth and never availed yourself of it, you could safely assume it would, if needed, be there.

Mireille and I were the two female assistants for now — the other woman had already gone off to deal with her family crisis — along with three men in their late teens: Vincent, who was, I soon discovered, nice but flippant and non-committal in the French way; Ralph from California, flippant and non-committal in the American way and not particularly nice; and Philippe, who was adorable — idealistic, gentle, very French with his Gauloises cigarettes, his scuffed sandals, and his shrug. It was his family who were giving us a house for the month of August.

At lunch, when Alain told the men I was going to live and work there for the summer, my strange new housemates stared. Jean-Joseph snickered and whispered, Emile continued to munch stoically while keeping an eye on me, Jean-Claude and Hughes beamed, and uptight Gérard got miffed about something and walked out. Maxime was so slow and incoherent in speaking, it exhausted me to try to understand him, and watching him chew, the food sloshing around his huge open mouth with its repulsive teeth, made me feel ill. Antoine started to shout and after lunch gave me an incomprehensible scribbled note. I stood trying to read it, unable to make out a single word, with no idea how to react.

Yet again, I found myself facing the question I'd asked so often on this journey, only with more urgency: *What in God's name are you doing here? This is a mistake*, my alarm bells sounded. *How will you ever make sense of this insane situation? Get out now!*

I went up to my room — our room — and scribbled a plaintive paragraph of despair in my diary. And then I went back downstairs and began my new job.

The first afternoon, I tailed the other assistants, watching how things were done, beginning to learn everyone's needs and habits. They discussed how to deal with the grim, always-angry Gérard, aggressive little Jean-Claude, huge, gentle Emile who was frightened of everything, very slow Maxime who was hated by the others. The kitchen sink got disgustingly clogged and had to be plunged, and the doors and shutters kept slamming shut in the wind, making a deafening crash in the high-ceilinged rooms. But even as I tried to find a bit of privacy and peace by escaping to the smelly toilet, a few moments to withdraw and connect to my past self, I felt something new, a voice inside saying, *This is important. Maybe you can do this.*

Bit by bit, I learned how the July days would unfurl. In the morning, helping any of the men who needed help to dress and eat. Breakfast — chunks of bread and jam dipped in a bowl of hot milk and chicory, delicious. Then, some days, errands and office work for Alain, but more often, into the workshop with the men. One of the foundational principles of L'Arche was the importance of accomplishment through participation in work. At the Moulin, everyone, regardless of mental or physical disability, was expected to contribute. Everyone had a job.

The challenge for each community — as well as in France, Mireille told me, there were now L'Arche communities springing up in Canada, England, and several other countries — was finding real jobs that could be managed by everyone. Our main work was assembling door handles for a local manufacturer. The various components sat in a row of baskets in front of us, and sitting around the table, piece by piece, we screwed them together and piled them up.

Hour after hour devoted to my bizarre new reality: sitting at a long table in the chilly workshop with its bare walls and concrete floor, assembling door handles with Emile the sweet giant, Maxime the battered epileptic, Jean-Claude the small fury, and the others. Gérard brought his transistor radio with terrible but better-than-nothing sound; we sang along to French bubblegum rock while the pile of parts in front of us grew smaller and the pile of handles grew larger. When Jean-Claude got stuck — even this mind-numbing work was mostly beyond his abilities — I went over time and time again to help him. And then someone would empty the basket full of handles; we'd get a new pile of parts and begin anew. We sat and worked and sat and worked.

In the evenings, after the meal and when the time-consuming chore of the dishes was done, we listened to music, read, went for walks. Of course, as the days went by, my scribbling self wrote a lot of letters and in my diary. *"Important things are happening to me on this trip. It feels as if soon I'll be able to write here about my work and the people I meet, the things I do and they do and the world we live in, instead of a continual exploration of my insecurities and my struggle to climb out of them."*

How soon was soon?

After my time on the road, doing exactly what I wanted to do when I wanted to do it, I found this new communal lifestyle exasperating. Now, at every single moment, there were all those dependent men and the needs of an entire community to take into consideration, no independence at all except within the confines of our time together. The relentless accountability of it all chafed, and I kept thinking, *I didn't sign up for this!* It was like a muscle I had to learn to use, thinking first of those in my care, rather than myself.

But day by day, I got used to going everywhere and doing everything with this unruly crowd. Now I was part of a much bigger picture, a participant in the flow of community, without sole responsibility for setting a course. It was like travelling with my family as a child, except that here, to my surprise, being part of a group was often a pleasure.

Still, when my first day off came around, I was relieved to escape for a bit. I went down the hill to visit Gail, feeling much more at ease now that, with my own home and work in Gordes, I was an active part of her world and understood the value of what she and Alain had been doing all those years. Though as before we studied the pages of *Elle*, gossiped, sang favourite songs from the fifties and sixties — *Never met a girl like my little Sheila/Her name drives me insane...* — and convulsed with laughter, I was no longer a tourist passing through. I belonged.

The men wanted to know about my life in Canada — "*Calada*" they called it — especially whether I had a husband. Why was someone as elderly as I, they implied, unmarried with no kids? They made me smile. There was sex beneath the surface of our community, I found, or at least sexual feeling. These were grown men, after all, with the bodies of men, living in close proximity with women; though we assistants never talked about their sexuality, and there seemed to be no instruction on this front from L'Arche itself, I knew instinctively that Mireille and I had to be careful. Despite his psychosis, which I hadn't seen in evidence yet, dark-eyed young Antoine was amusing and even, in his sullen way, attractive, and soon there was a kind of flirting going on between us. Caring, I called it. I cared for him, as I cared for the others. But though I didn't admit it, my body was attuned to him, and there was some heat. I knew it was wrong but couldn't squash it completely. After a week, Antoine gave me another scribbled note which, when deciphered, was about love, and then cornered me in the kitchen to ask if I'd read it. I said yes, thank you for the nice note. "I'm here in the community for everybody, and I like everyone equally," I told him, smiling warmly, flattered despite myself and not wanting to hurt him.

He turned away with a sneer. "You're too old anyway," he said and loped out. I felt an incomprehensible jolt of grief, almost like the hurt I'd felt in my other life when a guy I was attracted to had rebuffed me.

On good days, Jean-Claude was the radiant centre of the community, chanting a cheery "*Oui!*" to everything we said, banging on his broken stringless guitar, yowling garbled lines from his favourite songs and dancing wildly. Occasionally his mood plummeted and he was foul, a screaming bundle of fury and clenched violence. And then, just as suddenly, the fit was over, and he was his sunny self again. Childlike yet manly, with short legs, a big chest, and strong arms, he loved to play with little toy cars and regale us with solemn descriptions of his trips in them to the big city. All of us were "my friend" to Jean-Claude.

***

It was a lot of work to keep this obstreperous bunch going, and, as the weeks went by, I was embarrassed at how ill equipped I was to help. I'd made my way through nearly three decades with almost none of the practical skills that would make me useful here, including the cooking of chickens or anything else. I could not garden or knit or sew. I didn't even know how to clean properly, unlike my mother, who could do every housewifely thing and yet had not managed to pass on a single one of her skills to her resistant daughter. As a teen, to avoid ending up as a secretary, I'd even refused to learn to type and in my early twenties, when typing became a skill I needed, had to laboriously teach myself with a how-to manual.

Here, large meals needed to be cooked, rooms cleaned, clothes washed and repaired — my idea of a nightmare, these dull jobs, such a drain of time and energy. But watching Mireille shoulder her tasks and get them done well, without complaint, I began to consider domestic chores differently. It would be good, I saw, to be able to take care of myself — and others, too. These womanly skills were not necessarily boring and demeaning, it just depended how I looked at them. The male assistants were pretty inept, like me. But unlike them, I began to overcome my resistance and learn.

There was kitchen duty for everyone at lunch and dinner, helping to cook, serve, and clean. I didn't mind the clean-up but begged off any kind of cooking; the thought of making French meals for French people was nerve-wracking enough, not to mention preparing food for at least sixteen. Often visitors came and were always invited to eat with us — people from the village who'd contributed money or goods, potential employers or donors, some of them staring, shell-shocked, at the dinner table, as I had not long ago and did no longer.

Because despite the difficulties, despite the scenes, the mess and smell and noise, the waves of anguish and even revulsion that hit me regularly at the physical strangeness on all sides — Maxime shuffling out of the toilet with a streak of shit on his cheek — it did not take long for me to accept the disabilities of those I lived with. Some of my housemates — Vincent, Ralph, and Philippe — were men who needed a certain kind of attention and care. Emile, Jean-Joseph, and Antoine were men who needed another kind of attention and care. We were in this together; we all had jobs to do, and what mattered was getting them done.

Alain gave me important work on some mornings — the laundry. There was a lot of laundry in a house of a dozen or more, though I often also typed or filed in the office for him. And every afternoon — door handles, and sometimes a new job, sewing large wooden buttons on pieces of cloth. After the tedious routine of handles, being able to choose what colour and size of button felt hugely creative.

"*No faking possible here,*" I wrote. "*Get on with it and do it and watch and listen and try to help and actually help and do the dishes.*"

I copied a quote from Che Guevara and stuck it on the mirror in our room:

> *Permit me to tell you, at the risk of appearing ridiculous, that the true revolutionary is guided by great feelings of love. One has to struggle every day in order for that living love for humanity to be transformed into concrete deeds, into actions which set an example and serve to mobilize others.*

I didn't have to figure out what concrete deeds to perform to prove my living love for humanity. They were always, always, right in front of me.

On July 14, France's patriotic day of celebration, the community ritual, I was told, was to drive down to the village after supper to watch the fireworks. Though I'd gone on shopping outings with one or two of our wards, this would be my first time in public with the whole community. I wondered if I'd be embarrassed; we were so very visible, so peculiar. Instead, as the men emerged from the minivan and shambled toward the festivities, I was proud to be with them, proud to be an assistant to these damaged citizens. Thoughts of Mother Teresa flitted through my mind, both of us kind, magnanimous, overflowing with compassion for the less fortunate of this world.

Until Jean-Claude erupted. Something set him off — we never did find out what, perhaps that the fireworks were a bit late — and he launched into a horrifying fit. In full view of hundreds of Gordes villagers, he began to scream foul swear words, flailing his arms, trying to bite himself and rip off his clothes and then to punch anyone in the vicinity. His tantrum was not just distressing but dangerous; he might easily have injured someone else or himself. Several of the local men ventured closer to see if their help was needed.

Alain, Vincent, and Ralph managed to wrestle him, half-naked and shrieking, into the minivan and back to the Moulin. The rest of us watched the fireworks without pleasure, I overwhelmed with self-consciousness, imagining what the locals must think of these irresponsible young people, unable to control their loony wards. Though some of the villagers, I'd been told, were supportive of the community, others were hostile and suspicious; a scene like this would not help. People stared at us.

When we straggled back into the dark silent house, Alain said he'd given a tranquillizer to our enraged charge, who arose, next morning, blithe and serene. I realized that being Mother Teresa wasn't just about being kind. Sometimes helping others was a humiliating, unpleasant test.

***

After I'd been almost three weeks in the community, Gail and I begged for time together and managed to wangle a trip to Avignon overnight, to indulge in four activities at which we excelled: shopping, drinking, dining, and theatre-going. I bought my Cancer friend a dress for her upcoming thirtieth birthday and we went for dinner. There was no alcohol in the community so, in a huge adjustment for me, I'd gone without a drink for days at a time and appreciated more than ever the kick of beer or wine when I was able to fall on some, as I did during the *prix fixe* meal Gail and I polished off at a bistro.

That delicious taste of beer, the welcome warmth of drink spreading through me once more, brought back my life at home, and I confided in Gail something I'd recently realized: that it wasn't just my feminist principles that were the cause of my busy sex life there, but my job, the lifestyle that went with my job. We'd finish work on the Arts Club stage at 10:40 p.m. or so, I told her, and by 11:05, I'd be standing downstairs in the bar with a drink in my hand, gossiping with my colleagues who'd just done the same thing.

It took hours in the bar for the supercharged buzz of performance to wear off, and by the time it did, I was alight with the buzz of alcohol and possibly a drug or two. By 2 a.m., there was sometimes a guy around to be, in my blurry eyes, the object of my undying love. I had only two rules, really: One, no married men, ever; I would never harm another woman in my pursuit of a man, no matter how attractive. Two, I had to like him a lot, at least at the time. When I took someone home, it was always with the befuddled thought that this was the man for me forever and ever. In the harsh light of morning, I'd wonder what I could possibly have seen.

Gail was a virgin when she married; as she listened, her face was baffled, as if I was speaking Urdu. We'd spent our twenties in such different realities, it was a miracle we were still so close. And yet we were closer than ever.

And then we went to the *Festival d'Avignon*, one of the biggest theatre festivals in the world, to see the new production from Peter Brook, the brilliant British director now based in France. In London in 1972, I'd been lucky enough to see Brook's groundbreaking *Midsummer Night's Dream*, set in a luminous square white box with actors flying around on trapezes, Shakespeare's words never more clear. After the show, I'd walked out of the theatre feeling incandescent and weightless, as if I too could fly.

His new play *The Conference of the Birds*, performed in a twelfth-century nunnery, had a multi-racial, multi-lingual, multi-talented cast playing many different birds, telling a story based on an ancient Sufi poem. Gail and I were enthralled. Watching this imaginatively staged collective creation, my favourite kind of theatre, I felt the familiar call: this is what I do. This is what I love. How marvellous to see it while sitting beside my former acting colleague, both of us rejoicing in our brief hours of freedom.

After the play, we made our way through the packed city to visit a friend of Gail's, Sœur Marie de Jésus Christ, in the Carmelite convent where we were to spend the night. Sœur Marie, a small woman with her face almost hidden beneath a voluminous wimple, spoke to us from a *parloir*, we in one room and she in another, with mid-wall doors that opened in between and a counter below — a bit like a pub, I thought, as Gail and I leaned on the counter to chat and drink lemonade. She told us there used to be a double set of bars there, wooden and iron, removed only ten years ago, and confessed she was happier when the bars were in place; they added more privacy. Now the convent nuns saw people more openly and also had central heating and showers, luxuries "for the young people who are coming."

Sœur Marie told us she felt the call to the church when she was very young but thought her vocation was to nurse the poor, which she did for a while. Then she realized there was little she could do as a nurse and instead entered the convent. "I feel closer to the world through meditation and prayer," she said, "than I ever did when I was out in it."

Even though she was obviously sincere, that sounded like complete bullshit to me. I argued that surely the poor want someone not to sit around praying for their souls but to help them get bread and medicine and houses. Sœur Marie's contention seemed to be that lots of people were out there helping them with practicalities; her vocation was to pray. Gail told me a friend working with the poor in Honduras said she could only do her work knowing the Carmel nuns were praying for her.

Yeah. Sure.

I let it go. Some were do-ers, after all; some were thinkers and pray-ers. And some did nothing at all. It seemed a cushy life to me in the convent. Sure it was severe physically, six hours of prayer a day! But the nuns were protected by their faith, by endless rituals, by an enormous house with walls of stone owned by one of the richest institutions on earth. Almost no daily decisions to make, once the biggest one had been made.

Still, I envied her vocation, the absolutely surety of knowing you were doing what you were meant to do. That was exactly what I was looking for. Some kind of faith would be good, too, the comfort of having something vast and timeless to hang onto — a set of rules to guide you, to tell you what was right and what was wrong, even if you chose not to obey. *How easy*, I thought as I lay in a narrow bed that night, my friend asleep nearby, *to be handed a moral compass*. Without a specific faith, how to find a support system to give advice and solace? An outsider like me had to create her own, completely without a rulebook, except the universal rules I'd learned during my very brief time in Sunday school when I was ten: "Love thy brother as thyself," for example, was one I remembered and which was problematic. How to love my brother, whom I didn't like much sometimes, as myself, whom sometimes I liked even less?

Why didn't — couldn't — I believe in God? Any god?

Well, one simple answer for a start, I thought — because it would kill my father. Dad was an open-minded socialist who believed in peace, justice, and fellowship and had friends of all races and creeds. He was also a biologist who thought religion was a sop created for the weak and infirm of mind.

But I wasn't a non-believer just to please my dad. My own lack of belief in a grand design was not forced. It was simply unthinkable that there was something out there other than the random chaos of creation. What did Gail and Alain, clever, educated people, require from a religious belief that I didn't? Were they desperate for a tribe of fellow believers with the same values? Did they, like children, need to invent an imaginary friend, a white-bearded giant in the sky who created the universe and would whisk them to his lovely heaven after death? They were too smart and sensible for that.

Mostly, it seemed to me, we'd all been conditioned, brainwashed, in our earliest days, they by their Catholic childhoods and I by my atheist one. They'd continued, in Alain's case, or gone back, in Gail's, to a childhood certainty — "There is a God and I am loved." And I'd stayed where I was, figuring everything out for myself, without need for divine explanation.

It was hard to be alone on the outside, stumbling around in the dark, wondering how to make sense of the world and my place in it. Well — because. Just because. No answer possible.

"Love," said Sœur Marie, smiling at us next morning as we departed, "is the only thing that makes life worthwhile." I guessed for her, love meant Jesus or her fellow nuns.

And for me, what did love mean? To this vital question, I had no answer.

On the drive back to Gordes, my friend and I grew hoarse from talking and singing. Gail told me I should be a writer and President of the United States, and I extolled her knowledge of world affairs, her flawless skin, and her memory: she remembered the names of everyone she met, even in passing, whereas I could talk to someone five times and still be unable to address them by name. We realized, as we reminisced about good times since we'd been roommates, that discounting the celebrations at L'Arche, she had been to about three parties in all those years, and I to about three hundred. Not that either of us gained or lost much, either way.

As she dropped me off, Gail confessed that when I moved up the hill, her greatest concern had been my relationship with Alain, given the way he and I challenged each other, because now Alain would be, not just her husband and my friend, but my boss. "What if they fight and I'm stuck between them?" she'd worried.

But Alain and I got along beautifully. A decade older than the other assistants, I was keen, organized, glad to be useful. My boss was over-zealous and over-worked, but he was also thoughtful and practical and had a great sense of humour I'd only seen hints of before. To everyone's amazement, including my friend's and my own, he and I were a good team.

***

August was approaching, and with it not just our travels but my twenty-ninth birthday. The night before the actual date I was invited to Gail's for dinner, and as she dithered in the kitchen, I, the noble but irascible Leo, was soon in a foul mood. Why did people in Europe eat so ridiculously late? I hated being hungry and waiting endlessly for meals, and this night of all nights, I felt neglected and resentful. There I was, looking after other people day in and day out, and though I'd dropped a few hints, nobody had mentioned my upcoming birthday; nobody cared a damn about me. Me! Rage boiled up, and I marched into the kitchen, where my red-faced, frazzled friend, who'd refused any help, was bustling about. "For Christ's sake, what's taking so bloody long to cook?" I snarled.

Surprise! Gail was throwing a party for me. She'd invited Mireille and a few of their neighbours whom I'd met; she'd made Champagne cocktails and North American chili, and eventually, we had a grand celebration. I was embarrassed and relieved; she did love me, after all. For some time after, my dear good friend had fun teasing me about my crabby impatience.

That night, I pondered what I'd built during the formative years of my twenties: an uncertain fledgling career and a few good friendships. What else? No real love life, little money or confidence, nothing solid, just an ongoing struggle for meaning. Looking back on the last ten years did not make me feel good. But though the familiar ache of confusion and insecurity was still there, it did feel less hard and heavy — lightened, perhaps, by what I was doing now.

At the Moulin next day, there was a *fête* for the men who were going home for August and one man leaving for good — and also, I was pleased to find out, for me. Alain told me that regular *fêtes*, celebrations, were as important to L'Arche as daily work. Everyone sang *Joyeux Anniversaire* and gave me a card made specially and signed, legibly or not, by all. We ate and danced. Jean-Claude stood on the old stone wall outside, banging away on his broken guitar; Gérard lay on the sofa in the living room and ignored everyone; Jean-Joseph the cool, turning his back to us, danced alone; Maxime toured the room with his shambling, crooked walk; big Emile bounced up and down with hilariously resigned patience, eyes focused on the ceiling; and even Antoine, who usually hovered around the edge of our activities like a black moth, moved a bit closer. Alain danced with all the women and did an energetic, funny Charleston all by himself.

For a moment, I imagined my boyfriend Richard landing in the middle of this scene, gaping at the goings-on with incredulity and perhaps scorn. Two diverse, conflicting realities — my Vancouver-actress life and my L'Arche-assistant life — were co-existing inside me, though for now I had no problem tuning out the sparkly internal show-off who for some years had run things. Vancouver and acting seemed very far away, though I was eagerly receiving bulletins — who'd been given a good or bad review, who was doing what show, movie, TV series. Jobs I was missing, including an offer by mail from a youthful alternative company I'd been anxious to join, to do a show with them starting rehearsals in late August; I was sorry to turn them down. Friends reported that the TV episode I was in had aired, and my work in a radio play had been nominated for an ACTRA award, which I later learned, not to my surprise, I did not win. My dear Lani had been cast in a commercial as a pair of giant red dancing lips. The real world, my real world, out there somewhere.

Back here, door handles. Dealing with Maxime's falls and Gérard's nasty temper and Ralph's infuriating laziness. It was like landing in a big family in which every single member, including me, was nutty and needy. We assistants showed our flaws when we were disagreeable with the men or each other; when we avoided work that had to be done, leaving it for someone else; when we complained about something that couldn't be changed, or made fun of someone behind their back: one of the men, one of us, Alain. Even Mireille, though I loved her, was too self-sacrificing, I thought. Philippe was weak and scattered, Alain rigid. And I — anxious, edgy, too quick to criticize others and myself.

"Simply living in community celebrates what it is to be human," Jean Vanier liked to say. Unfortunately, being human was the problem.

My parents sent a birthday card with a very welcome cheque and an announcement that the oldest son of a dear French friend of Dad's was getting married in the south of France in September. They'd be coming to visit.

Hooray! I wrote back to thank them and to ask my dad if I could borrow some more money till my income tax rebate came through and I could pay him back. I didn't expect him to make me do so, though. *"Consider this a grant from the Kaplan Council of the Arts,"* I joked, *"to assist me in the exploration of Europe. Thank you for your support."*

I was contemplating returning to Greece — the Peloponnese this time, or the island of Ios — and maybe Italy too, after my August stint at L'Arche was over. Late September and October was the best time there, I'd been told, most tourists gone and the weather and produce at their peak. But I'd need some money to get back on the road as well as to get home, and my tiny salary would not stretch into savings. Plus — I knew my parents didn't mind helping, once in a while.

"I'm a bit trepidatious (?) about August," I wrote to my mother, *"six mentally retarded men and us, their assistants — two French 19-year-olds, a pimply Californian and me - in a tiny cottage in the Massif Central. Make a great film, eh?"*

Or not.

One evening after supper, as I sat smelling the lavender and roses in the tangled Moulin garden and thinking about the upcoming reunion with

Mum and Dad, a painful memory emerged from the shadows. In 1974, my father went on sabbatical for a year to do research at the Institut Pasteur in Paris; my parents sublet an elegant apartment on the Boulevard Raspail, and I flew over for a short visit. It was heavenly to meander around that divine city where my family had lived ten years before. Alain and pregnant Gail had left their two-year-old firstborn with Alain's parents and driven to Paris for a visit with us all.

My parents, friends, and I were chattering during dinner when, over a plate of my mother's *boeuf bourguignon*, my father and I became embroiled in a war of words about feminism, the revolutionary movement that had just hit my twenty-three-year-old self, as well as the entire Western world, with full, life-changing force. I had only recently, while reading my new bible, *Ms. Magazine*, heard "the click," the moment a woman realized how unbelievably sexist our society was, how unjust and skewed to men. "We women," I said, pointing my fork at Dad, the male chauvinist pig, "have always been held back by an unfair, repressive patriarchal system designed to thwart and deny us at every turn!"

It was thrilling to hear these challenging, articulate words coming out of my mouth.

"What exactly has been denied to *you* by the patriarchy, my dear?" he shot back, swilling his glass of wine. "On the contrary, you've been offered limitless opportunities. Since you didn't take them up, perhaps you're just resentful of the audacity of men. Perhaps you and your noisy feminist sisters should stop whining and just get on with it."

How quickly and completely he silenced me. I was twelve years old and defenseless once more, his words like blows. *Sarah Heartburn*, was what I heard. *Spoiledselfishlazy. She's the culprit.*

I excused myself and headed for the kitchen, where I burst into tears. Shortly afterward, the door opened, and there was Dad, looking for me. When he saw me huddled in a chair, he knelt in front, his face stricken, and took my hands in his. "Bethie!" he cried. "What's wrong?"

He spoke as if he'd draw his sword and slay the vile person who'd harmed me in any way. Only, of course, it was him. For years and years, it was him. He had no idea, he never knew, what was wrong.

When Gail and I talked about the occasion later, she couldn't remember my father saying anything out of the ordinary. But I knew what I'd felt, what I'd so often felt: that I was frightened of him and detested him and loved him more than breath. My hope that one day, perhaps, he'd find me worth listening to.

Thinking about Dad made me cry sometimes, still. Wiping my eyes, I bent in the grey light of dusk, picked a bouquet of lavender and held it under my nose, inhaling the gorgeous aroma of Provence. And then went inside to tidy the living room, check the kitchen to be sure all was put away, finish some filing for Alain in the office. To make sure all was well on the very small planet where I now lived.

***

The night before we were to leave for our vacation, I walked down to Gail's to say goodbye. Alain was still at work, so I helped her give the kids their supper. They were particularly rambunctious, enough to make me rejoice, once more, in my peaceful, childless state. After the meal, my friend sat on the floor, dreamily folding a toppling heap of laundry, smoothing little pants, T-shirts, and skirts and arranging them in tidy stacks, while a tornado of children raged around her. More piles of things lay on the dining room table and in the middle of the floor, piles that had collapsed and formed other piles — toys, newspapers, magazines, books, letters, bills, dead flies, dead leaves from shrivelling houseplants, crumbs dribbling from bread baskets. Her husband was driven and self-righteous but also the indispensable engine that kept everything on track. She was vague, floating above the chaos, unassailable and yet the centre around which the other four revolved.

A few days before, I'd been thrilled to see Gail and Alain holding hands. No matter what we saw from the outside, there was affection and respect, their own kind of love. Just as Gail needed her husband's gravity and drive, Alain needed her easy-going lightness and warmth. It worked. *How can we ever understand someone else's marriage?* I thought. *Look at my parents.*

At last the children were in bed and all was quiet upstairs, and we poured another glass of wine and began to talk, as we always did, as we always had, about the existence of God and what was in style this season according to *Elle*: wide pants, long flowing skirts, blouses with bows at the neck and puffy sleeves, not that she and I really cared, but it was good to be aware of these things. We discussed the poetry of William Blake and Canada versus France and our parents and our siblings and the passing of time. Martin Buber. Marvin Gaye. Margaret Thatcher, the newly elected British Prime Minister who, as a rare female head of government, we hoped would bring a gentler kind of politics to the world. Though we agreed that did not look likely.

Gail cocked an ear upstairs. "I'll just go check," she said, and I followed with impatience — hadn't these children taken enough of our time tonight? She went into the dark messy bedrooms, smelling of pee, baby powder, and sleep, silent except for sighs and snuffles. My friend was not usually a demonstrative mother; it was a pleasure to watch her tend her sleeping bairns, quiet for once. She tucked the sheets around Charles, slid Rachel's blanket away from her nose, kissed the top of Miriam's head. Nestled in their cots, they were perfect, with downy skin and solid little bodies, each so luscious and so different. Straightening up, Gail looked at me and smiled.

I was leaning against the doorframe, taking in the scene, when a force slammed into me so hard that I nearly fell backward against the door. A thought, startling and urgent, hit me in the chest. A child.

I had to have a child.

My own child.

I knew it with as much certainty as I'd ever known anything: I wanted a baby. The need burned into me; I was absolutely sure. I had to press my back against the door to keep my body upright.

Gail walked right by me and down the stairs. How could she not notice? Surely I must look different. But no, she registered nothing. Back in the kitchen, I didn't tell her about the revelation since I didn't understand it myself. But shortly afterward I left, and in bed that night, bewildered, I tossed from side to side. First a crazy voice had suggested I leave the stage, and now a fist had punched me in the solar plexus and ordered me to have a baby. What the hell was going on?

If I weren't an actress, how would I earn a living? And even if I decided to go ahead with the lunatic baby idea, how would I ever conceive? I had never, not once in my decades on earth, met an eligible heterosexual man I'd fully admired and respected, let alone longed to marry. If I wanted a child, I'd have to conceive and raise it, somehow, alone. And that would be impossible with no money, maybe no job, and definitely no sperm.

Wait a minute – I didn't even like children. Was I going mad?

NINE

Hands in the mess

On the day of our departure, we packed up the minivan, loaded in those who were coming — a few of the men had gone home to their families for the August break — and set off, driving north into the heart of France.

I'd practiced a few times, but still, being at the wheel of a big van full of precious life was nerve-wracking in a strange country where everyone drove too fast. I'd earned my driver's license only a few years before and didn't have much experience on ordinary highways, let alone French ones. So I sweated the whole way, even with Mireille beside me giving directions. I drove too fast and then too slowly.

"*Pas de problème*," said Mireille with a wan smile. "*Tu conduis bien.*" She was fibbing. But we made it.

When we arrived, Philippe, who'd gone on ahead and would be living not with us but with his family, met us and showed us around. His village was as picturesque as could be, clusters of small houses with red tile roofs, cobbled streets, a village square with a burbling fountain in the middle, an ancient stone church with a high pointed steeple, even a café with — yes — red checkered tablecloths. *If Walt Disney'd had a fantasy about the perfect French village,* I thought, *it would look like Le Theil.*

Philippe took us to our home: La Volière — "the aviary" — an eighty-year-old farmhouse in the middle of a sheep field. Built by his great-grandfather for his wife, it had been uninhabited for years. We spent two days scrubbing and dusting, getting rid of cobwebs, ants' and birds' nests, and a million dead flies, moving in bits of furniture, including a dining table fashioned from a door on trestle legs covered with a donated piece of oilcloth. There were four bedrooms, kitchen, dining and living room, with rough wooden floors and rough wooden chairs. To my shock, there was no bathroom or indoor toilet, only a bidet, and in the field outside, an outhouse colonized by a big wasps' nest that had to be removed by local firemen, though not before Gérard got stung and howled. There was no shower or tub; we'd have to go swimming to bathe. There was no stove, only a small electric burner and a pressure cooker, and no fridge, just a cool basement. If I'd known before we left that our living arrangements would be so primitive, I would not have come.

But the house was awash in light, the windows huge with white shutters that swung shut after dark to enclose every room. In Gordes, I'd asked Mireille, who'd seen the house, if it was old, and she replied no, not really — but then her family home, I found out later, was a 350-year-old chateau. With typical optimism, I'd imagined our farmhouse home angular and modern, small and dark, uncomfortable and ugly. It was the opposite of those things; it was rustic, it was livable, it was glorious. And here we were to stay for the month of August, four assistants and six handicapped men in the middle of a flock of sheep.

No work, no door handles, just exploring the region — excursions, swimming, sightseeing. The main work, of course, would be getting food on the table. This was France.

Our first Sunday, I drove my devout companions to the musty village church and, while they were at mass, passed the time in the café, drinking coffee and reading. What a scene — their wives at prayer, the local farmers in their industrial blue jackets and overalls were gossiping and guffawing, smoking Gitanes and drinking red wine or *pastis*, one with his arm through two loaves of circular bread, like enormous brown bracelets. When we got home, a neighbour appeared at our door with a basket of fresh lettuce and beans.

As our first week went by, I found it difficult to believe that the stranger in the café, the busy woman living in a community of handicapped men in a pasture at the edge of an authentic French village, was *moi*. It was hard to write letters home about my new life, it was all so new. The simple pleasures of the senses that France was so glad to provide flooded me daily with happiness: our milk came warm from a spotted cow named Pollux at the farm next door, our eggs, dusted with dirt and feathers, straight from the hens; the six fresh baguettes we went to the village to buy first thing every day, the fresh cheese, fresh fruit and vegetables, some of which we picked ourselves, the smell of hay and flowers, the baaing of our neighbours the sheep. The ease and simplicity of our days. We shopped and cooked, walked in fields and woods and visited local people, especially Philippe's huge extended and welcoming family.

Under Mireille's constant supervision, I took up knitting and produced a clumsy scarf and then a loose woolen vest I was so proud of, I took it off only on the hottest days. Finally I plucked up my confidence and volunteered to cook; after a few iffy concoctions, including a mushy attempt at Gail's *courgettes farcies* that almost everyone refused to eat, I amazed myself by taking a rabbit that had been skinned, cut up, and given to us by the farmer and preparing a rabbit stew in red wine sauce. In the pressure cooker. With freshly-picked mushrooms, rice, and *petits pois*. My stew was the best dish I'd ever tasted. My housemates ripped off slabs of bread and wiped their plates clean.

I found myself easing into an unfamiliar state of tranquility and contentment. How could I not, with swallows slicing through the hazy, sweet-smelling air, the nearby barn full of their nests, the cries of fledglings through the day? The garden of the farm next door ablaze with DayGlo dahlias. At dusk, the flock of grazing sheep, nearly motionless, soft grey, the colour of the house itself, the sun low over the fields, the sleepy drone of bees in clover, Pollux next door lowing to be milked, her bell clanking. The full moon like a spotlight on the harvest field as we stood in the stubble, watching the harvester whirring and churning, up and down. Walking to the village, single file along the path through the fields, stopping to watch ducklings in a pond and Maxime falling in. Visiting Philippe's uncle's farm for a cold drink of syrupy water and going for a swim in his pond, as piglets, chickens, rabbits, cows, and calves surrounded us and stood watching. Asking his grandmother, who'd lived here all her life, for her advice on a medical issue, and her getting out the thick dusty *Larousse Menagère* given to her as a wedding present in 1928. "And I use it still!" she said.

One Sunday, I attended mass with the others in the decaying little 600-year-old church, the wheezing organ played by one of Philippe's aunts, Jean-Claude bellowing hymns and beaming at M. le Curé, the village priest. All of us gathered afterwards in the square outside with Philippe's family and neighbours, to hear the latest scandal and talk politics. Our Sunday afternoons we passed quietly at the house, and I noticed that wherever I was, Antoine would find me. One day, as I lay reading on a blanket in the field outside, he appeared and lay beside me, his presence a disquieting comfort. I told him he was handsome when he smiled, as he was doing more often, and he smiled again. My insides gave a little lurch.

Rainy evenings we spent at home with the fire burning — Antoine drawing; grumpy Gérard listening to his radio as always; Jean-Joseph embroidering the word "KARATE" in gold thread across the back of his jean jacket or poring over the Catholic sex education magazine he'd bought; the table littered with cigarette butts, coloured pens, bread crumbs, delicate Limoges demitasse cups we'd found in the kitchen cupboard, and pots of the wildflowers I'd picked in the fields as we walked.

All this heavenly calm was regularly punctuated by cries of rage and other sounds that drove me mad: cries, belches, farts, banging, squealing, howling, cursing. It rained for days, and almost everyone caught a cold and was wretched. Maxime, our scapegoat, fell over and shouted because I wasn't watching him carefully enough, then roared with a swollen ankle when someone pushed him down again. Glowering Gérard refused to leave his bed, swore at us for trying to pry him out, and on one outing, fell out of a window. Antoine was smiling one moment and foul-tempered the next. Jean-Joseph vanished for most of a day, leaving us deeply worried and about to launch a search party before he reappeared without explanation, humming, wafting about like a sprite in his own private universe. Jean-Claude played one note for hours on the recorder, and when the others shouted at him to stop, he shouted back, "*La vie tartiste!*" — the life of the artist — and kept tooting. It poured so hard one day our planned excursion had to be cancelled, provoking him to scream, over and over, "*Chier la pluie!*" Shit the rain! Following the advice in a book about drug addicts, I made him a *tisane* — an herbal tea — and took him outside to walk up and down under an umbrella, until his temper cooled.

And yet, none of this pushed me over, or even close to the edge. I'd come to understand that no matter how violent their tempers or how annoying their quirks and habits, all these men faced life with a deeply disarming honesty, a guilelessness the rest of us couldn't even approach. Our handicapped friends read us. They saw us because they looked right into our eyes. They could tell if we recoiled, if we were faking friendliness, if we'd rather not be there. They could not fake anything themselves; pretense required too much sophistication.

I knew now what Jean Vanier meant when he talked, in an interview, about the moving vulnerability of the handicapped and dispossessed, the inevitable change of heart in those who open to them. He wanted his work "to reveal to those who are humiliated that they are precious; that we are all human, precious and loved. Where the poor are, there is mess. Keep your hands in the mess and there your heart will change.

"L'Arche wants to be a sign that peace and unity are possible — if we all give priority to compassion and service."

Compassion and service — not qualities much valued in the business I had temporarily left behind. And that was true in our own tiny society as well, there in the farmhouse, where far too often we fell short of both. Most of our daily disputes stemmed not from the men but from us, the assistants; Mireille alone was always attentive and kind. On bad days, Philippe was disorganized and impractical, Ralph selfish and indolent, Vincent petty and humourless — and I, testy and judgmental. Though I struggled to be tolerant, the habits not just of our handicapped housemates but of the male assistants irritated me to distraction, even their attempts to make music. Philippe played boring love songs on the guitar and sang excruciatingly out of tune; then Vincent would take the guitar and bang out the same riff over and over really loud with an amplifier. And then the record player would blast out tedious French pop. I chewed bits of Kleenex and stuck them in my ears by day, and at night too, as sometimes the bleating of the sheep was so loud, it woke me up.

One day, I understood what some of the music signified: Mireille and Philippe had fallen in love. It was adorable. I wanted their romance to work out, two dear sweet people, but they suffered. O the sadness of young love, so very young, he nineteen and she twenty; was I ever that dewy and naive? I gathered they couldn't be together because Philippe was committed to continuing his education in the fall and Mireille to keep working in the community, perhaps for the rest of her life. They couldn't see a future together, so there was great sorrow. Their pain made me feel very old. And then there were many even sadder songs sung very flat, that made me want to howl at the moon.

But still, moving along the peaceful — the relatively peaceful — track of our days, we kept our hands in the mess; we lived with our demanding housemates, we cooked and ate and did the dishes three times a day as we figured out how to make it all work. I was down to one or two cigarettes a week, and my skin was clear and shining. Even my pulse rate felt slower. A word from my past kept coming back — loose, pronounced "looz." There'd been a skilled movement coach at one theatre company, a Polish mime who taught us to keep our bodies limber; like my fight instructor B. H. Barry, he told us one secret of life was to know how to work hard and stay relaxed at the same time. "Keep looz!" he'd shout, as he pummeled us to release the tension, shake our clenched jaws into softness, force our rigid shoulders to drop. "Looz looz looz!"

Here in Le Theil, I was starting to feel what he meant. Both body and mind were beginning to untighten, learning the grace of being loose.

One lunchtime I undertook the demanding chore of making omelettes. They weren't *baveuse*, not quite runny or creamy enough as demanded by the French, but not bad. Omelettes almost *baveuse* for eleven people — and the cook was me. Then I went out to peg our laundry on the line, watch it flap in the wind and sun, take it down, fold and distribute sweet fresh shirts, pants, towels, sheets. A new kind of contentment.

It rained. And rained and rained. We tried to keep the lid on restlessness and anger by teaching and playing chess, painting pictures, visiting chateaux, abbeys, churches. To our dismay, one thunderous afternoon Gérard gave himself a haircut that left chunks missing from his scalp. That same day Antoine discovered how much he liked ironing and spent hours laboriously tending to our newly dried clothes. It was a marvel to see him so serene.

The sun came out at last, the men went fishing — "*Trois heures pour rien!*" grunted Emile, when they returned — and we all played a riotous game of badminton in the neighbour's field, among the cows.

***

Philippe borrowed camping gear from his family and proposed that for a summertime treat, we take the men two by two on a mini camping trip. We pitched the small orange tent in a field a ten-minute hike from the farmhouse, and the first night, Vincent took Gérard and Antoine. The following night, Ralph went with Jean-Joseph and Maxime, and on the third and last night, it was my turn to sleep there with Emile the friendly giant and Jean-Claude, the manic man-child.

Emile was phlegmatic — always, on the surface, at least, unflappable — so as soon as we'd crawled into our sleeping bags, he was fast asleep, sputtering gently on one side of me. On the other, Jean-Claude chatted and buzzed, crawling to unzip the front flap and look at the stars, excited and speedy as I tried to settle him down. And then the storm started.

At first there were just droplets pittering on the canvas tarp to add to the adventure. I peered out; the clouds massed against the night sky looked far away. The first bone-shaking crash of thunder, however, was too loud to ignore. Then came stabs of light, rumbling explosions, rain hammering our little ark. Four wide eyes stared at me above the sleeping bags. Determined to appear unconcerned, I babbled about ordinary summer storms, though I was really thinking *Jesus Christ get us out of here!* and longing for my safe, dry apartment back home.

"Isn't this exciting?" I sang. "Won't the others be jealous when they hear about our adventure?" While the world outside continued to flash and groan, the tent to quiver, and the rain to seep in under the door flap.

Emile turned over and went back to sleep, but I could hear Jean-Claude gasping with fear. In a burst of empathy for the poor little man, I moved my sleeping bag nearer his and took his shivering body in my arms, making soothing noises. "*Ça va bientôt passer*," I murmured — this will be over soon, it's all right, don't be afraid — stroking his hair and brow, liking the Pietà we made in my mind's eye.

I wondered if Gail had ever endured an epic storm like this when camping with the children. But then, Alain would know what to do in any situation — one reason, I could see, it'd be nice to have a husband around sometimes. *Though really,* I thought, *how often do you need a man to protect you from a storm outside your tent?*

The tarp held, and gradually, to my immense relief, the apocalyptic booms and flashes faded to silence. When Jean-Claude was at last slumbering peacefully, I pulled my arms away, congratulating myself on my nurturing abilities and Philippe on his good strong tent, and turned over to try to quieten my heart. We'd survived, were not even a bit wet; despite my own fear, with two dependents counting on me, I had not lost my cool. How good it'd felt to offer consolation in a crisis, to comfort a frightened man by holding him tight. There was no doubt I was a capable woman. If I could successfully look after someone as problematic as Jean-Claude, I could be someone's mother one day, no?

It felt like something big and rich and wise was growing in me, a fund that hadn't been tapped yet.

Next morning, walking back over the sodden fields, Jean-Claude insisted on locking his arm around my waist. As the others gathered in the warm kitchen to hear the dramatic story of our night, my small friend remained pressed to my side. "The storm was terrifying, but we were very brave," I began, when he interrupted.

"*Couchn tente,*" he kept repeating, "*caressen cheveux.*" Sleep in tent. Caressing hair. He stroked his own hair to show how I had touched him. I explained that I'd soothed Jean-Claude who'd been so scared. "Beautiful friend," he beamed at me.

"*Ma copine,*" he crooned over and over — my girl pal, my buddy — as he kept trying to take my hand. When we went out as a group, Jean-Claude elbowed his way beside me, telling the others in his choppy language that he and I were going to move to the city, and he would drive a truck. Though I turned away again and again, he would not leave me alone. The next evening, as we dried the dishes, Emile and I began, laughing, to dance together. Jean-Claude stormed in, wrenched me away and pinned me to his short strong body, trying feverishly to dance. It took two assistants to pry us apart.

At last I understood. Jean-Claude knew that men and women in love sleep in bed together, and so had we. He and I had spent the night touching, side by side, and were now, to him, a couple. *Ma copine* also meant my girlfriend.

I had toyed with him. Reaching over to take a simple man with limited understanding in my arms, I'd thought only how good it would feel for us both, in a scary situation, to hold a warm body close. I hadn't considered what that gesture would mean to him and was now aggravating the hurt by pushing him away again and again, eventually hiding in my bedroom with the door closed, hoping he'd forget.

He did not forget. "*Amour toi chante amour toi belle cheveux toi,*" he called, searching for me. "*Moi jeune homme.*" Love you sing love you pretty hair you. Me young man.

Mortified, I explained to the others what had happened. "I simply thought I'd stop him being afraid," I said. "He's like a little boy to me." We all knew that holding someone in my arms had calmed me as much as being held had him. "Holding is human," I protested. "Everyone needs to hug and be hugged."

Especially me, I thought. Most of my one-night stands had begun that way — not with a desire for sex but with a ferocious need to be wrapped in someone's arms.

But this was different. I apologized for my thoughtlessness, and for the first time, we had a good discussion about the undercurrent of sexuality at L'Arche, about our own crucial responsibility to make sure no feeling ever flamed into action. I saw that my interactions with Antoine were not innocent, as I'd wanted to imagine, but dangerously flirtatious, and stopped. After a few days, distracted by other excursions, Jean-Claude eased up, though his singsong call "*ma copine*" still followed me everywhere.

I swore that Jean-Claude's *copine* would never be careless again with another man's feelings, or with love itself.

I began to think hard about love — spiritual, emotional, physical. About how recklessly over the past few years, desperate to have and to hold, I'd given away my heart and my body, sleeping with unsuitable men and pining ravenously for other unsuitable men. If I really was going to have a baby one day, a thought I'd tucked away, deep down, but which was still there, all that would have to change. A child needed a father, a family, and so to become a mother I'd need real depths-of-the-soul love with a life partner. And for that to happen, I knew I had to undertake the most difficult love of all — for my own flawed and hopeful self.

A new, surprisingly easy resolution: I would not sleep with another man unless I wanted to bear his child. Which, as far as I was concerned, meant a lifetime of celibacy, because I'd never once met a man with whom I wanted to share an apartment, let alone create a human life. From now on, thanks to what I'd learned from Jean-Claude, I would reclaim my own body and live, perhaps forever, as celibate as Sœur Marie de Jésus Christ. "*The end of adolescent love,*" I wrote in my diary, "*all that stupidity and need and greed.*"

That evening as I sat knitting and listening to Vivaldi in our living room, a gasp of sheer joy burst from my throat. *The seventies are ending*, I thought, *and with them, my sex life. What a relief!*

I remembered the director of a show I was in, who'd tried to get me to sleep with him. When I turned him down, he'd said, sneering, as I got up to leave, "You know, Beth, 'independent' is just an upbeat word for 'lonely.'"

"On the contrary," I replied, walking out the door. "'Lonely' is just a negative way of saying 'independent.'"

On the flyleaf of my Dutch diary, I'd copied out an apt quote by Louise Weiss, a French feminist writer. "*I am never alone,*" she wrote. "*Always in good company. My own. And that's enough.*"

From now on I'd be independent, in the most positive sense of the word. Self-sufficient, always in good company. A truly liberated woman.

It was time to deal with Richard. We were writing still to each other, he more often than I. But I did not want to pretend any longer. It took me several starts to find the right tone for a "Dear John" letter, but in the end it was, I hoped, as kind as I could make it. We'd had a wonderful time together, I wrote, and I was grateful for all he'd done for me. But I had changed on my journey and wanted, when I got back, to make a fresh start. I knew he'd find a better partner and hoped we'd always be friends.

All I felt was the release of being honest, more or less, and free.

To my surprise, as the doors of my body closed, the windows of my heart swung open. Each day I felt more profoundly linked to the men in my charge, who were so beautiful. I learned the main reason for Gérard's sour moods: he'd been abandoned as a baby by his family and had grown up in a violent, overcrowded institution. Antoine's parents were *clochards*, homeless beggars, and he too was raised by the state. I learned the physical causes — a kind of autism compounded by psychosis, brain damage caused by a difficult delivery — behind Jean-Claude's manias and Emile's slowness.

Most of all, what I now understood, when I looked at both the men and my fellow assistants of L'Arche, was that, in one way or another, we are all handicapped. Some of us manifest our handicaps in ways that are immediately visible, in our bodies and faces, how we move and speak. Others successfully hide what Vanier calls our "wounds" behind limbs that function and are labelled normal. But we all have handicaps.

"We are all broken," he says. "We are all vulnerable and poor and broken."

And if there is a more important lesson than that, I do not know what it is.

***

As the date of our departure back to Gordes loomed, I didn't want to leave our retreat, attached not just to this great country and its people, but to its *terroir* — its land, its very soil. Like everyone around us, we ate only what was in season, and I felt a new healthy connection with what was on my plate and in my mouth. One day, passing a doctor's office, I asked to use the scale and found, once I'd worked out how to translate kilos, that I'd gained weight since leaving Canada and so was fifteen or so pounds more than I wanted to be. But I wasn't battling my appetite, struggling to eat less and torturing myself with deprivation and recrimination. There was no point when everything that touched my tongue was delectable. Yet I wasn't overeating. The food was too good to be wasted. It too demanded respect.

A neighbour dropped in to give us a basket of plums and a pot of honey made by the bees in his fields. Plums just off the tree, dark and juicy, and golden clover honey smeared on a crust of warm baguette. Each bite better than the last.

To thank Philippe's family and others in the village who'd been so kind to us, we organized a day of festivities we called *Journée Americaine* — American Day. Ralph and I did our best to conjure up American treats with French ingredients — potato salad, Caesar salad, and especially hamburgers — exotic fare for French families who rarely ate with their fingers, let alone hot grilled meat stuffed into a kind of bun. I made an emergency run to a nearby town to search for one essential ingredient: ketchup. Naturally, our guests, especially Monsieur le Curé, our guest of honour, and Philippe's parents, siblings, aunts, uncles, and some of his twenty-five cousins, arrived with overflowing baskets of food.

After dinner, we explained the rules, formed teams, and played a hilarious game of baseball, French people swinging, flinging, leaping about with no understanding of where they should throw or run to, no idea what bases were, our men especially taking off in all directions, charging madly to the edge of the field and waving their arms in victory. We played with a child's rubber ball but a real bat the young farmer next door had brought back from Idaho, where he'd lived for six months on a massive American dairy farm. He saddened me when he confided that what he liked most about life in America was wandering into the kitchen to eat when he felt like it. "The family just opened the fridge and took something out — whatever they wanted — and sat anywhere, even in front of the TV, and just ate," he said, marvel in his tone. "No effort, like here, every meal so much time and work. It was so casual and easy."

I wondered how many of his compatriots might eventually agree and what that would mean to French cuisine, and thus to France itself.

On our last afternoon, my housemates drove to the nearby town to see *L'Anarque*, the dubbed version of *The Sting*. The other cinematic choice that day was a film called *L'Ange Guardien* starring Margaret Trudeau, the estranged wife of the Canadian ex-Prime Minister, which everyone, understandably, rejected. I stayed home alone and spent the afternoon sitting on the steps in the sun, glad for the sweet breath of hay in my lungs, watching the sheep and the shining white cows next door, reading decades-old *Paris Match* magazines I'd stolen from a barn and writing in my diary about the month in Le Theil.

At the start of my twenty-four-hour-a-day interactions with these new physically and mentally impaired friends, I'd expected to be my usual self, intolerant and even repelled. But in dealing with the world of L'Arche, I was finding in myself an empathy I hadn't known was there. Perhaps this kind of depth was not often called for in the theatre, or perhaps I just hadn't bothered to unearth what was in me. Sure, there were whole days that were exhausting, and times I felt trapped, out of touch, anxious to know what was going on back in the real world, where it mattered. Times I thought the slowness and weirdness of my housemates would push me round the bend. But mostly, there bloomed inside a new self-assurance and openness. I was too busy looking after other people to spend time judging myself.

Without question, some kind of magic was at work.

No way to escape it, we had to pack up and set off south, back to Provence. It made me sad to see our beautiful La Volière boarded up, shuttered and empty, an abandoned shell once more. *Admettons* — admittedly — Provence was hardly an unpleasant place to land. But after the long drive back to the Moulin, I was out of sorts at first. Why was I in the metropolis of Gordes, so crowded and hectic after my village? Where were those little grey-white clouds, my sheep?

When Alain and I met in his office and discussed our summer travels — a resounding success on both sides — the issue of my prolonged visit came up. We'd already decided I'd stay through the end of September, when my parents were coming to visit. He wondered if I'd hung onto my dream of returning to Greece afterwards.

"Another time," I said. "Now it's my turn to make a proposal."

I asked if I could continue at the Moulin until the last possible moment — early November — to get me back to Vancouver just before rehearsals began. Being stuck here in an ancient house full of *handicappés*, I told him, was driving me crazy.

And there was nowhere more important for me to be.

TEN

We are all broken

A few weeks after our return to Le Moulin, Gail had big news: she'd just discovered she was pregnant. Everyone went on and on, how wonderful, big families are a blessing, Alain loves kids, etcetera. But I was outraged and launched into a rant. This was 1979! Birth control was easy to find and use! Four children under the age of eight was preposterous for a woman who could barely cope with three. And what about the poor planet, over-populated, crawling with humanity — more than four billion people now, they said. Four billion! Did they even think about that? How irresponsible and selfish. One — or at most two — children was right and natural. More than that was just wrong.

"Perhaps," said Gail, grinning and patting her stomach, "I'll make you this baby's godmother."

"Very funny. You can't just keep getting pregnant forever to avoid figuring out what you want to do with your life," I shot back, thinking again of my mother and her proud announcement that my birth had shown her why she'd been put on this earth. I was sure Gail didn't think of her babies in that sweeping, self-immolating way; she certainly had no desire to lose herself in her kids the way Mum did. Then why did she keep having them? I could think of only one answer: Catholics.

The universe provided another answer. The following weekend, walking to do an errand in the village, I passed Gail's house, and there in the yard was Alain, beside his shadow, little Charles. The man was bent over, fixing the vacuum cleaner with a screwdriver, showing the boy what he was doing; their faces were identical, serious, intent. As I watched them, father and son, like twins, another thought hit me smack, crack in the gut. Of course — there it was in front of me, the reason to have children: not just to tuck sweet sleeping creatures into bed at night, but more importantly, to share with the world something of who and what you are. Your genes. To transmit your genes.

I had not just love but traits, talents, abilities I'd been given by my parents and ancestors that it was my duty to pass on, gifts to give to the future. To my child. My most fundamental and important job on earth, like every other living creature's, was to replicate my genes and live on in my descendants.

A baby.

One baby.

At most, two.

Father and son looked up at me and waved as I stood smiling from one to the other. And then they went back to work, and so did I.

***

Every morning before breakfast, whoever wanted to in the community gathered in the tiny Moulin chapel to say the Lord's Prayer. Standing pressed against the others in the cramped old mill, lit by candles and dusty sunbeams shining on a makeshift altar, moved me profoundly, as did the prayer itself. I found myself repeating it at odd times during the day, like a poem or a mantra. Like — well — a prayer.

> *Notre Père, qui es aux cieux,*
> *Que ton nom soit sanctifié,*
> *Que ton règne vienne,*
> *Que ta volonté soit faite sur la terre comme au ciel.*
> *Donne-nous aujourd'hui notre pain de ce jour.*

Pardonne-nous nos offenses
Comme nous pardonnons aussi à ceux qui nous ont offensés.
Et ne nous soumets pas à la tentation,
Mais délivre-nous du mal,
Car c'est à toi qu'appartiennent le règne,
La puissance et la gloire, aux siècles des siècles.
Amen.

Amen.

Though I would never admit it to Gail, my time in Catholic France, in a Catholic community, was beginning to give me an inkling of the comfort and power of religion, or of religious ritual, anyway. Not all the men went to mass in the village on Sunday mornings, but most did, along with almost all the assistants, and I started to go with them. Though L'Arche was a religious institution, I gathered there were a few other atheists working in the communities, but perhaps no other half-Jews attending mass on a regular basis.

A former assistant, Ken, who came to visit the Moulin, told us a moving story about his time working at the first L'Arche community in Trosly. A devout Protestant, he had gone regularly to mass but like me did not go up to the altar for communion. One Sunday in church, André, one of the handicapped men, was standing beside him. "André spoke rarely," said Ken, "but when he did speak, we listened. He was a man of great wisdom."

After André returned from taking communion, he tapped Ken on the shoulder. "*Si on ne mange pas,*" he said, "*on risque de mourir de faim.*" If one doesn't eat, one risks dying of hunger.

His words had a powerful impact on Ken, who soon after converted to Catholicism. "A strange choice," he said, chuckling, to me privately later, "because as a gay man, I've chosen a religion that rejects everything about me. But it was something I needed to do."

I too was greedy for spiritual nourishment. But sustenance would not come from swallowing a slim wafer and certainly not from the Catholic Church or from a god in whom I did not believe.

Until recently, faith-based rituals symbolized nothing more for me than family struggle. When I was ten, my mother started to take me to church every Sunday. Baptized and raised Church of England but with no religious ties as an adult, she had a vague sense that I should know some of the hymns she'd sung as a girl in her father's village choir. As an important bonus during these troubled times in my parents' marriage, her decision to take me to church tormented my father, who feared losing his impressionable daughter to the power of religion. Mum and I would put on our Sunday best hats, coats, and white gloves and go off with the neighbours to All Saints Cathedral, while my sneering dad took my brother on some marvellous Sunday adventure involving ice cream.

But the Sunday outings with Mum did not last long; the dogmas of Christianity made no sense to me, even at ten. My father had just told me about the Holocaust, ripping my heart out, and at Sunday school, after listening to the dull, grey-haired teacher intone about "the greatness of the loving God," I put up my hand.

"If God is so loving, Mrs. McNeil," I asked, "why did he allow the murder of six million Jews?" She stared at me with panic in her eyes and had no answer. To my dad's delight and my mother's chagrin, I never went back.

The Gordes church, the first I'd attended regularly since All Saints, was ancient and ugly, its interior gloomy, cloudy with dust and incense in the dim gold light of candles. I came to love my Sunday mornings there — not the service or the sermon and constant talk of Jesus, which were meaningless and irritating, but the ritual of sitting in structured contemplation, every week at the same time, thinking about the seven days since last Sunday. What had transpired? What was good or bad, wise or unwise? What had I learned?

I still could not understand the need, or even the ability, to believe in an invisible all-powerful being. But I saw the importance of a few weekly hours of ritual and routine, thought and prayer. "*It's like a kind of spiritual stocktaking*," I wrote one Sunday after church, sitting under an olive tree at the edge of the cliffs overlooking the Luberon

Valley. And realized as I did so that even what I wrote in my diary now was different. I was trying to savour words and ideas, making sure, before jotting them down, that they were truly what I wanted to say. I resolved to make time on Sundays, and if possible the rest of the week too, for writing.

Since early childhood, sitting with pen and paper had been one of my greatest joys. When I was six, we lived for a time in England, where I'd preferred stationery shops to toy stores. At eleven I won a national essay-writing competition and was awarded a set of Encyclopedia Britannica Junior; the reporter sent by the *Halifax Mail Star* to interview me asked what I wanted to be when I grew up.

"An actress and a writer," I'd replied without hesitation, to his condescending amusement. It was true; I was equally keen on acting and writing, it was just by chance as I grew older that work in the theatre had taken precedence. But then, acting provided a structure, a schedule, an actual paycheque, meagre as it was, whereas the literary life, I suspected, was frighteningly solitary; no one told you what to write or paid you for trying. I'd been to school to train as an actor. Where could you train to be a writer?

I'd brought a few notes for stories or essays with me on this trip, though despite jotting streams of letters and journal entries, I had not opened the ideas folder once. But one night, at the table in the quiet dining room, I got out an essay I'd started in Vancouver about keeping a diary, launched with a quote from Anne Frank: *The nicest part is being able to write down all my thoughts and feelings, otherwise I'd absolutely suffocate.* Though I didn't know how to end it, I worked on it until it felt more solid.

Keeping yourself company on paper

It's like a pressure build-up, that's the only way I can describe it. The cause can be extreme, like fury or grief or the heartbreak and euphoria of love, or it can simply be an idea I need to mull over or an event to examine. Or, often, a list of my own defects. When something hits, I deal with it by writing it down. I'm an analytical person who needs to transfer life experience from gut, through brain, down the arm to paper. To a diary.

I have kept a sporadic but constant journal from the age of nine, starting at Christmas 1959 with my best present, a gold lamé one-year diary with tiny lock and key. There has never been a set routine. Long periods, months, have gone by when I don't write at all, and sometimes, during especially fraught times, I have written several times a day. If I want to find out what I was doing in August 1967, the Summer of Love (travelling with my parents in California), or August 1975 (acting with a hippie troupe in a village in the Kootenay mountains), I can dig through and find out. My past is stored in dusty boxes under the bed.

And other people's pasts too, since my family and friends — and enemies — are also chronicled. I sometimes go to anniversaries or birthday parties carrying an excerpt about them, their deeds and misdeeds. This habit has caused some concern. Others are not as keen as I to remember.

But I think it's a lucky family that has a chronicler, the one with the travel notebook, the letter writer, the family eulogist, the keeper of the family stories and most likely the family photographs and mementos as well.

Why do diaries matter? Diaries bring comfort and sanity, truth, therapy, companionship, insight, friendship. They mean taking time to ponder and process. We diarists are trying to make sense of life by keeping track. As events go whipping by, we can hang on, slow time a bit by taking note. I figure things out in a notebook. I keep myself company on paper. And I continue to write because I do not know how to live any other way. I cannot take a trip without chronicling it, cannot go through an experience without noting it. A kindred spirit once told me he has kept a diary every single day since he was nineteen. "I need to feel my life has some meaning," he said. "That makes sense to me, all those binders, side by side."

Do he and I assume we're more interesting than everyone else? Absolutely not. We simply need to experience life twice: once as we live it, and then again in thoughtful retrospect.

People who know of my habit say, "Aren't you so busy writing, you're not actually living? Don't hang onto the past," they say. "Don't dwell. Let things go and move on!" In most lives, after a momentous event, happy or sad, frightening or wondrous, the impulse is to register it — perhaps tell a trusted friend or write a letter or call a family member — and then, yes, simply move on.

And then there are diarists.

I never understood why I've had this particular writing bug since childhood, until one day my mother handed me a thick manila folder. "I thought you'd appreciate these," she said. Inside were stacks of small notebooks that turned out to be the travel diaries of both my grandfathers. My American grandfather Pop sent my mother his daily diary about a tour through Europe with a new girlfriend after my grandmother's death. My English grandfather meticulously chronicled all his trips, starting with a visit to us in Halifax when I was one year old, during which my father contracted polio and nearly died, an event barely mentioned in the tidy pages.

As I read the ballpoint script of both my grandfathers, I wondered: Is the need to process one's life on paper genetic? Have I simply inherited the journal gene?

Doing the editing work I'd always loved, sitting in a quiet room crossing out and adding, moving words around, finding the exactly right ones, I wondered if writing went to the core of my being in a way acting did not. But writers, I'd heard, made even less secure a living than actors, who were already on the margins. And come to think of it, here at L'Arche I was earning almost nothing at all. Why couldn't I have a skill or a calling that involved a decent wage? It was as if I was allergic to money.

What was I meant to do on the earth? How to take the package that was me, with all my deficits and plusses, my flaws and my gifts, and use it to become a more valuable human being, while also managing to eat?

And while I searched for the answer ... door handles, dishes, laundry. I resolved to do my daily chores with more grace; it was important to make work as pleasant as possible, because it had to be done. Hating it, sometimes, as I did. Tedious fiddly stupid. But it had to be done. Didn't someone at Sunday school say, "God is in the details"?

As I sat pondering art in my diary, Antoine appeared at my elbow. He'd been watching me again. "*Tu racontes encore ta vie, toi? Tu te fais encore des soucis?*" You still telling about your life? Still finding things to worry about?

We smiled at each other. There was friendship between us now, nothing hidden. But he knew me better than I'd realized.

***

In mid-September, my parents appeared. They'd arranged to spend two days visiting us in Gordes, which included treating Gail, Alain, and me to a bang-up dinner, and then I'd take off with them for nearly a week. The three of us would drive to Perpignan, where Dad had a colleague who'd invited us to stay; then we'd make our way to nearby Carcassonne for the wedding of the oldest son of Dad's friend Jacques.

My boss had kindly granted me the time off. Mind you, if he hadn't, there would have been trouble; I couldn't wait to spend time with my parents. As I prepared myself — steeled myself — for their arrival, I wondered if I loved my absorbing parents a bit too much. Was it even possible to love your parents too much?

What mattered most right now was not their unique coolness but that they'd have money. Rich people who loved me — what could be better? Not rich per se, but a hell of a lot richer than I. After a few months of devotion to the poorest of the poor, I was ready for some serious indulgence.

They rented a car in Avignon and made their way to Gordes, where they checked into their hotel. I ran down to greet them — hugs, exclamations, my mother so lovely with her piercing blue eyes that looked right through everyone, most of all me. My voracious dad, even hungrier than usual for every kind of sensual experience, including, always, huge quantities of food and wine in his mecca, France.

We drove up the hill to visit Gail and Alain. They'd known Gail since our university days and loved her, as everyone did, and now they also loved her very French husband and children, whom they'd met on a previous visit. My mother had brought the things I'd requested, unavailable in Provence: most importantly, for Gail and me, a pot of Skippy peanut butter and bags of Dare oatmeal chocolate chip cookies. For the kids, classic English-language children's books like *Winnie the Pooh*, and for Gail, the latest *Doonesbury* compilation, the most recent Jackson Browne record, her favourite Cheezies.

Unfortunately, Mum had forgotten something I'd requested for myself: those sticky yellow strips that hang from ceilings to trap flies. The French did not believe in screens on windows, and the clouds of flies buzzing constantly and landing on the food drove me mad. But I'd have to live with them.

As we drank an aperitif — a superb local Muscadet — and as Gail crunched the bright orange treats and licked the neon dust from her fingers, we had a noisy discussion about French politics, philosophies, drivers, cuisine. Mum told again the famous story of how the first time she and Dad came to Gordes, they'd forgotten Gail's address, just knew she lived on the main street, so had walked along peering into windows. "And then we saw a living room that was something of a tip," she said with affection, "and we knew we'd found it."

Gail laughed as loudly as the rest of us. Being teased about her housekeeping skills, or lack of them, did not bother her at all.

Religion was not a topic my parents broached with Gail and Alain. Not just a wishy-washy searching-for-meaning atheist, like me, Dad's ferocity about all organized religion included the Judaism of his own heritage. "If you're a religious Christian or Jew," he once said, "you must be either a moron or a schizophrenic." Obviously he understood even less than I my friends' need to believe in a deity. But we had a great deal else to talk about. Then we all went up to the Moulin. My parents had been invited for dinner.

Years ago, hearing about Gail's commitment to L'Arche, Dad told me that when I was being born, and nearly four years later my brother, he'd sworn to himself that if something went badly wrong and his babies came out with severe deformities, he'd have found a way to end our lives. "Nature makes mistakes," he said, "but that's no reason to inflict a life of terrible deprivation and suffering on some poor unfortunate." He made clear it was the baby's pain he was addressing, not his own.

But this was the exact opposite of the philosophy of L'Arche — that God, or nature, makes no mistakes; that each person is precious, and everyone, regardless of abilities, is here for a reason, equally deserving not just of life but of a home and work, respect and comfort, belonging and love. My geneticist father's words had not surprised me; I was used to his dispassionate scientific point of view. He'd shown his empathy for the world in his own way, including endless hours of volunteer work with Ban the Bomb, the March of Dimes, committees dedicated to furthering science and encouraging peace.

But it was shocking to realize that in this instance, I was sure my brilliant father was wrong, and I wondered what this encounter with the physically and mentally disabled would mean to him.

Maxime with a friend.

One of my favourite moments before our communal meals was when we all joined hands and sang a short song of prayer. It felt like a new kind of blessing to see my parents seated at our long table, hands linked with Emile and Jean-Joseph, Gérard and Antoine, listening to us sing thanks for the food, for the day, for each other.

Through the meal, my mother was a natural, smiling at everyone. Dad was uncharacteristically quiet, his usually animated face withdrawn, even pained, as he contemplated his tablemates over our simple meal. Perhaps, I thought, his scientist's brain couldn't see past "nature's mistakes" to the noisy human beings beside him, with personalities as strong as his. It occurred to me that my father had once been severely handicapped himself. When Dad was twenty-eight, he'd been afflicted with polio that left him completely paralyzed from the neck down. Only his tremendous drive, his fierce will to live, had brought him back from the brink of death — or at the very least life in an iron lung or wheelchair-bound paralysis — to standing and walking almost normally again. I was thirteen months old when he came home, weak, thin, on crutches, from the hospital. My father and I learned to walk together. Perhaps the physical deficits so in evidence around him brought that terrifying time back.

Despite the pleasure of sitting at table with my parents, I was jabbed by a sudden flashback. The good, plain food in front of us and the loud conversation churning on all sides brought back mealtimes in our Halifax home, which were torture for my young self, a fussy eater forced to consume vile things like Brussels sprouts and meatloaf that made me gag. My brother, who loved food, was held up as a good child with an appetite who ate everything without complaint, which made me resent his favoured status more. Family conversation at mealtimes seemed to revolve around what was still on my plate and my flaws generally, or else there were terse arguments, overt or seething beneath the surface, between my parents. The opinions and thoughts of the children at the table were not of interest. A friend, knowing of my folks' strong left-wing views, had once said, "Your dinner table must have been a minefield of discussion," and I realized that our dinner table was a minefield, all right, though not of discussion.

But one of the vital features of L'Arche was the importance of gathering for lunch and dinner at a long table where everyone was heeded, no matter how difficult it was for some to speak or even to make sense. Breaking bread together was essential; so were listening and participating and being heard. We all had the right to be heard.

Dad said nothing afterwards about our dinner companions, and I did not ask if he'd changed his mind about the value of a visibly damaged life. My family chatted incessantly, but rarely about the things that mattered most.

The next day I took my folks around the village and nearby countryside, pointing out the beauty of it all, proud of being knowledgeable enough to be their guide. That night, Gail and I did our best to improvise evening wear, and leaving the kids with a local teenager, we set off with Alain for a meal in the hotel's two-star restaurant.

As we entered, the maître d' recognized my father immediately. A few years back, when my parents had first come to Gordes, they'd also stayed at the Mayanelle and dined at its restaurant. The maître d' told us he had not forgotten Dad's gusto, his loud appreciation of the food and especially the wine. As he handed us the menus, he said, "I have something for you, monsieur," and vanished. We were mystified. He returned cradling a bottle that he displayed triumphantly.

"*Le Chateauneuf-du-Pape blanc est prêt,*" he said. My father nearly burst into tears.

We learned that on Dad's last visit, when he'd also treated Gail and Alain to a sumptuous meal here, he'd asked for this relatively rare white wine from a regional vineyard famous for its reds. The maître d' had informed him that the *blanc* he had in stock was unfortunately not ready to drink. And now, years later, he'd remembered the request and produced the perfect bottle.

We ate a superb four-course meal, ending of course with the cheese tray — *brebis* and *banon*, Chaumes and Reblochon, Camembert and Roquefort. "Disappointing," said Alain of the Roquefort, lying perfectly sliced on his plate, "not worth trying." And several desserts, accompanied by Alain's favourite Perrier-Jouet Champagne. We sat overlooking the cliffs on the other side of Gordes, watching the sky turn yellow, mauve, then black, our table by an open window through which the breeze grew milder and sweeter as the evening wore on. Everyone was jovial; neither of the couples spent time niggling each other, as they were wont to do — at least, my mother and my friends. Dad had huge flaws, but he did not niggle.

Back at Gail's, stuffed and amicable, we sat outside in the dusty courtyard, drinking Alain's Armagnac and looking up at the Milky Way, the great speckled path across the night sky easy to see from our mountaintop village. The meal, which cost less than $100 for the five of us, showed me once again exactly why my father was so enamoured of this magnificent country.

My parents and I set off, heading due west. I was glad for a break from door handles and the intensity of communal life, happy to be chauffeured around France, everything paid for. We three knew each other so well, finishing each other's sentences, repeating old jokes. Dad loved to crow my line from *Medea* in falsetto, to great hilarity: "WHITHER SHALL I FLEE … FROM MOTHER'S KNIFE?"

As we discussed France and the French and reminisced about Halifax, I reminded them of my time in Grade Five with Miss Hewitt, a desiccated crone who took an instant dislike to me. That year she was forced for the first time to teach French, and at the end of term, Dad had come with the other parents to an open house, to hear us proudly chanting:

LA FEN EH TRA. THE WIN DOW.

LE POO PEE TRA. THE DESK. That one made us children laugh.

LE STORE. THE CUH BOARD.

LE LIV RA. THE BOOK.

I thought Dad would be pleased because he loved the language so much, but at the end, I could hear him in the hall loudly complaining to the principal. "… not even the slightest comprehension of French, the most appalling accent, and she's even teaching mistakes. 'Le store' means a window blind, not a cupboard. It's inexcusable."

Miss Hewitt heard it too. And from that moment on, my fate in Grade Five at Tower Road School was sealed. Dad thought Miss Hewitt hated me because she was anti-Semitic. I thought she hated me because something about me was hateful. My year in her class was so wretched, my mother sent me to one of the only child psychiatrists in Halifax, a cold, unskilled man who made the situation worse.

We all laughed about it now.

Before long, despite the welcome familiarity and affection between my parents and me, and the pleasure of never having to open my wallet, I found it hard, just as in Ottawa, to be dependent again. Here I was in the back seat of the car listening to them bicker, as I had during my youth, including our travels fifteen years before in France. Just like now, I'd sat looking at the back of their heads as they argued about the route, the itinerary, and especially the way Dad drove — fast, like a Frenchman.

"AAAAAH — Gord, slow down, you nearly hit him!" Mum would shriek, pressing her foot on an imaginary brake. My father, his mouth a thin line, ignored her and zoomed ahead. I was fourteen again, appalled by the repetitive drama in the front seat, helpless to make things better. Why stay married when marriage was such unceasing mutual torment?

But on the other hand, I thought, paraphrasing Alain, would they be better off alone? Decidedly not.

In all my growing-up years, Dad and I had almost never been alone together, but this trip, when I moved to the front seat so Mum could fall asleep stretched out in the back, he and I had a chance to talk. He brought up his work, not his teaching but the experimental work in his lab, and told me for the first time that his whole scientific career had been based on a hypothesis about yeast genetics that turned out to be false. "It happens often in science," he said, and that he didn't regret those wasted years, which almost certainly meant he would never win what he coveted most, a Nobel Prize.

"But real talent," he said, as we rocketed down a typical French road lined with stiff elegant plane trees, "is knowing when to stop, or at least change directions. I learned that the hard way."

Respect and sympathy washed over me. I loved sitting beside him as he drove with his usual skill, so thrillingly fast.

He told me he'd recently heard a simple expression that had profoundly altered his thinking. "A French friend told me about examining a job offer," he said, shifting to a higher gear as we sped up, "using the words *Choisir, c'est renoncer*. To choose is to renounce. You choose that, and therefore the door closes to this. If you decide to have this, you cannot have that. For a long time, I lived as if that were not the case."

It made me smile to imagine my father finally coming to terms with the limitations of being mortal. He did want everything. But now, it seemed, he was growing up. I tucked his story away to note later in my journal.

"Have you ever thought, Bethie, about the creation of the universe?" he asked.

"O Man of Science, I have not," I said, one of my teasing nicknames for him. "Tell me about it." But then Mum woke up, and our tête-à-tête was over. When my mother was around, all family communication was channeled through her. It was a gift to have had even fifteen minutes of my father's undivided attention.

Dad's professor friend in Perpignon lived in a sprawling old farmhouse, renovated and luxurious with a huge garden and several spare bedrooms. The night we arrived, the meal, eaten outside under a grapevine arbour, was endless, course after delicious course crowding the Provençal tablecloth with everyone getting merrily drunk under a star-strewn sky. It ended, as dinners with Dad in France often did, with them all singing dirty songs with forty choruses.

Quand je meurs, je veux qu'on m'enterre
dans une cave où il y a du bon vin...

When I die, I want them to bury me in a cellar where there's good wine. On and on. My mother was the only one not drunk, not singing. Her face was closed. She pulled me aside.

"I can't bear it," she said, "Dad, these interminable rich meals, I won't last two days here. Why don't you and I take the car and go off by ourselves? Let's drive to Spain. It's not far."

I did find my father's cascades of fluent French a bit much. But the food and wine were good, the hosts friendly, the house beautiful, and we were going to spend the days exploring the walled medieval ... No, we weren't?

As usual, I came instantly to Mum's point of view. Dad was obnoxious and impossible. Of course we should escape together to Spain.

He was surprised when Mum told him. "But —" he began to say, and then stopped. Perhaps, I thought, he was going to say he wanted us all to be together; that he wanted a chance to spend time with me. But perhaps he wasn't thinking that at all and just wanted to eat and drink with his pals. No point debating, because Mum had decided for us both.

She and I waved goodbye next morning and set off in their rented car, leaving Dad behind to sing as many drunken songs as he wanted. We had better things to do.

Now, long hours in the passenger seat beside my mother, who liked to tell me her secrets. She was especially eager to bring me up to date on the saga of her former lover, the Frenchman Marc, husband of a scientist called Monique who'd worked with Dad in his Ottawa lab.

While I was at theatre school in London, Mum had come from Canada to visit and to ask if she and Marc could use my bedsitting room for a weekend. I'd thought their affair, which she'd described to me in graphic detail as it was happening, was long over; Marc's wife Monique had had a nervous breakdown after the birth of a son, and she, Marc, and the baby returned to France. In 1972, Monique was still recovering from electric shock treatments in a convalescent hospital near Paris, and the exuberant bearded Marc was coming to London to spend the weekend in my room, in my bed, with my mother. Why didn't they go to a hotel? Such a practical solution didn't even occur to me, or, I guess, to them.

I arranged to crash at a friend's so they could have their tryst. My mother was almost fifty, Marc was twenty-eight, I was twenty-one. How lucky I was to have such a hip, youthful mother who, though she loved her husband, could make room in her heart and her bed — and even in my bed — for other men.

While we prepared my room for Marc's arrival, I confessed to Mum how solitary I was finding the year in London, how arduous the regimen at school. And then I blurted all about my passion for Ron, a sternly self-disciplined fellow acting student, straight, for once, who was pining for the prettiest girl in our class, Wendy who wore false eyelashes a foot long. As we put clean sheets on the bed and I packed a small suitcase, Mum listened sympathetically to my tale of heartache. I told her how at Christmas, my grandfather had given me two tickets to Handel's *Messiah* and Ron had accepted my invitation to come, but nothing had come of our date.

I didn't divulge the details — how the music was so stirring that though I didn't want him to see me with puffy eyes and red nose, I couldn't keep myself from weeping. Afterwards, as we stood at the edge of Piccadilly Circus watching the neon whirl of taxis and double-decker busses, I decided to be forthright. Looking straight ahead, heart bashing through my chest, I said softly, "Ron — I like you a lot, you know."

There was a pause that felt like the end of time, as Piccadilly glittered and roared in front of us. And then Ron said briskly, "Well … thanks for the ticket, Beth. I'd better get home."

I did not expect to be loved. And perhaps, I was slowly beginning to realize, I chose my love objects poorly over and over again, in order to prove that true.

Though thinking about it later, I did wonder if he'd even heard what I said.

As we drove to Barcelona, Mum told me that though she and Marc still wrote and loved each other, it was clear he had moved on to affairs with other women. She and Dad were hoping to see the couple on this trip; Monique, who'd made a full recovery and was working at a lab near Paris, was one of Dad's favourite colleagues, and Mum was always keen to spend time subtly flirting, still, with Marc. My mother and father, I learned, had never talked about my mother's obvious affair, though Dad would have to have been deaf and blind not to notice his wife's ecstatic demeanor, the fact that she suddenly looked ten years younger. Once again, my parents in avoidance mode, managing to get through. Well, why not? Avoiding discussion of their problems must work for them. This trip was a celebration of their thirtieth wedding anniversary.

When it was my turn to tell, I informed my mother about the summer of the sheep, Jean-Claude and the tent, about some of the problems with the assistants and the men; we discussed Gail's strained but stable marriage, her house, her kids. Though it was highly unusual for me to hold information back, I did not tell Mum my thoughts, too new and fragile, about a baby or my vow of celibacy.

We found a small hotel in Barcelona and rented a room with single beds side by side; we visited the bizarre mishmash of the Sagrada Família, ate, giggled, walked. Not too much walking; Mum had a "bad heart," and she had to be careful. I never understood how someone with such a bad heart could have phenomenal energy one moment and the next, collapse onto the nearest bed or sofa and instantly fall asleep. It was a great gift she had, effortless sleep, which, like her homemaking skills and her effortless charm with men, she had not passed on to me.

We were sisters, Mum and I. She had two actual older sisters who lived far away, so I'd replaced them. I was happy to do so. She enjoyed confiding in me not just about Marc, but about her previous lover Hugh and the passionate, doomed affair that had blossomed in London when I was six and had briefly torn apart our family.

But I did not want to hear any more about the long-gone Hugh. Or Marc either, for that matter. Or about her good friend Maureen, a married woman with three children who'd apparently fallen in love with Mum and had tried unsuccessfully, when the two of them went on vacation together, to seduce her.

And she told me a great deal about Dad. She complained that my father was bad at managing money, that he was selfish, his needs always coming first. "I follow him from conference to conference and wait on him hand and foot, like a groupie," she said. "What should I do?" It was like watching a woman's consciousness being raised right in front of me, as she realized that three decades as a traditional wife had severely limited her options. But this wasn't just any woman discovering Women's Lib, it was my mother, and the man she'd leave, if she decided to go off and find herself, would be my dad. He might be a chauvinist in her eyes, but he was my father. So complicated.

I listened with sympathy and tried to intone words of wisdom without encouraging anything drastic. Mum had come late to the click we young women heard when we turned into feminists. I wanted her to be fulfilled and happy, but not, if possible, at Dad's expense. He needed her. We all needed her.

"You've come a long way, baby," went the saying. But only some of us had.

One dinnertime, as we sat outside eating tapas, she told me how demanding my dad was sexually. She said my brother had been such a huge baby that giving birth to him had stretched her vaginal canal, which made sex unsatisfactory for my father. "We used to joke," she said, chuckling, waving an oily sardine on a toothpick, "that he was playing his violin in my cathedral."

So she'd had surgery to tighten that area, which helped. Sometimes, she informed me, my insatiable father woke her up in the early morning to have sex.

Part of me was delighted to have such an intimate, adult friendship with my vivacious mother. Another part did not want to know these things, not at all, not not not at all. The mother I preferred to see, the one her friends adored, was authentically generous and caring, musical and open, full of life. There was another mother too, invisible to those outside the family circle — needy, self-centred, suspicious, thoughtlessly intrusive. It hurt too much to acknowledge that one, especially as no one else knew she existed. So I pretended, with great success, that she was not there.

As Mum drove us back into France, I thought about one of the most important talks I'd ever had with my father, another journey he and I had made together in a car. Dad had also come to visit me in London. We'd borrowed my neighbour Holly's car and driven north to the Edinburgh Festival, where we saw several plays. Dad was so tense and impatient that I demanded he take off his watch; startled at how easily he obeyed, I was elated to watch him slow down and relax. We continued on to the Isle of Skye where he bought me a green Fair Isle cardigan that I wore for years, until it was lacy with moth holes.

And all that time, all the hours I rode beside him, I could not say a word about the secret burning inside: my mother and Marc. I had to find a way not to mention it, and so at every restaurant and bed and breakfast, I crammed my mouth with food. Once, when we stopped at a petrol station, I snuck into the shop to buy two chocolate bars and hid in the bathroom to gobble them down. Anything to keep my mouth closed about something that mattered so deeply to us both. There was a barrier between my father and me, a wall resembling my mother.

On the last leg of our journey, as we drove back south to London, Dad cleared his throat. "Bella Pupikina," he said, his eyes fixed on the road, his voice somber, "I know in the past, for some time, I was hard on you, and I'm sorry. I did love you, all those years. I hope you know that."

I sat beside him, hardly believing what I'd just heard. Hard on me? I thought of the time in New York, visiting his family, when he'd smacked me for disagreeing with him, and my outraged aunt threw a pot of food at his head. Or when at seventeen I was nearby as my parents argued yet again about my brother, who was flunking out of high school. Dad had whirled away from Mum and pointed at me. "There's the culprit!" he'd barked. "She's the one who's the cause of so many of our problems."

His remark was so devastating, so unfair, I didn't know whether to rage or weep, so, as usual, I fled the room and did both.

And yet, most confusing of all, what Dad had just said was true: despite his fury, I'd known, all those years, that he loved me. The older I became, the more the secret bond between us strengthened. In some ways, we were alike. And now he had even apologized.

"That's good to hear, Daddy," I said, gazing away from him at the miles of identical row houses flashing by. "Thanks." I didn't know what else to say. Later I wished I'd brought up those unhappy years, explored more deeply what might have been other causes of his wrath back then. But the moment passed.

"I love you, Dad," I said.

"I love you too, Pupick."

When Mum and I got back to the Perpignon farmhouse, I couldn't help thinking of my father as a demanding sex maniac. At the same time, I was glad to see him, glad my mother had someone else to talk to, for a while.

***

Jean-Louis's wedding near Carcassonne was a friendly gathering. After the ceremony, to my father's delight, came a lavish French feast. Though it had been many years since he'd spent time with Jacques's son and had barely met his bride, Dad stood up to propose an eloquent toast to the young couple, with a few salacious *double-entendres* in his flawless French that had the whole room guffawing. He was very good at animating a room. One of his best skills.

Meanwhile, my mother was beguiling the men at our table. Watching her, I wondered if there was a signal some women sent out, like a high-pitched tremor only dogs could hear, that said, "I am soft and helpless and you are so strong and brave, please tend to me immediately."

I despised her feigned weakness, her fluttering. But it worked; they heard her, and tend they did. Whereas, I thought, my signal to men said something like, "I'm scared of you yet desperate for you to love me. Can you figure out how to handle that as soon as possible?" For some reason, my secret message didn't make guys jump up and rush to my side.

They pushed back the tables; it was time for dancing, and, heaven, they were playing hits of the fifties and sixties. I looked around but could see no cute single Frenchmen to dance with, and when "Rock Around the Clock" came on, I could no longer sit still. "Come on, Dad," I said, pulling him to his feet. My father didn't know how to jive, which was good because I didn't either. But we could both twist and gyrate and stomp. At the back of my mind, I wondered about his thin legs, the muscles weakened or destroyed by polio. But nothing impeded his movements. He was completely unselfconscious, twirling, flinging his arms into the air, and so was I. We were a team, a matched set of dancing fools.

When the song ended, we were both breathless, red-faced, and sweaty. I looked around. Everyone else had stopped dancing. The roomful of wedding guests, including my mother, had formed a circle around us, and they began to clap.

Dad and I grinned at each other. He took my hand, and we bowed.

ELEVEN

The time to think box

My parents were heading north to Paris to visit Monique and Marc. What an encounter that would be — Dad with his former colleague and her husband, my mother's former lover. Honestly, it was like a French farce; I was glad to bid their complications goodbye and get the train back to the simplicity of life at the Moulin. Happy to be back in my room with Mireille, flinging open the shutters in the morning to look down at the quiet village, the soft light of Provence, the chateau pink in the morning sun, the Luberon mountains dark against the horizon. Listening to the bell tower clock which sounded all day, telling us the time at half hour intervals, and to the autumn wind, so vicious and well-known that it had a name — the *mistral* that tore through our bones. I pulled on my favourite work clothes, a pair of baggy jean overalls, and started peeling a hillock of potatoes. I was home.

Alain had found us new work, assembling sachets of lavender, much nicer than door handles and buttons, and shortly after my return, he launched an important new initiative: finding work outside the community for the men. Jean-Joseph was sent to apprentice with a housepainter, which was a good fit, but when Emile went to work the *vendanges* — the grape harvest — the irate farmer drove him right back, shouting at Alain about the useless *handicappé*. Luckily Emile did not hear the intolerant man. At least, we rushed to distract him and hoped he did not.

On my first day off, I walked to the Abbaye de Sénanque, a much-photographed twelfth century Cistercian abbey tucked in a valley beneath the hills, in the middle of a vast field of lavender; though the mauve crop had been harvested, the intoxicating scent lingered in the air. As I wandered through the 700-year-old rooms, it struck me that in Canada, nature, or what God had made, was magnificent, but what man had made was almost entirely ugly. Here in Europe, one could not help but celebrate the divine gifts of human creativity — buildings, art, even food. Food for the soul.

I'd come to the Abbaye in late afternoon; at dusk the monks, who still lived and worked there, filed into the chapel for vespers, so I sat to listen. They lined up on either side of the plain darkening room and sang Gregorian chant, overlapping harmonies reverberating from the ancient ivory-coloured stone walls. *It's easy*, I thought, *to understand dedicating your life to God when you hear hallowed music in the stillness and solemnity of an ancient chapel*. The experience was so transcendent — the music, the building, the lavender, the light — I thought I'd glide out the windows and levitate into the crimson sky above Gordes.

Instead I walked back to the Moulin on a cloud of song, to discover that Antoine had had a tantrum and broken some dishes, and the milk for the morning had gone sour. None of it mattered. I made a *tisane* as Alain had taught me, sticking bunches of herbs fresh from the garden — camomile and mint, *verveine* and *tilleul* — verbena and linden — in the pot, letting them steep in boiling water and stirring in a spoonful of local lavender honey, so sweet and delicious I spread some thickly on one slice of bread and then another. Too much pleasure.

But the serene aura of Sénanque vanished later in bed, as full of recrimination I kneaded the rolls of flab on my belly. After all this time in France learning healthy habits, why was I still not in control of my eating? Why did this soft body cause me so much torment, when it was the only one I'd ever have? In my early teens, it was just there, disdained because it had only provided me with small breasts; boys desired what they saw in *Playboy* magazine, and I was deficient in that area. Otherwise, my body was merely a satisfactory machine beneath my head. Until in an instant, that changed.

With the wind pushing at the closed shutters and Mireille sleeping silently, curled up like a dormouse, I replayed my troubled history with food.

It started in university in 1968, as I stood by the snacks table at a party in a basement rumpus room. "How much do you weigh, anyway?" he'd asked.

Eighteen with long straight hair, wearing a formfitting dark green wool dress knitted for me by my mother's best friend, I was drinking beer and crunching on chips and dip and other treats when the boyfriend of a petite, stylish classmate came over and gave me a concerned pat on the shoulder.

"Beth," he said. "Stop eating."

I froze with a mouthful of bread and cheese.

"I noticed you spending a lot of time over here," he went on, and asked about my weight. In that instant, following my foremother Eve, I bit the apple of consciousness. Until then, I'd never had a moment of anxiety about the pounds on my body. Waif-like models had not yet gashed a hole in my psyche. For me, the desirability of thinness was simply not on the radar. I replied to my friend's question without hesitation, because I'd just been for a check-up.

"A hundred and forty-three pounds," I said. A good weight, according to my doctor, for a teenaged female nearly five foot nine. "Why?"

"Whoa!" he exclaimed, chuckling and raising his eyebrows. I looked at his midge of a girlfriend who probably weighed fifty pounds less, and, just like that, I felt like a hulk, a bloated giant with quivering mounds of belly and hips. I left the party, went home to change into a looser dress, and came back to stand again by the snacks table. This time, I was secretive as I slid food into my mouth.

Instantly, the cyclical pattern was set: a desperate need to eat — not celery, fruit, or salad but bread and peanut butter, cheese and chocolate — followed by rage, self-loathing, and a resolve to improve, the back of my diaries filled with columns of calorie calculations which might or might not have been correct:

Pizza: 200.

Cheese and crackers: 300.

Stick of gum: 5.

And then other kinds of lists, like the one where you kept track of portions: *Bread IIIIIII; Meat IIII; Fat IIII; Fruit II. Veg III. Wine II.* Those didn't work either.

While the guests conversed outside at the end of my twenty-first birthday party, a dinner hosted by my parents in their garden, I stood in the kitchen gobbling leftover chunks of my mother's famous cheesecake from their plates.

That summer, before going off to theatre school, I fasted for days to lose weight quickly, so I could begin this important year slender and confident. But as the months passed in London, I felt so alone and lost that only food afforded solace. The sole items of nourishment ever allowed in the small fridge in my bedsitting room were yogurt, lettuce, and Cox's Orange Pippins, the best apples ever. When I got hungry, which was often, I would climb through the house's communal bathroom window onto the roof and in through my neighbour Holly's bedroom window. Skinny Holly from South Africa, who worked in finance and was always at the office, stocked chocolate digestive biscuits, buns, cheese, all kinds of delicious things. I would devour her treats, then go out to buy replacements and leave them on her doorstep. Luckily, she was amused by this odd arrangement.

I expanded. For one role at school, my costume grew so tight before we opened that the frowning seamstress had to let it out. The director frowned too.

The day I ate half a loaf of Holly's bread before rehearsal, I felt so disgusting and disgusted, it occurred to me that I should try to rid my body of the excess. In the freezing school bathroom, I knelt by the toilet and stuck my finger down my throat. I had never heard the word "bulimia," did not know this sordid activity had ever been carried out by other girls; I thought I'd invented it all by myself. But in any case, I could not do it; it hurt. I never tried again, just got fatter and wore loose shapeless clothing to hide the bulges, even, for a long time, a plaid maternity top. When I went to a London doctor about a plantar wart, he looked sharply at me as I peeked around the door and sidled into the room. "What are you so afraid of?" he asked. "Why are you hiding your body?"

I had no answer. How had he instantly sussed out my shame? In his practice, I realized, he must have witnessed many self-conscious, starving girls. In the early seventies, almost all of us young females in the Western world felt the same excruciating pressure.

Up, down, down, up; I spent my twenties ballooning and shrinking, from a scrawny 130 pounds at one point to a bulky 175 at another, as awkward and self-deprecating as Lynn Redgrave in one of my favourite movies, *Georgy Girl*. Vancouver casting directors called me when they wanted a "big-boned comedienne," but then, for a sexy role, I would lose weight fast, feel svelte and desirable — Charlotte Rampling, here I come! — and just as quickly gain it all back, and more. I wrote in my diary that my first play would be called "*The Loneliness of the Long-Distance Eater. A character sits in the kitchen and eats continuously for an hour. The curtain falls. Critics compare it to Beckett and Pinter.*"

On my worst days, the mirror told me my bum, belly, and thighs were jiggly and repulsive, and yet my pathetic breasts, a woman's most important sexual attribute, were still — how was this possible? — way too flat. I cursed skeletal Twiggy who'd ruined the lives of so many of us with appetites and normal womanly curves. My lack of will power, and the body that was the result, filled me with contempt.

One day I was moved to read something Eleanor Roosevelt had said: *"No one can make you feel inferior without your consent."* Why had I consented to feeling profoundly inferior, not because of being a horrible person, but because I wasn't capable of starving myself into the stick-like weight approved of by fashion designers and *Vogue* magazine?

How to have the courage to throw the harsh judgment of my peers — and more importantly my own — out the window?

Could I develop that courage? Nothing mattered less at L'Arche than those despised extra pounds around my middle. Couldn't I learn to just enjoy food and not obsess? To love my own miraculous, magnificent body?

Perhaps I could. Perhaps, one day, I would.

***

Gordes grew colder. I spent many evening hours knitting myself a thick sweater, undoing and redoing and casting on again. By day I was absorbed in the urgent daily concerns of the community — the always backed-up sink and the freezing atelier, personality struggles and nasty disagreements among the assistants, serious fights among the men, their new and on-going health problems and budget issues and what, oh bloody what, to cobble together for our daily three-course lunches and dinners.

At night, before picking up my knitting needles, I spent a lot of time writing letters to Canada and poring over the ones sent to me. After his humiliating election defeat, poor Pierre Trudeau was enduring the very public demise of his marriage; a friend sent me shocking tabloid pictures of Margaret at trendy Studio 54 in New York, one of her sitting on the floor in a mini-skirt, clearly not wearing underpants. A nude beach in Greece is one thing, I thought; a Manhattan club full of photographers is another, and she the mother of three little boys and still the first lady of Canada. I felt sorry for Pierre.

A Vancouver director sent me the script of a new play by one of my favourite playwrights, the Quebecois Michel Tremblay, and an offer to appear in it the following March alongside Janet and two other dynamo actresses. "*Shiver me timbers*," I wrote to my mother, "*the thought of spending five minutes in an elevator with those three is frightening enough, let alone a play.*" But when I read the work, I didn't like it at all, the playwright haranguing the audience about injustice to artists in his native province, and with relief, I declined.

Gail lent me a book about the making of Peter Brook's *Conference of the Birds*, the play we'd seen in Avignon, and I read it hungry for information about this inspiring director and his troupe. But what emerged was not at all what I'd imagined. The book painted the picture of a man who, in search of some elusive catharsis, had dragged a bunch of talented, eager actors around Africa, subjecting them to all sorts of tortures: heat, disease, exhaustion, playing improvised material under unbelievably difficult circumstances. It was disillusioning.

If even world-famous Peter Brook was confused and heedless, where were the good directors doing theatre as it should be done? And what was the place of women in all this? I'd noted in my diary something Simone de Beauvoir had once said: "*As long as [a woman] still has to struggle to become a human being, she cannot become a creator.*"

Was that true? If it was, why would a young woman bother to attempt creating anything at all? *But despite our struggles, Simone, women do create*, I thought. In my minuscule way, though almost nothing tangible remained, surely I had created something. Audience members had told me what my work meant to them, that I'd made them laugh, cry, think. That was a gift worth celebrating, no?

The *Three Sisters* director Kathryn, an artist I liked and respected, also sent a letter, telling me we'd start work in mid-November with a week of improvisation, diction classes, and lectures about Russia. My actress self, buried beneath cooking pots and sachets of lavender, stirred again. Kathryn hadn't told me yet which part I was to play, but

I'd guessed. Probably not the oldest sister Olga, I was too young, or the youngest Irina whom I'd played at theatre school; now I was too old. "Moscow!" Irina was always sighing with her sisters, longing for something she would never have. "Moscow!" I longed to play Masha, the starring role, but she wasn't right for me; I was not a romantic lead, not a leading lady. So that left Natasha, the petty bourgeois wife of brother Andrey.

Let the sisters whine; I could be a bitch if need be. It was delicious to contemplate, and part of me itched to get back to work, my real job of learning lines, creating a persona who was both me and not me and making an intense bond with a group of fellow artists, which would last only until the show ended.

But all that was far away, in my other life. Right now there were howls from the living room to deal with.

Along with the daily quarrels and screw-ups, we faced one mounting problem: Jean-Claude was in crisis. Among other issues, he had grown to dislike his name. "*Moi grand monsieur!*" he'd rage. His explosions had become more frequent and violent; small body wracked with fury, face blotchy and red, he'd throw things and attack the others. I was relieved to hear from the psychiatrist who visited the Moulin once a week that this was provoked by something long buried inside and not from a recent trauma in a tent. He advised us that Jean-Claude should return to the large mental hospital where he'd grown up, so his medications could be adjusted in a safe environment.

Mireille and I visited him there, a concrete, factory-like institution, two thousand inmates in clinical halls with locked doors, a barrage of bright lights, a loud TV set blaring. In the cavernous visiting room, Jean-Claude looked more than ever like a lost child. But, "*Ma copine!*" he called, when he saw me. And then — "*Beaucoup peine moi.*"

Most of the men at the Moulin had lived here, some for many years. As we drove away, I felt a profound sorrow for those who had survived that desolate place and for those who were still there.

Just before Jean-Claude's return, Alain had an interesting idea: since he didn't like his own name, what if we tried calling him by another? When he arrived back, already calmer on new meds, Alain asked him what name he'd like to be called now. Jean-Claude chose the name of a compassionate L'Arche assistant who'd stayed a few days at the Moulin: Tom. We all called him Tom, and incredibly, it worked; the spasms of rage stopped. Jean-Claude was angry. Tom was not.

In mid-October, I suggested we invite our Gordes friends and neighbours to a new kind of celebration. Based on the success of our *Journée Americaine* in August, why didn't we teach the locals what Hallowe'en was? Ralph and I did our best to explain to baffled French faces what the rituals of October 31 meant *chez nous*. Playing dress up and eating candy sounded good to everyone.

Finding costumes, inventing games, carving pumpkins, and making prizes consumed our evenings. I decided to produce a little play. The French love that kind of thing, I'd found; in any kind of gathering, including at L'Arche, someone or a group would likely perform a silly skit. The challenge here was presenting any kind of theatre starring my cohabitants, who were opinionated, stubborn, and, to put it mildly, erratic. Alain suggested adapting a La Fontaine fable, but instead I cobbled together a rudimentary script, based on the talent I had — "The Lost Princess." Emile, usually antisocial but now eager to be a star, was cast as a princess who got lost on a journey and had various encounters, giving me a chance for a few random scenes with some of the other men. Our heroine ended up in the loving embrace of her family — a scene in which everyone could participate. It was Emile's idea to be a princess rather than a prince; he wanted long hair. We found a big piece of material that would wrap like a skirt around his huge frame and equipped him with a straw hat from which dangled two long braids of yellow wool. He was enchanted.

When it came to costumes for the rest of us, not for the play but for the party afterward, I proposed that my fellow female assistants and I dress up as Charlie's Angels, looking forward to approximating the magnificent sweep of Farrah Fawcett's puffy hair. But my French colleagues didn't care for this idea and went their own way. On the night, most of the men ended up wearing women's nightgowns, and the women wore men's pajamas; Jean-Joseph was hilarious in a little girl's dress, his hair in pigtails. Alain appeared in a strange get-up; he wore a bathing cap covering his head and a thick scarf wrapped several times around his neck. When I asked whom he was portraying, he took me aside.

"A thircumthized penith," he said.

Behind us, Tom was singing at the top of his lungs, banging like Elvis on his wrecked guitar. Emile, who after the disjointed performance of our playlet had graciously received the applause as his due, was chewing the apple he'd just bobbed for, still wearing his straw hat and long blonde braids. In the dining room, Maxime was devouring my attempt at pumpkin pie, his broken teeth covered with orange paste.

How could I ever leave this place?

Yet there were bad times still with no escape, long difficult hours when I was in a foul mood, swimming in self-pity, furious at Alain's self-righteousness, Ralph's indolence, Vincent's passivity, working myself into a rage at the men, at myself. Some days it seemed everyone in the community was cranky and mean-spirited with exhaustion, strain, *la merde*. Autumn was windy and wet; the roof leaked and the house flooded, the minivan broke down, the men glowered, Gérard and Tom embarked on several noisy fistfights, and everyone, as usual, was mean to Maxime. Several times I thought I'd run screaming out the door, not just because of the noise and mess, but more, the pressure of constant, unrelenting caretaking, the limitless patience needed.

And yet, even as I exploded with irritation, I knew these annoyances were an ordinary part of the day, the way life was here; things would soon settle, and we'd be fine again. It helped, mind you, that I didn't have much more time at L'Arche. The end of my work here was not far off.

One night, the last straw — in a high wind, the electricity and heating conked out, and we were left in freezing darkness. After our charges were in bed, I rooted around in the pantry, found a dusty bottle of *cerises à l'eau de vie* — cherries in brandy — and snuck it into our room, where all the assistants, wrapped in blankets, ate the marinated fruit by candlelight and regaled ourselves with stories of how we'd murder the men.

I was still *enervée* — exasperated — the next day; I just did not want to be in a cold old building surrounded by damaged people. I'd had enough, I wanted to be normal. Normal! Alain wisely sent me out for a walk, and I went straight to Gail's, who, though hardly anyone's definition of normal, at least spoke comprehensibly and chewed with her mouth closed. The children were at school, the house quiet, and she cheered me up with a cup of tea and a chat in my own language, in complete sentences, with a grown-up. We reminisced about the William Blake class we'd both taken at Carleton with a favourite professor, and she pulled out a book of Blake's mystical poems and paintings to examine. We discussed whether she looked better with short hair or long, and boys we'd loved and lost, and the importance of faith.

Gail helped me touch base with myself. I regained a sense of perspective and went home. That night, I had a dream in which I, a lifelong arachnophobe, deliberately touched a large hairy spider with my foot.

As my stay wound down, my best friend and I had little time together, though we did make a quick trip to the Carmelite convent in Avignon for a last visit with Sœur Marie. To entertain her, I showed her the sweater I'd just finished knitting; after weeks of work, it had giant shoulders that would drown a football player. "Perhaps," she said, wiping away tears of merriment, "you should put it on display somewhere."

I gave my misshapen creation away. Knitting, it seemed, was not my calling, though I was glad my efforts had made the sweet nun laugh. Almost worth all those hours.

I had come to an even greater appreciation of Gail's courage in throwing herself headlong into a foreign country — and a foreign family. Her in-laws, Alain's snooty parents from the *haute bourgeoisie*, I now knew, did not like anything about her, not her wondrous laugh, her kind heart, or her generosity. They were grateful for the grandchildren she was heaping upon them, but that was all, and they did their best to snub and exclude her at every opportunity. Yet it was clear she'd never return to Canada even to have her babies, as several of her North American friends also married to Frenchmen had done, and she would not force a split from Alain's exasperating family, which I'd have been tempted to do. She just carried on with her bouncy children and her fussy, duty-ridden, remarkable husband. I still did not envy her for a moment, but more than ever, I admired her.

My mother had left behind a *Harper's Bazaar* magazine, and during one of my visits, Gail read aloud that the new miracle formula for the over-thirties face was chicken embryos. "Hmm," she said, inspecting her skin in the mirror, "where in beautiful downtown Gordes do you suppose we can procure some chicken embryos?" As always, we choked with laughter.

As I left to make the uphill trek to the Moulin, she gave me another book, a self-help book I'd never have chosen for myself: *I'm OK — You're OK* by Thomas Anthony Harris. I copied a particularly pertinent quote from Paul Tillich into my notebook.

He wrote that grace *"strikes us when year after year, the longed-for perfection of life does not appear, when the old compulsions reign within us as they have for decades, when despair destroys all joy and courage. Sometimes at that moment a wave of light breaks into our darkness, and it is as though a voice were saying, 'You are accepted, accepted by that which is greater than you ... Simply accept the fact that you are accepted.'"*

Simply accept the fact that you are accepted. What a beautiful sentence. What a beautiful, impossible thought.

Closing the book before bed, I brought back an experience during my family's stay in France in 1964. Just after we'd arrived to spend a year in Europe, my father had sent me off on a two-week camping trip with a group of French-speaking girl guides, reasoning that this would immerse his daughter in a new language and help her learn it quickly. The whole experience had been a horror for me; I, a fearful girl who hated camping, found myself on my fourteenth birthday in a tent in a field in the French Alps with a group of strangers, avid hikers speaking a language I did not understand and doing vigorous things I loathed doing. Despite the guides' kind efforts, I remained as wretched at the end as I'd been at the beginning.

On our last day, all the newbies, even *la Canadienne*, were given an adjective. Mine was *pressée* — in a hurry, impatient. My impatience had been a shortcoming, a character flaw since childhood, as I rushed to scramble away from where I was to somewhere else, which would surely be better. I'd had a lifelong fantasy of being special, one of the chosen few, given gifts to accomplish great things for mankind. I saw now that this elevated feeling meant I never really landed, was never fully present in a specific time and place. Instead, I was waiting to be elsewhere, somewhere more important, to fulfill my mission, whatever it was.

The hippies went on about "Be Here Now," but I'd always rather "Be Somewhere Better, Thank You."

At the Moulin, there'd been no time, no possibility of holding myself apart and above; like everyone else, I had to plunge the sink, hang up the laundry, dry the dishes. If I was special, so were Tom and cranky Gérard and all the others. We all had a place, and perhaps even a mission, on this planet.

But now I also saw that being *pressée* had its advantages. Well-organized, with a strong dislike of wasted time, I'd worked to change the way chores were done in the kitchen and the office so they functioned better, to everyone's advantage, a legacy that would last long after my departure. *Efficace* — effective, efficient — a new adjective had been applied to me here, one I liked much more.

Fifteen years after the guides, I'd not only survived a sojourn in a French field but had flourished there.

Ithaka gave you the marvellous journey.
Without her you would not have set out.
She has nothing left to give you now.

And if you find her poor, Ithaka won't have fooled you.
Wise as you have become, so full of experience,
You will have understood by now what these Ithakas mean.

I didn't know what my journey had meant. But it had indeed been marvellous, and I was full of experience and even wiser. Definitely wiser.

***

At the end of my stay, I knew Alain would bring me in to his office and ask me to speak in front of all the other assistants about what being at L'Arche had meant to me. This was an important L'Arche tradition. I wrote in my diary that my concerns before coming to the Moulin had been correct: I was not a saint or even a particularly good person. But as I wrestled daily with my insecurity, my temper, petty resentments, and fears, I was now also aware of myself as good-hearted, *efficace*, a good organizer and team player with other important assets, like empathy and a sense of humour. What was needed in this place was obvious: patience, hard work, love. Even if sometimes I wasn't so good at the first two, I knew now I had a lot, really a lot of love to give.

What I'd managed to contribute had helped, had made a positive contribution to a tiny piece of the planet. I was valued here, not by being beautiful or successful, but by having something worthwhile to share. I was valued by men who were themselves, on the surface, neither beautiful nor successful. In fact, their looks had frightened and repelled me once. Now, theirs were the most unguarded faces on earth, and their affection and trust meant everything.

Unlike Mireille, there was no notion in my mind to devote myself to this work; I would be glad to return to Vancouver and fulfil my obligation to do the Chekhov play. In these months far from my profession, I'd realized how much there was to appreciate about the theatre, which did contribute, in its colourful way, to bettering the world. Of course, what show business accomplished for good was not as immediately discernible as aiding the handicapped. Human beings most needed food and shelter and loving kindness.

But, as I'd learned in Greece with its ancient amphitheatres, people had always needed to better understand their own lives by seeing other lives played out before them. At its best, the theatre brought spectators together for a communal experience that gave them insight into human needs and emotions. It reflected their own humanity back to them, showed them themselves in a clearer light.

And not just the theatre; I brought back other transcendent artistic experiences that had enriched and transported me, like watching the exquisite ballerina Suzanne Farrell dance, weightless as a beam of light. Truth and clarity and rapture were the gifts given by great artists.

I, too, was an artist, returning soon to my art. The productions I'd been in recently had fallen short of the mark, but that didn't mean great art wasn't worth trying for, again and again. Though the voice I'd heard in the theatre at Delos also stayed with me: maybe a life not on the stage but somewhere else. Seat E9.

When at last I stood in Alain's office with the others and was asked to speak, I was afraid of sounding phony and self-important, but I did have a lot to say. I told them the experience of living here with them, brief as it was, would shape the rest of my life. That it had shed light on my strengths as well as weaknesses and made me think for the first time, hard, about my ideals and code of ethics. I'd learned that my powerful need to share, to love, and to hold was not an impediment or a distraction in my life. It was, in fact, my life.

That living by loving is not a feel-good adjunct to more important things — ambition, getting on, moving up. It is the most important thing. Figuring out how to be a patient, compassionate person is a life's work. At least, my life's work.

"It's a skill I had to learn — to make sure everyone was included and heard. To pay attention like that, and to truly care, as much as is humanly possible. And just to be cheerful. Cheer is needed here. It helps keep everyone afloat. For me, being with handicapped people was like being with children — I had to learn how to do it, how to be myself, not a performance, not an effort, just me.

"Something so different is required. Not brilliance or clever conversation or creative feats, but being fully there with an open heart, dealing with medical issues, psychological issues, paying attention. Getting through another day with as much grace as possible."

I turned to my boss, with, of course, a tear or two in my eyes. "A lot has happened in such a short time. I'm beyond grateful, Alain, that you offered me this opportunity to slow down and unearth what's inside."

Alain liked that. He said when interviewing possible assistants for the Moulin, he looked not necessarily for people of great faith but for those who were flexible, thoughtful, honest. He'd asked me to come to L'Arche knowing I'd be strong and competent, able to do the work. He didn't know if I'd be able to grasp the joys and move through the tough daily problems of communal life, or to take on the struggle of living in close quarters with disability.

"Not everyone gets it," he said. "Some can't cope, and I was concerned at first. But you learned fast. L'Arche called something from you that you didn't know was there. You didn't have to entertain, just to be."

High praise from a man not given to compliments. He opened a bottle of St. Émilion '65 someone had brought to the community as a gift, and we all drank a toast to my future.

The handicapped men and my fellow assistants had seen my soul at its best and at its worst. They didn't care about my career, my reviews, failures, and successes, my missing cheekbones and squishy belly; they knew only the look in my eyes, the expression on my face, the tone of my voice, the work of my hands. And that was enough.

I simply accepted the fact that I was accepted.

The following night, the Moulin's Canadian assistant, who happened to be me, cooked a meal for eighteen people: a big pork roast in the pressure cooker with thyme and rosemary from our garden and cloves from the braid of garlic hanging in the kitchen, with gravy and freshly-made applesauce, accompanied by pasta in a gruyère sauce and steamed green beans with parsley, followed by salad, cheese, and a dessert of apricots in *crème fraîche*. The beans were overcooked and the gravy a bit lumpy, but still — "*Pas mal du tout*," I thought, as I sliced another bit of Camembert and watched my family eat.

On my last day, misty-eyed, I went around writing everyone's birthdate in my notebook — Antoine, February 23; Maxime, May 4 — determined to send cards from wherever I was. The community gave me a poster of the Abbaye de Sénanque, on the back a few lines or at least a scrawled signature from each of them. Vincent had written, when translated, "*The league of alcoholics is happy to count you from now on as one of its active members and wishes you a good trip prospecting in Canada.*

"*May the sun shine always in your eyes and in your heart,*" wrote Jean-Joseph the charmer. "*I will always keep your face in my thoughts.*"

Emile gave me the French fisherman's sweater I'd once admired, the real thing, white with dark blue stripes in heavy wool, much too big but just right. "Every time I wear it," I told them all, wiping away tears, "I'll be back here with you." I gave Emile a hug, and his impassive face beamed.

I made special time for a goodbye with Tom. His eyes, as they often were, were squeezed nearly shut by the size of the smile on his face, his mouth stretched as wide as it would go. His little body hurled itself at me, as he threw his arms around my waist in a strangling hug. "*Ma copine!*" he said, his face buried in my chest. For a moment I had to struggle for breath, not because of the tightness of his grip, but because I was overcome with love.

I didn't have any illusions about my place in his life; I was another of the many assistants he'd met and would meet, who'd grow to cherish him and do their best to keep him safe and make him happy. I was pretty sure, though, that none would spend a night clasping him in an embrace. I still blushed to remember how thoughtless my impulse had been.

My small friend didn't know, as the rest of us did, that smiles don't have to take over your whole face. He didn't know how to do anything in a careful or socially acceptable way. There he was, intellectually and physically deficient and as full of *joie de vivre* — as well as anger — as anyone I'd met. *If Jean Vanier had not created L'Arche*, I thought, *the great fire that is Jean-Claude would almost certainly have been extinguished.*

How blessed I was to know this man, to have been taught by him. How to tell him what he meant to me? There was no way, only to hug him hard and pledge to write. Promise never to forget him, a promise it would be easy to keep.

Finally, I took down the Che Guevara quote and put it in my diary along with the Cavafy poem. *One has to struggle every day in order for that living love for humanity to be transformed into concrete deeds.* To show love through action required daily effort. That bit of wisdom felt like a bright new room in my soul.

It was tough to take my leave not just of Alain and the community but of my dearest Gail — and her children too, whom I'd grown to like and look forward to seeing, feisty, entertaining small beings, all three, with the independence of kids twice their age. And the growing bump, the mystery of what kind of person the next member of the family would be. I still thought it was not just absurd but morally wrong for anyone to bring a fourth child into an overcrowded world. But if someone had to do it, it should be this family.

In June, I'd arrived for a week's visit with Gail. Over four months later, she drove me to the station in Avignon and stood waving goodbye. "S-A-R-T," I turned and called out to her. "I know how to spell it now!"

And got on the train — not with a large disorderly group to care for, who'd care for me. Alone.

ACT THREE

The true pilgrimage consists in coming home.

—Ursula K. LeGuin

TWELVE

Rich with all you have gained

After landing in Toronto, I stayed a few days to get caught up with theatre colleagues and friends. During a visit with Hillary, my childhood schoolmate, she announced with a shining face that she'd just secretly married her long-time boyfriend; I was the first person she'd told. It was hard to reconcile the seething tomboy I'd known since Grade Four, then the ferocious feminist working at Radio Free Women who had no time for dating, with the demure thirty-one-year-old wife shyly, proudly, showing off her ring.

Moving right along.

I took the bus to Ottawa for yet another quick visit with my parents and, not coincidentally, to go to the family dentist who would send his bill to Dad. I'd paid my own dentist bill once in Vancouver but preferred my father to do so, and Dad did not complain. I knew I'd be truly grown up when I paid for my own dental work. Not anytime soon.

It was good to be back in Canada, and yet one foot remained planted in France. After living for months in another language, I had to adjust back to my own tongue, my own country. I loved this land, but Canada looked like a gangly adolescent, bland, and, except for the countryside, hideous; it hurt my eyes to look at ugly cityscapes, garbage, billboards, blaring shops, badly dressed people, absurdly big vehicles, buildings of every style mashed together with no aesthetic sense, no coherence or taste. France was a compact, cultured, shrewd old lady in comparison, with hundreds of years of knowing how to do things correctly. Not just the etiquette of passing a salad bowl, but more importantly, how to prepare and enjoy mouth-watering repasts to be eaten slowly, enriched by conversation. And, reflecting on my flight out of Paris, how to build a metropolis of pale, graceful, six-story buildings with almost nothing to offend the eye.

But after a few days, I relaxed into my homecoming, happy to acknowledge that my fellow Canadians were so much less uptight than the dignified, stuffy French who could not eat soup at lunchtime. Around me, I felt a gratifying sense of space and limitless possibility in this nation comparatively without history, at least for its settlers, and thus without strings. I appreciated Canada's informality, its casual open-faced people, soft toilet paper, glasses of fresh cold milk, endless helpings of peanut butter on brown toast. But no villages of ivory stone, no sheep or chateaux, no baguettes and endless varieties of pungent, room temperature, correctly sliced cheese. I was bereft. Yet overjoyed to be home.

As I spent time with friends and family who knew the old Beth, I struggled to hang onto the new one, the one I hoped was deeper, quieter, less dependent on attention and praise, more grounded in confidence and serenity. Surrounded by people who I felt expected something from me — anecdotes, snappy talk, wit — my blood rose and my heart beat so fast I'd hyperventilate and feel lightheaded and breathless. As I caroused and gossiped and told funny stories, I felt the new Beth already slipping away. Determined to get her back, to make sure she did not get buried or lost, I'd leave the social circle, step into the shadows, and close my eyes.

Notre Père, qui es aux cieux
Que ton nom soit sanctifié...

I was back at the Moulin in the early morning with Alain, my fellow assistants, and my teachers, the men. I saw Maxime lifting his thick pinky finger daintily, like the Queen, while drinking his *tisane*. I thought of furious Antoine's well-guarded cupboard with every single thing he owned locked inside; of how powerful the pull was once between us. I remembered Jean-Joseph's dreamy eyes; Tom's smile when I hugged him goodbye; Vincent my fellow assistant in his exercise shorts, running, running; the noisy lunches, the long quiet hours in the cold atelier. I tried to anchor myself there.

While I was in Ottawa, my dad had an important appointment. He'd been selected for a local half hour television series that interviewed Ottawa notables. His segment, because of limited studio space, was scheduled for eleven at night.

Mum was in bed so I was pleased to accompany my tired father, who'd already spent a long day teaching and working in his lab. Dad was shown into the studio and I to the control room. I watched behind soundproof glass as he joked with the makeup woman and the cameramen; the hostess was soon rolling about with laughter. *Dad*, I said, though he couldn't hear. *Stop! You're wearing yourself out.* It horrified me to watch him, because I saw myself too — the performing seal, the animator, the clown who had to make everyone in the room at ease. There was our role, Dad's and mine, being played out before my eyes.

Sure enough, by the time the cameras started to roll, after midnight, my father's voice was hoarse, and the fatigue was plain in the shadows under his eyes and the strain on his face. He did his best, but his sparkle and wit were exhausted. The interview was okay if you didn't know how much more he was capable of. But nothing like him at his best.

On the way home, though I'd clapped him on the back and said, "Great interview!" I decided to speak up.

"Dad, I hope you don't mind if I say this. You put so much energy into entertaining the people in the studio that when the cameras were turned on, you were spent."

It was the first time I'd dared to critique my father to his face. But this needed to be said.

On he drove. "So, *nu*?"

"I wondered if it occurred to you to hold back, even a little. To save yourself for the taping."

"Save myself?" His tone was incredulous. "No, Bethie. It did not occur to me." He chuckled. "What a wise old bird you are… Save myself." As if the thought had never dawned on him.

Perhaps it would now.

It felt good to make people laugh. But one day, I thought, Sarah Heartburn too might take off her red clown nose and save herself.

***

Vancouver. At last, home to Cosyland with the million-dollar view — though in fact the mountains, beaches, forests, and ocean were impossible to see through the grey haze because it was mid-November and raining non-stop. My poor cat had obviously been traumatized by the man who'd sublet and was skittish and trembling. Lani had recently returned from working at a carnival in Santo Domingo and knew how to say, "Buy my volleyballs! Hit the back of the barrel!" in Spanish. She told me raunchy stories about her work as a pair of dancing lips, until the ad was declared obscene and taken off the air. Other friends heard I was back and called, but no one was much interested in my journey, in my time at L'Arche. Which was just as well, because I found it hard to discuss, the experience too profound to be glib about.

I went to the theatre, a brand new space on Granville Island, to sign my contract — I was indeed playing Natasha, the lower-class outsider — and ran into Matthew, a tall, friendly young man who managed both the theatre building and one of the companies that performed there. I'd met him a few times before going away, had found him agreeable, attractive, and attentive to me, but a discreet enquiry let me know he was married, and that was that. Now there was, as before, a nice buzz between us. And then someone told me that over the summer, Matthew had separated from his wife who was living with someone else. His marriage was over.

That was interesting but meaningless. I was no longer interested in relationships with men. *Point final*, as the French said. Period.

Rehearsals began, not just for any play, but for Chekhov, like the Himalayas for an actor, a daunting uphill challenge. There was a huge cast, but Natasha's scenes were mostly with Andrey, the three sisters' weak-willed brother who would become her husband. Andrey was played by George, who was considered by many, including me, to be the best actor in town, nearly a genius, extremely talented and conscientious. Almost too conscientious, I sometimes thought. A gay man with not much else in his life beside his profession and his long-term partner Bart, a nascent director, George felt that acting demanded and deserved everything, and if you didn't feel that way you were beneath contempt. I struggled to make sure he understood that I cared too. Not as much — no one could care as much — but a lot.

The maelstrom of rehearsals: trying to figure out what this great Russian playwright, dead for seventy-five years, was really saying, what the director wanted, how to cope with so many fellow actors and their peccadilloes. I tried to pretend this was another kind of L'Arche community, that I was another kind of assistant dealing with a group of damaged artists and their complicated handicaps. Instead, I felt myself falling back into the usual anxiety, the terror of failing, thrashing through a parade of theatre nightmares. We all had them, dreams of stepping onto the stage naked or not knowing what play you were in or forgetting your lines. If you did a bad job in another profession, well, it was a bad job. If a theatre actor did a bad job, it was in front of hundreds of people night after night, with the possibility of public humiliation in the newspapers. What a lunatic career.

Yet I was doing my best. George and I worked so hard on our scenes, I thought perhaps he was pleased with me. I was a little in love with him. More than a little. I'd once seen him in a zany play where he first appeared as a madman lying in a bathtub; only his feet, propped above the sides of the tub, were visible. He had stolen the show with his toes. That was talent.

Matthew was around a lot, dropping in after rehearsals. Most nights, he was working late at the theatre — he was always working — and he started to offer a few people, including me, a drive home in his little red truck. I noticed how considerate he was with Belle, the older actress who played Anfisa, the maid. In her heyday not that long ago, Belle kept reminding us, she'd starred as soulful sexy Masha. Now, demoted to the dumpy family retainer in headscarf and apron, she was sustained by the mickey of vodka in her purse. Matthew helped her out of the truck and up to her door.

He always drove me home last, and we'd sit in the truck for a bit and talk. He asked one night if I wanted to go have something to eat sometime. Sure, I said. So after one rehearsal, we went for Chinese food. Though he was serious at work, he had a playful sense of humour at dinner, and we laughed a lot. I told him about L'Arche and found, to my astonishment and delight, that he understood perfectly what L'Arche was about because he had a brother severely handicapped with cerebral palsy. Matthew talked about his brother Dan — how, growing up with a sibling one year older who couldn't move about or feed himself and talked only with great difficulty, he'd felt he never had the right to complain about anything because his brother had so little. I thought that was beautiful. It felt hugely important to meet someone who grasped what I'd just been through; to talk, not just about work and friends, but about a subject with deep meaning for us both.

Our fortune cookies came. Mine said, "*Change, travel and variety featured.*" I liked that message. Matthew cracked his open, unrolled the little rectangle of paper and grinned. His said, "*Change, travel and variety featured.*"

Maybe this restaurant only had one message in its cookies.

When we got outside, we saw it had snowed, and Vancouver was covered with an unaccustomed coating of soft, silent white. In the truck, in front of my place, we sat watching the snow and said good night. We did not kiss, and I did not invite him up. I would never do that again. I was going to be celibate forever, and anyway, he was too nice, too ordinary, for me.

Only much later did he tell me that on the way home, a few blocks from my apartment, his truck ran out of gas. He didn't dare come back and knock on my door, even to ask to use the phone. "It would have sounded like such a phony line — 'I ran out of gas!'" he told me. So he'd trudged through the snow in his shoes, trying to find a gas station that was open at midnight.

On my next day off, he took me skating. I hadn't skated in years, and he was smooth and fast, steering me skillfully around the ice and taking me afterwards for hot chocolate. Another time, after rehearsal, we went for pizza and started to talk about travelling together at some point, as friends. It felt like I had a guardian angel, though it was clear, I finally had to admit, that he was keen on me and open to more than friendship. He made his interest so obvious during our pizza date that as we drove home, I told him, as if casually mentioning a health issue, about my vow of celibacy. I didn't want to embarrass him by pushing him away, just to let him know romance for me was out of the question.

Too bad we didn't meet earlier, I thought, although he reminded me uncomfortably of a boyfriend I'd had for a brief time in Victoria. A student and bartender who rode a motorcycle, which was fun, gentle Brian lived in a funky little house on the edge of town, and he liked me a lot. One morning, while I slept, he went to the nearby woods to pick blackberries. When I awoke, he brought me a mug of strong coffee and a stack of hot buttermilk pancakes doused in fresh blackberry sauce. *Such a sweetheart!* I thought as I lay feasting in his sunny bedroom.

I dumped him.

The memory of how poorly I'd treated Brian reminded me of something Groucho once said: he didn't want to belong to any club that would accept him as a member. At twenty-four, I couldn't respect any man who cared for me; love had to mean struggle, denial, rejection. Pain. I wondered if that had changed.

"*A nice straightforward guy has sort of adopted me*," I wrote to my mother. What would my snobbish, cosmopolitan parents say if they met my small-town friend, who drove a truck and had hardly travelled?

The rehearsal wars continued. I mentally divided the many actors into two camps: the neurotics and the shallows. There was no question where I belonged, but surely, I reasoned, there was a happy medium between fretting constantly, complaining to the director, and worrying the thing to death, and on the other hand, simply doing your job, making easy choices, and going home to drink vodka and watch TV. There was certainly a middle ground, but I didn't know how to achieve it. Before the first preview I had an argument with the director, not about my work but about my friend Marlene's. Marlene was flailing about trying to find her way, without realizing she was making the experience more problematic not just for herself but for the rest of us too. I fought to defend her, and the director snarled, "Your playing nursemaid to needy people does not help anyone and gets in your own way!"

What's wrong with helping people? I thought. *That's what I do, what I did at L'Arche. It's not permissible here?*

Was kindness a liability in the theatre? How could I transfer what I'd learned, who I'd become in France, into this dramatic world?

But later I thought about her words. There was a big difference between watching out for Jean-Claude, who genuinely needed assistance to navigate, and Marlene, who didn't. I should figure out the difference between the two, I, who seemed to need to take care of everyone. Because God knows, there were a lot of people in the world who really needed care.

Who'll care for me? Don't I need to be looked after too, sometimes? The subversive thought stole in. I squashed it.

When we moved from the rehearsal hall into the theatre, a whole new set of problems arose: our enormous company had to cope with each other not just on stage but in the one dressing room that was far too small for such a huge cast. We were sharing the narrow area with a children's company production, which ran during the day, of *The*

Wizard of Oz and had a rack of infuriatingly bulky costumes that occupied much of our already limited space.

But battling for excellence and truth was worth the effort because *Three Sisters* was such a stunning piece of writing. I was reading the one-act play I'd do next, by a local playwright who had a hard time getting two characters through one meaningful hour. Chekhov took eighteen characters through four years of their tortured Russian lives, each line ringing with authenticity. And despite the difficulties, I was rediscovering a certain pleasure I'd known in my earliest acting experiences, when I'd played the wolf and the selfish princess for Mrs. Stanbury. Insensitive, vulgar Natasha was the villain of this piece. There was fun and freedom in that.

After the second preview, which had been frustratingly slow and awkward with problematic set changes and a hundred misplaced props — and me saying to myself, "George is so good, what am I even doing on this stage with him?" — we neurotics all headed out to the bar to fuss. Matthew stopped me and asked if instead I wanted to come with him; he had to deliver the costumes to the seamstress to be finished. I thanked him and said no, we had too much to work out. How not to trip on the goddamn Tin Man costume on the way to the stage. What to do about that appallingly complicated scene in Act Three, after the fire. And why don't they just pick up their bloody cues? George was getting lots of detailed direction from his partner Bart that was the opposite of what our director wanted, and once again, I was caught in the middle.

Halfway to the bar, as George the chief neurotic ranted on, I stopped. "It's just a play," I thought. If George had heard me say that, it would have meant the end of our friendship.

"I forgot something," I said to my friends. "See you later." They barely noticed. I turned around, breathing in the cold night air, the sea gleaming black a few yards away, and found Matthew locking up.

"Changed my mind," I said, and we climbed into the truck.

Listening to George seethe, I'd realized once more that I would never be like him and more importantly, did not want to be, did not want his killer instinct and burning intensity of focus. I could never lose myself to that degree. He'd told me once about working with a virtuoso British actress who, he said, was a deeply unhappy alcoholic, struggling for balance and even for sanity. From watching her with the greatest admiration for her craft, he'd resigned himself to the fact that there is no happiness in making great art.

But I wanted happiness.

I'd heard a similar story about a well-known Canadian actress who needed a bucket placed in the wings because before she went on, she always vomited with nerves. Janet had to conjure up the deaths of her children in order to cry on stage. I tried to imagine a lifetime of doing those excruciating things to my body and soul, but now knew I could not and would not. It was just a play.

I thanked dear Matthew for the drive, hugged my cat and collapsed into bed. One day, I'd confide in this good new friend my doubts about the theatre. But for now, I had a living to make.

The night of the *Three Sisters* opening, I was very nervous but this time in a different way: it was Chekhov's beautiful play at stake rather than my career, and that carried me through. The harsh critical voice was there, as always, in my head — *You weren't as on as you should have been at the end of Act One! You drove too hard through the top of Two instead of the subtle approach you and George worked out!* After that scene, I felt I'd blown it for Natasha; she'd started so high, she had nowhere to go, and I was angry at myself. But I did not sink to new depths of terror and self-blame as I usually did, as I had on the opening night of *Shadow Box*.

"I'll do the best I can for this play tonight," I said, and kept going. Though I felt my performance was workmanlike and uninspired, I did not take the curtain call bow with my usual sick feeling of failure. I'd done my best.

At the opening night party, friends told me how fabulous I'd been, which I did not for one second believe. Handing me a bouquet of tulips and orchids, Shayla said, "How could you even think of giving up acting?" Matthew told me he'd known all along it would be good. With his tall form hovering nearby, I felt safe.

What mattered most was that the stressful horror of opening night was over; now we could get on with the real work of going deeper. The reviews were positive, one with a big photo of me and George. Who can understand these things?

My old boyfriend Richard called to congratulate me and tell me he was depressed because it was his thirty-third birthday, his car had a flat tire, and his business was yet again going under. I reminded him that the Soviets had just provoked the anger of the U. S. by invading Afghanistan, a volatile situation that could well produce a third world war. So we might as well be happy.

Looking out at the mountains with the purring cat once more a warm weight on my lap, I thought about the nearly gone seventies, so full of bizarre events. The end, to my father's immense satisfaction, of the horrific Vietnam War and, after the shocking revelations of Watergate, of Richard Nixon, the worst, the absolutely worst American president imaginable. Heiress Patty Hearst turning into a gun-toting revolutionary. So many murderous cult-leading weirdoes like Charles Manson and, just this year, the demented-looking Ayatollah Khomeini who'd deposed the Shah, though of course what went on so far away in Iran would never affect us. Many horrors. Sometimes I regretted being a reader of newspapers, even if I didn't comprehend what I was reading. Wiser to focus on the antic brilliance of Monty Python. "This parrot is *dead*!"

***

New Year's Eve 1980, the start of a whole new decade. After the show, rather than rushing off to a party, some of us — the neurotics — sat around the dressing room. Matthew, who'd been in the audience yet again, came in to join us. Someone produced two bottles of harsh local Similkameen wine, someone else had bought a bottle of cheap bubbly. Belle had leftover tuna salad, George and Bart dug out cookies, Matt — now that I knew him better, I could call him Matt — brought some prop Melba toast; like the loaves and the fishes, a humble feast emerged. We moved to the stage, where we set up the big table used in the dinner scene and sat around it, drinking and telling stories. George came over to give me an urgent lecture about my career. "You have to sell yourself — sell out and make people want you and know your name!"

"Sure, I guess so," I said, though I had no idea how to do that.

Nick picked up a guitar used in the play and began to strum, and we sang along, lit only by prop candles until Matt turned on the stagelights, low. We talked about how we got into the theatre. Each of us, it turned out, was an imaginative, often lonely or unhappy kid who used fantasy and invention to build an alternate world.

This is the best of the theatre, I thought, *the camaraderie, courage, and imagination actors have and give to audiences and to each other.*

But even as I toasted my colleagues with Similkameen, I knew that if necessary, I could find such warmth and community elsewhere; that I had found it in an ancient building in the south of France. Though the work here meant a great deal, I'd discovered something that perhaps meant even more. While my castmates sang and played spoons in a stirring gospel chorus, making an unforgettable party out of nothing, I withdrew to the silence inside where what mattered was moral fibre and recited my French prayer. It felt as if the top of my head was lifting off as that space opened up, the sacred space made by contemplation and breath.

When I opened my eyes, Matt was watching me. We looked at each other across the table and smiled. What a very nice man. Handsome. Too bad.

At midnight we all shouted, "Happy eighties!" and sang *Auld Lang Syne* with our arms linked. We drank toasts to peace and brotherhood and kissed and hugged each other in that dramatic actory way. Last year's drunken New Year's Eve flashed through my mind, the TV party, the ridiculous cheese tray in my purse. I was more grounded now. Was that temporary? Or real?

Later, Matthew and I found ourselves sitting side by side, the others teasing us because they assumed, just by our body language, I guessed, and the rides home, that we were dating. I didn't bother to inform them we'd embarked on nothing more than talking, skating, and pizza. While our companions sang and traded bits of gossip, he and I reminisced about an event we'd both attended the winter before, a weird alternative theatre "happening" in a cavernous church hall like an echo chamber. While we were all sitting cross-legged in a circle watching solemn actors do incomprehensible things, Belle the chainsmoker had blown up the silence and destroyed the pretentious Zen mood by hacking her lungs out. Separately, it turned out, Matt and I had both been forced to stifle our own explosion of laughter.

As we sipped the dreadful wine and nibbled crackers, he told me a story about Jack, a sweet but flaky director whose next show he was producing. Jack, he said, had come to him with a pressing special request that a door be built in the set. "But," Matt had protested, "there's no door in the script. No one comes in or out. The budget is small and we can't afford to build a door that's never used."

"I must have a door!" Jack insisted. "To give the audience a powerful sense of …" — Matt imitated Jack waving his hands vaguely in the air — "… *lockedness*."

"Lockedness!" he repeated. It was Jack exactly, impractical, befuddled Jack. My friend and I laughed aloud at exactly the same time in exactly the same way — with insight and a touch of exasperation but mostly with affection. Lockedness.

At that moment, my heart split wide open. It hurt.

When the party wound down, once more Matthew offered to drive Belle and other inebriated cast members home in his red truck. At the end, as usual, it was just the two of us, pulling up to my place and sitting outside with the motor running, as New Year's Eve celebrants streamed out of the Hot Jazz Club. But this time, at last, I understood who was there beside me, even if I still wasn't sure who was there beside him. Everything had changed. He knew it too.

I turned to him and he to me. Without a word, he put his arms around me, and we kissed. It was a long kiss, a long, soft kiss. The world vanished, dissolved, except for the place where his mouth touched mine.

When we stopped, he did not take his arms away, his arms around me. And I fell, sensed myself falling, plunging into a silky warm cave underground, never to surface again.

"Matthew," I said, "would you like to come up to Cosyland and meet my cat?"

And although he was allergic to cats, he did.

In the morning, all that mattered was when we'd be together again.

THIRTEEN

Choisir, c'est renoncer

Love. Love love love. Everything I'd dreamed of was opening up in a cloud of rosy perfection. The man. The bliss of us. I turned instantly into one of the people I'd resented when I was single, who use the word "we" incessantly, like a weapon. "We are doing …" "We'll be going …" "We think …" Or two names spoken as one: "MatthewandI" or "meandMatt." The thought of doing something, anything, without him, after years of getting along perfectly well on my own — no. *Pas possible.*

I loved everything about my man — his long pale lanky body and open face with wide high cheekbones, blue eyes, and light brown hair. I loved his playful sense of humour and the red truck that mattered so much to him. He let me take the wheel once, and I drove for miles with the safety brake on. "You could have fried an egg on the hood!" he laughed when telling a friend about this misadventure. He understood engines; his father was a skilled auto mechanic. My father wouldn't have known what to do with a carburetor if it jumped into his arms.

"She did that to your truck and you didn't get pissed off? Wow, that's true love," said his friend.

Yes, it was.

We were as inseparable as two people with busy lives can be. I was now rehearsing and, after the Chekhov closed, performing in the festival of new plays Matt had produced. He was doing two or really three jobs simultaneously — running a theatre company as well as a theatre building in the midst of an expensive renovation and fundraising for both. If he wasn't travelling on business, we slept most nights at my place; only once in his stark, almost empty bachelor's bedroom. Just a few months before, he had moved out of the apartment he'd shared with his wife of seven years. I learned bits of their story: she was his high school sweetheart; they were young when they married, too young, she eighteen, he nineteen. All their friends had done the same. But he'd had to work long and hard to pay for university and student loans and to get ahead, and she complained bitterly that he was never around. In August, while I was communing with sheep in a French village, he'd grown suspicious and one day followed his wife's car. After waiting a bit, he walked into the flat she was visiting, to find her in bed with an actor.

Matt moved into a house with George and Bart. He assured me that though his wife said she still loved him, their divorce was underway.

Good news for me.

As I learned more about him, I grew more aware of the profound differences in our backgrounds. Despite my parents' socialist inclinations, I was firmly middle class. He'd grown up in a crowded bungalow in a small B.C. town. His stories told of a childhood skating on ponds and swimming in lakes — hockey, bicycles, and milkshakes, hot dogs on the barbecue, hot rods roaring up and down Main Street on Saturday night. *So Canadian!* I could hear my mother say approvingly, with her usual touch of condescension. There was brother Dan, the one with cerebral palsy, then Matt and three younger brothers, five boys in a family with limited financial resources, further impoverished by Dan's medical needs.

I felt spoiled and lucky to have enjoyed the comfortable homes and relative ease of my well-travelled family. Our frames of reference were poles apart. And yet there we were, together every possible moment, day after day going by in a fog, intense, spectacular.

Our friends said we were meant for each other. I wrote to my parents about the great love affair, he to his. This was official. We were permanent.

***

In late February, Matthew and I decided to get away on a trip together. He had always wanted to visit New Orleans, and when I saw an ad for a special deal — cheap flights to a number of southern states as long as you always went through Atlanta — we agreed to go; I was between shows, and with a lot of holiday time due to him, he could just manage ten days off. Since we'd be down south anyway, I proposed we also visit my eighty-eight-year-old grandfather Pop in Florida.

I spent many hours arranging all the flights and accommodation. Hard to believe that so soon after my long solo trip, I'd now be travelling with my lover. My life partner.

We drove to Seattle, parked the truck in one of the long-term parking lots, and flew through Atlanta to New Orleans, where for the first few days in our guest house on Bourbon Street, we made such vigorous love that we wore ourselves out and had to back off for a bit. I took a photo of Matt blowing up a condom and batting it around the room like a kid with a balloon. In a daze, a haze of lust and love, we wandered hand in hand among the lacy silver and black balconies of the French Quarter and took streetcars that were not named Desire but should have been.

Late one night, we had our first big fight. For more than an hour, stuck in a jazz dive in a remote and very poor part of the city, we could find no cab or bus to take us back downtown. Frantic with worry and impatience, I made snarky remarks about his inability to get us out of there, while he, resentment simmering, tried methodically, which to me meant far too slowly, to commandeer a ride. For the first time in our weeks together, we snapped and growled. But eventually we got a taxi back to the French Quarter, and the storm passed.

We were a unit, a twosome, an inseparable pair. I realized that, unlike my many chance meetings in Europe, I was encountering no locals or fellow travellers while on the road with Matt because the two of us were so absorbed in each other. Bliss.

Looking idly at a map of Louisiana, I was startled to see a town called Kaplan. Imagine, Kaplan, Louisiana! "Perhaps founded by a distant relative," I said, grinning, with a new plan — we had to visit. We rented a car, he drove, I navigated. Kaplan, it turned out, was not a casual jaunt but nearly 170 miles from New Orleans. We chatted and listened to music; he liked country and Western, which I emphatically did not, and when I told him about my immense passion for the Beatles and, less so, for other British groups of the sixties, he said, "I missed the sixties. I was working." I wondered if that was meant as a rebuke, but no, it was just a fact.

Finally, we sat in companionable silence for hours as endless flat miles of small-town America, Cajun country, flew by. It was a very long drive for a few visual jokes — photographs of me in front of the Kaplan police station, the Kaplan post office, Kaplan High.

I managed to buy a postcard and some Kaplan stationery but, though Matthew did not complain, I worried that this was too idiotic a stunt.

On the way back, we stopped in the small town of Henderson to eat at Dean and Dave's Diner, where I insisted we grab the opportunity to order the local specialty, crawfish pie. Where else would we get to eat crawfish pie? It was salty and pungent but delicious. As I dug into mine, Matt tested his gingerly. Then he put his fork down and took my hand.

"Beth," he said in an odd, strangled voice. I froze, hardly daring to breathe. Was he breaking up with me? Was I already too much, overwhelming him? Surely not, he'd given no indication ...

"This isn't very romantic," he said, "I'm not on one knee, I don't have a ring, but ... will you marry me?"

Not a moment's hesitation. Yes! Yes yes yes yes yes yes. Never, except in my most romantic teenaged dreams, had I imagined feeling so cared for and desired by such a good man. We kissed, and I joked, wiping away tears, that he'd popped the question today because here was a woman important enough to have a whole town named after her. We couldn't set a date yet; "I have to get divorced first," he said, grimacing. Though it pained me to do so, I felt compelled to ask if he was moving on too soon; after a decade with his girlfriend then wife, he'd been separated only a few months when we got together.

"What do you think?" he said, to my relief. I knew the answer.

Next day, on Rue Royale, we went into Rothchild's Antiques. The engagement-type rings were too expensive so we chose an antique bracelet for me, a plain gold bangle, as a token of our commitment. I would never take it off.

After our flight, via Atlanta, to Tampa, we rented a car and drove, not to Sarasota where Pop and my grandmother Nettie had lived for decades, but to his new home in Sun City Center, an artificial town exclusively for seniors. After Nettie succumbed to Alzhcimer's, Pop had moved to an apartment in Sun City, where Matt and I were going to stay for a few nights in a guest room. Dad had warned me on the phone when he found out about our visit. "It's like a giant geriatric playground," he said. "And there are almost no Jews." A huge change for my father's father, who'd spent his life in New York and then Sarasota surrounded almost exclusively by Jewish business associates and friends.

I told Matt about Mike Kaplan, second-oldest boy in a family of impoverished immigrant Jews from a *shtetl* near Minsk, who in America, through very hard work and clever business deals, had risen to become a successful dress manufacturer. My grandfather had put his two youngest brothers though law and medical school and had bought his two sisters a piano, since all well-raised girls needed to play. On one of my visits to him in my early twenties, after he'd extolled the virtues of the new miracle fabric, polyester — "No ironing!" — Pop was eager to buy me the modern woman's dream outfit, a pink polyester pantsuit. Instead, sticking to my bellbottoms and faded second-hand dresses, I'd asked for and received what I wanted most: a portable electric typewriter.

Snappy in his usual pastel polyester golfing garb, Pop met us at the door of the apartment complex; he was stooped, looking frail but still vigorous, and anxious. Even before greeting us, before introductions, he said urgently, "I'm going to introduce you to everyone as Mister and Missus."

"What for?" I said.

"You know these *goys* — they won't approve of you sleeping in the same room if you're not married. So I told them you got married."

"But Pop, no one cares these days, it's 1980! And anyway," I said, waving my bare fingers around, "I don't have a ring."

"That's not a problem — you're a modern couple, you don't believe in rings."

We kept running into grey-haired people to whom he introduced us as man and wife. They'd obviously heard all about me daily since Pop moved in; he kept all my good reviews carefully folded though falling apart in his wallet and whipped them out at any opportunity, as well as articles about Dad's scientific, academic, and activist achievements and the triumphs of his younger son Edgar, a world bridge champion. And now this young actress they'd heard so much about was suddenly married? The *goyish* eyebrows shot up.

We met Pop's girlfriend. The man once married to the daughter of the Jewish Shakespeare was now happily coupled with Marie Beauchamp from Trois-Rivières, Quebec, a diminutive French-Canadian who worshipped him and was very sweet, unlike my grandmother, who was not sweet at all.

After a day being shown the excitements of Sun City — handy golf course, stimulating arts and crafts, the challenging fun of shuffleboard — and dinner at 5.00 p.m. in a restaurant stuffed with more columns and statues than all of ancient Greece, Matt and I retreated to the room Pop had rented for us, with two single beds this newly married couple had to push together, and batted around some more balloons.

The best part of our Florida trip was watching my intended play chess with my dear ancestor and letting him win. The two became best friends. As we packed to go, the old man took me aside. "I always thought you'd fall for someone like your daddy," he said, "but instead you've fallen for someone just like me." I smiled to think there was any similarity between Pop, the hard-nosed, workaholic Jewish businessman in his pale yellow golf pants and pale pink golf shirt, and Matthew, from English and Scottish stock like my mother, hardworking producer of new plays, the *goy* from small town B. C. in his plaid shirt and jeans.

And then Pop turned to Matt. "You're getting a terrific wife. She's a jewel, she'll add sparkle to your life."

Pop had always been offended by my impractical lifestyle, my thrift store clothes and lack of financial acumen, my singleness. It gave me immense pleasure to note that finally I had made him proud not just as an actress, but as a woman.

On the way back home, Matt and I had to walk, one last time, through the warren of tunnels under the Atlanta airport. Each time we'd gone through, we had to pass a table selling right-wing bumper stickers and big buttons with messages like "*Conservative — because not everyone can be a freeloader,*" "*Guns don't kill people, abortions do,*" and "*Feed Jane Fonda to the whales.*" This time as we went by, my rage boiled over, and I stopped to face the two square-jawed young men with buzz cuts behind the table, wanting to make a rational point about their vile intolerance. Instead, what came out of my mouth was a strangled, "I hate you! I hate you!"

"Perhaps you could be a bit more articulate next time," Matt said dryly.

After floating in bliss for more than a week, my new fiancé and I faced a big problem as soon as we landed back in Seattle: neither of us could remember where we'd left the truck. We must have been given a parking tag of some kind, but we hadn't the slightest idea which of us had it or where it was. My body was rigid with tension and guilt; we were already tired with a long drive across the border ahead of us, Matt had to be at work early in the morning, and this glitch was surely my fault. Even though I had organized this entire trip from beginning to end, I had not organized this. Matt was white with fury. I'd let him down.

Standing in the airport, frantically going through our wallets and suitcases, we were both so overwrought, we might have split up right there. But I found the piece of paper at the bottom of my purse and apologized for not being better prepared. We drove home in weary silence, and he dropped me off and went to his place. I wondered briefly what it would be like when we had no other place to go; when it was just the two of us, in our own home, forever.

It would be heaven.

My mother was startled when I told her the great news. "Are you sure?" she said. "It's so sudden!" My parents hadn't even met this man yet, and we were engaged. So unlike me to be decisive and independent. I was growing up. No, I was grown up. I was going to be a wife — and a mother, maybe, one day. Matt, three years younger, only twenty-six, hadn't yet thought about having children. We'd discussed it, of course, concluding that neither of us was ready and, for the time being, that we'd be scrupulously careful, using both condoms and spermicidal foam. "A baby one day, of course," he said, "but not until we're settled and I've achieved what I want to achieve in my work."

Thinking about my parents' marriage and my own to come, I tallied up the contrasts with satisfaction: though we'd been a couple only a short time, Matt and I already enjoyed a rare kind of togetherness. We were dear friends who trusted each other completely, would always be honest, never sneak around having affairs. I would always make my own money, never be dependent like Mum. He would always consult kindly, not make snap decisions or be a tyrant as Dad sometimes was.

One day, I knew for sure, we'd have a daughter who'd grow up to be my best friend, just like I was to my mother. Only I would try not to need her too much or confide in her things she did not want to know. But when our baby girl arrived, my man would not be in a high-pressure, soul-destroying job, like Dustin Hoffman in *Kramer vs. Kramer*, a powerful movie we'd just seen about what happens when a woman frees herself from an oppressive marriage, leaving her workaholic husband to look after their child. Matthew and I would both work and raise our daughter, equal partners, side by side. We just would.

Perhaps my parents would even learn something healthy and new from us.

***

It was time to move in together. Another miracle: an apartment became available where Shayla lived in Vancouver's West End, a square old eight-storey building in which each one-bedroom flat had many windows and a dignified dining room paneled in oak. Though it was a bit too expensive for us, we took it. I had a drink with Shayla to celebrate.

"I hardly recognize you these days," she said. "Even your voice has changed, gone all soft and girly."

"Thanks," I said, glowing.

"No, I don't mean it's necessarily a good thing," she went on, "to turn into someone completely different when you fall in love."

What was she talking about? Of course I was different; I was now a woman with a life partner. *She must be jealous*, I thought.

I still could hardly believe that here was a man who liked me just as I was. He liked my body just as it was, too, with its curves and flatnesses where once I'd thought they shouldn't be; the days of obsessing about my weight were over. We felt the same way about many things, both of us left wing but not dogmatically so, atheists who honoured others' spiritual paths and were seeking our own. When we discussed the choices our friends were making, we came to the same conclusions, and we were amused by the same things. *Lockedness.*

The one area where we truly differed, besides our taste in music, was our finances. I realized that for Matt it would be impossible to work at a place like L'Arche, to give up paid employment for a job, however idealistic, with almost no financial return. He had slaved to go to university, the first and so far only member of his extended family to do so, and was careful and businesslike. I was careless — not extravagant, I didn't fling money about on fripperies or buy expensive things, but I had never kept vigilant track of my money or made a budget. I was either making enough to keep myself afloat, or I wasn't. In an emergency, as there'd been in France, I could always "borrow" from my parents.

Matt had no such cushion. He joked that I was a Volvo and he was a Chevrolet. I wondered, once or twice, if it was in fact a joke.

On our first night in our new home, I couldn't sleep, was wide awake at dawn and so was he, maybe because my restlessness woke him up. He proposed a walk by the water, now only a few blocks away. At 6 a.m. the tide was going out and flocks of sea birds skimmed the water; little fires had been lit along the beach to get rid of driftwood, and sculptural logs gleamed in the early light. We walked, silent. I thought, *It won't be easy, this adjustment to being a permanent couple, living together. Under my happy front, I'm just as insecure as ever. Yet this kind, capable man loves me.*

I stopped to give him a hug. We stood motionless on the beach, our arms around each other, as the sun inched up the sky and turned the water gold.

Back in the apartment, we faced the thrilling task of combining our worldly goods and creating a home. I quickly found out he was an obsessive neat freak, and he found out I was not. After the pandemonium at Gail's, I was living with the opposite extreme; Matt's pants, shirts, and shoes were so precisely lined up, it looked like there'd been an army inspection in our closet. He told me he'd done much of the housework after the birth of his youngest brother, when his mother went back to work. "If I'd vacuumed, she'd lift up each chair," he said, "and run her finger around the bottom to make sure I'd done it properly and moved the furniture."

That explained his compulsive neatness. My family always had a cleaning lady, whom my mother treated like a dear friend and sat drinking tea and sharing secrets with. I hadn't touched a vacuum till moving to my first apartment. Volvo. Chevrolet.

"I didn't have a childhood," Matt explained. His brother Dan, exactly a year older, needed a huge amount of time and attention. All his nightmares were about Dan. "I got out of bed one night to go to the bathroom," he told me, "and found him, freezing cold, in a heap on the floor. He'd fallen out of bed, and no one heard his cries. We lived with constant concern and guilt."

He knows how to look after a helpless being, I thought. So stable, an authentic Canadian whose great-grandparents on both sides were Canadian and who had spent all his growing-up years in the same small town, with aunts, uncles, and cousins from both sides. So unlike my family, my American father and British mother moving us from

Halifax to London to Paris to Ottawa, with no extended family in Canada at all. He would make a wonderful, solid dad. Though that was years away.

I was playing house and loving it — washing a man's underpants and socks, planning and cooking meals, entranced by the wonders of domesticity, thankful I'd taken a crash course in these tasks at the Moulin.

"*My heart leaps when I'm cleaning and pick up his moss green turtleneck sweater,*" I wrote, with typical cool restraint. "*We still spend as long as possible each day entwined around each other. My Matt is the dearest, softest, sweetest, wisest, most adorable of men.*"

Our move had shown me — and my extremely neat housemate — just how much paper I was hauling around, box after heavy box of chronicles, diaries, stories. Opening a few file folders, I was surprised at how seriously through the past decade I'd taken my development as a writer, scribbling extensive notes about interesting people or situations, commanding myself to notice more detail for potential essays or articles, many of which, like the diaries story in France, I'd begun but never finished.

When he saw me lost in stacks of old prose, Matt pointed out that his alma mater, the University of British Columbia, had the only Creative Writing Master's degree in Canada. "Why don't you look into it?" he said. "You say you want to do more writing."

Taking a writing course had never occurred to me, but he was right; feedback and the companionship of peers would be invaluable. Though I wasn't sure how I'd fit something else into my life, I decided to at least give it a whirl, and after making enquiries with the department, I compiled a dossier of more than thirty pages to send as an application. Into the manila envelope went published articles and theatre reviews, scenes I'd written for a collective creation, three monologues created and performed for Dad's good friend David Suzuki's CBC radio show, even a funny poem I'd just written about my partner's carpentry expertise, that began:

You'd think that they'd been fashioned by elves,
But no, it was Matthew constructed those shelves.

Selecting material from the overflowing boxes and file folders, I saw that almost everything I'd written, except the drama stuff, was autobiographical non-fiction. Though occasionally I'd tried writing fiction, nothing had come of it; all that issued from my pen were true stories. This wasn't a surprise; I'd spent countless hours since childhood chronicling my days, so the fact that other writing flowed from my life and not my imagination made sense.

But given the personal, idiosyncratic nature of the material sent to UBC, I had no confidence that it was good or even acceptable as creative writing. They'll think it's trivial and banal, a sloppy mess, I thought, and it will hurt a lot when they say no. But I sent it anyway.

***

I was considering two offers for my next job, revelling in the choice, when Matt told me he had a business proposal.

"Actually, it was George and Bart's idea," he said, as we sat at our small wicker dining table, my fiancé ploughing through a large second helping of my approximation of Gail's *coq au vin*. "They've always wanted to do a production of the British comedy *Love on the Wing*, directed by Bart with George as the guy, but they've never found the right actress for the female role. They think you'd be perfect for it, and they've asked me to produce it."

How flattering, and what an opportunity — Matthew's own production starring me and George, directed by Bart, who didn't have much experience as a director but had a lot of opinions and ideas. I skimmed through the "two-hander" — a play for only two actors — about the reluctant love affair between a crabby birdwatcher and a needy stewardess, a hit in the West End and then on Broadway, and was satisfied it was funny enough with a great part for me. Matt went to negotiate with the Arts Club artistic director Bill, who said he'd be happy to have us in his theatre through the summer and, we all hoped, on into the fall. Matt got the rights for the play, and we were on. Our dream was that we'd actually make a lot of money, and Matthew could start his own production company.

Once more it was hard to believe this was I, soon to start rehearsing a hit show produced by my future husband, living with him in a sunny apartment, lying in the same bed every night except when he was away for work. I'd never had anyone beside me for more than a few nights. But Matt didn't thrash about or snore. Nothing felt better than being spooned, his front warming my back, his arms around me until I pulled away to sleep, curled up on my own side. Though we were both too shy to talk about what we did or did not want to do in that bed, what we each gave and received was tender and solicitous. It didn't matter that I was far more sexually experienced, because with him, I was starting afresh. He was my first real lover, my first man, and our lovemaking was beyond anything I'd ever imagined.

"*I used to be afraid of cold, of hunger, spiders, my parents — both of them —* " I wrote jubilantly, as I waited once more for Matt to come home from work, "*of being unlovable, too smart, too ugly, too crazy, too silly, too fat, too emotional, too vulnerable. TOO MUCH.*

But now I'm not."

While my inner world felt sublimely fortunate, now I had time to sit at the wicker table every morning to read the *Globe and Mail*: Iranians holding fifty Americans hostage; hideous horror stories emerging from Cambodia. But it was spring, and Vancouver was bursting with friendship and family and feeling. The swans on nearby Lost Lagoon were nesting; pink and white apple and cherry blossoms and magnolias were spilling onto streets and lawns. A few of my friends, suddenly, were pregnant, including my American cousin, one year older, about to give birth to her first child.

"So Matt and I," I wrote, "*will one day have babies and not talk about the third world war.*"

***

There was something new to worry about. My mother was scheduled for open heart surgery to replace the aortic valve damaged by a childhood bout of rheumatic fever. All of us in the family had lived through decades dreading the weakness of that valve, the inevitable failure of Mum's heart, its need for repair; and now the time had come. We delayed *Wing* rehearsals so Matt and I could go to Ottawa, he for a brief visit, and I to stay until she got out of hospital. My father and brother were both away, returning just before the operation. So this time, Matt would meet only Mum, which was good. I was still worried about this first encounter, because my parents were overpowering, and Matt, though the accomplished holder of a Master's degree, was in comparison an innocent.

But mostly, I was anxious for the two people I loved most to get to know each other, wanting Mum to adore him as much as I did. I joked in my diary that Matt was so like Mum that when he and Dad eventually met, I hoped my father wouldn't fall in love with him. For that matter, I hoped my mother wouldn't either.

Of course, she was crazy about him, a good listener four inches taller than she. She twittered and fussed, stuffing him with huge plates of her beef stew and homemade bread and pinning him with her riveting blue eyes.

The second afternoon, after a morning tour of Canada's capital in my parents' Volvo — a detail that made Matt grin — the three of us had just ordered lunch at a restaurant downtown when I noticed a couple who'd been my friends at university and excused myself to move to their table and get caught up. We chuckled as we remembered a decade before, sitting on their battered Crippled Civilians sofa in front of a little black and white TV to watch the Americans land on the moon, after which we'd smoked a joint and raided their fridge with the munchies. Now they had two children and government jobs and hardly even drank.

When our food arrived, I moved back to our table, noticing Matt's tense face and wondering if Mum had said something negative about me, or him, or us. When she rose to pay the bill, he blew up. "How could you just walk away and abandon your mother who's going in soon for major surgery?" he said, his jaw taut, eyes cold. "She might die, and you're over there carrying on at the top of your lungs, as usual."

I froze, breathless, as he berated me. How could the man I loved express such scorn? But my mother overheard. "Don't be silly, Matthew," she said briskly, taking us both by the arm. "I don't expect Beth to dance attendance on me every minute. Her life has to go on."

She didn't mean it. She did want my life to stop while hers was threatened. It was my pleasure to be her handmaiden, as I'd always been. But though Matthew had said nothing I hadn't, at bad moments, thought about myself, his outburst bruised me deeply. *This is who I am*, I wanted to say. *If you don't like this friendly, noisy, show-offy person, we're in trouble.*

I put the thought far, far away and did not bring it out again.

He flew home, Dad and Mike returned, and Mum went into hospital for prepping. Though the surgery was not uncommon, there were still considerable risks, and I marvelled at her spunk. At home, she was always complaining about some malady or other, but in hospital, with nurses and us at her beck and call, she was radiant. Her room was full of flowers, including a dozen red roses sent by my fiancé, which pleased her a great deal and me even more, though on our tight budget, we certainly couldn't afford such extravagance.

The night before the surgery, Dad and I finally had to leave her, arranging to telephone early next morning, just before she went under. At 7 a.m., I pulled on my dressing gown and went into their bedroom where Dad was just waking up. We talked to her briefly from the bedside phone; she was dopey from the sedative but resolute. After we hung up, I pulled back the blankets on Mum's side of the bed and climbed under the covers beside my father. We lay side by side. "If something happens, Dad," I said, tears trickling, "I'll be there for you."

"That's very sweet, thanks, bella Pupikina," he said, patting my arm. He did not look comfortable. "But all will be well. She's in the best possible hands." I knew this was an odd situation, that probably I should not be in bed next to my father, and yet it felt right. We were going through this nightmare together, and he should not be alone. My close presence should be a comfort to him.

He got up to get ready for work, and I went back to my room to pray.

Notre Père, qui es aux cieux …
Please God, let her live.

Later that morning, Dad, Mike, and I drove to the hospital. I imagined the surgeon's hands inside my mother's ribcage, wrapped around her heart. And then there he was in his long white gown, at the door of the waiting room. He stood looking at us and time froze, the three of us staring at him, his face grave. A few hideous seconds. "Sylvia has pulled through just fine," he said.

Of course she had.

I stayed, playing Florence Nightingale for a week, until my partners in Vancouver insisted I come back to work. Mum needed me, she owned me, but from now on, she'd have to find another devoted nurse. I was pretty sure she'd have no trouble doing so.

***

Rehearsals for *Love on the Wing* began in a flurry of goodwill, with an article in the newspaper, accompanied by a photo of the four of us. We were a funny-looking group — Matt very tall and fair, George like a mischievous toothy beaver, short with a prominent nose and a receding chin, Bart as suave as a matinee idol with his stiff white smile, and hating-the-camera *moi* in my green Fair Isle sweater. Besides being in awe of George's talent, I liked him a lot, and he'd always seemed to like me. Our offstage friendship helped a great deal as we began work on a two-hander where all that happened was the ping pong back and forth between two flawed characters. Our chemistry made it work.

It wasn't long, however, before cracks appeared. Though charming one-on-one, Bart and George as a working team turned out to be rigid and humourless — problematic traits when rehearsing a comedy, albeit a dark comedy about two losers who on the surface revile each other. My director and co-star had been a couple for many years and were tightly in synch about everything. Their chief focus now, it turned out, was my "acting problems." Bart let that bit of information slip the second day, as we blocked scenes in the rehearsal hall.

"One reason George and I were so eager to do this production," he said, grim, wooden, "is because it's an ideal vehicle for us to tackle your acting problems." This had largely to do, it seemed, with my approach to the job. To me, the play was a light-hearted comedy I'd do my best to perform with skill and pleasure, but which would not take over my life. I had a life, as I saw it, full of friendship and curiosity and love that fed my work as an actor, and they did not. During rehearsals, they wouldn't see friends or do a single thing they felt would interfere with their focus. Each moment of this flimsy play was to be explored as profoundly as Chekhov, and anything less was not just unprofessional, it was the sign of a despicable incompetent.

How dedicated, I thought at first. How over-the-top obsessive, I thought a week later. But as the criticism in rehearsals grew more intense, I felt myself slipping back into the old self-deprecating paranoia. It was easy to re-admit the dark voice insisting that the shallow person Bart targeted was the true me — *spoiledselfishlazy* — and that the confident, hardworking woman who'd bloomed at L'Arche was an aberration.

I tried anew to immerse myself as profoundly as my co-workers, but the poisonous atmosphere did not improve. One night as I sat alone at home — Matt was as usual working late — I willed, I forced myself to pull out of the downward slide. *It will damage both the production and me*, I thought, gazing out at the lights of the West End high-rises, *if I don't believe anything good about myself. For my own survival, I should start now. Because I'm not going to get any help from these guys.*

We had to make this work; Matt's future as a producer was riding on it, and maybe even our future as a couple — could we actually break apart over this?

One afternoon, after we'd moved rehearsals to the comfortably familiar Arts Club, I took Bart aside to try to clear the air. I told him his tone was patronizing and insulting, and his blatant disrespect for me was damaging the show. That as he proceeded in his fledgling career as a director, he'd find that actors work in many different ways, almost all of them different than his.

"I have to find my own way to playing her," I said. "I'm not a puppet, not a machine you can turn on or off. I have ideas too."

"I'm responsible for how this show looks and runs," he said sharply. "The major decisions are mine and you have to trust me."

"I can't trust you if you show no respect for me. We all have insights to bring," I said, wishing that George, skulking nearby, would jump in on my side, sure that he would not. "You discover stuff and so do I and together we make the show. Can you not respect my process?"

"Oh yeah right, your *process*," he said with a smirk and walked out of the room.

Preview night was agony, the worst night of my life. This was my biggest role so far, so much riding on it, all eyes on me and George for nearly three hours, both my personal and professional future decided in three long acts without a net. Lying on the floor of the dressing room trying to breathe, I felt hot, cold, delirious. The tension electrifying my body was so great, I wanted to die.

The stage manager's calls came: "This is your half hour." "Five minutes." "Places please." Though my head was whirling, I managed not to throw up. George and I hugged and went to our respective spots, the lights came up, he was on stage doing his thing, the laughs began, that welcome warm rush of sound, I walked out into the hot glare and — it was like swimming, I knew the strokes and just powered myself along. My colleague and I worked hard side by side, more laughs rolled in, the right kind of silence during the serious bits. It was fine. My relief was incalculable, except that the next huge challenge, the following night's opening, was just ahead.

But the opening show was even better. Afterward, as I took off my makeup and wig, my body ached all over, as if I'd just climbed a mountain and was standing on top with a flag, my very own flag.

The reviews could not have been better, for the production and the performances. One critic said that George and I worked "*splendidly together, both offering well judged, highly appealing performances that make the script look a great deal more significant than it actually is.*"

No kidding, I thought.

Another wrote that our characterizations were "*about as fulfilling and well-rounded as you can reasonably expect from either role,*" that the teamwork was "*beautiful to behold.*" And the third, that the actors provided "*just the right amount of buffoonery balanced by the more serious underlying message that two lonely people can indeed find true love …*"

Bill was excited about the possibility of a long run. Our first production was launched. We'd pulled it off.

Matt's parents drove in from the Okanagan to see their son's first effort as a producer and to meet his new roommate. After having supper with Matt and then seeing the play, they came back with us to the apartment to have dessert and spend the night. What pressure, to impress my future in-laws as an actress and, more importantly, as a homemaker. We'd both scrubbed, dusted, and polished, and I'd written to ask Mum for her famous cheesecake recipe, which I'd made that morning, following her instructions to the letter. Encased in its round metal pan with a thick topping of blueberries, it looked beautiful. After half an hour of panicked conversation, at least from me, the time came to slice my *pièce de resistance*. But instead of slipping out in a firm wedge, the pieces ran liquid like soup, and I, already nervous, had to serve dessert in cereal bowls with spoons. It tasted good, but what had gone wrong?

Luckily, my low-key future in-laws did not seem to mind. They were genial and friendly but not effusive. "Very nice, dear," was all Matt's mother said about the show. She was tall, big-boned with a strong body and face. The boss, it seemed; her gentle, humorous husband deferred to her. He told a funny story, that once he was watching TV when his wife came in and threw a sweater into his lap.

"Connie," he'd said, "am I cold, or are we going somewhere?"

I'd never met anyone like them. *Please find me acceptable*, I prayed.

When I called Mum the next day to find out about the cheesecake — "I've no idea what went wrong," she exclaimed. "What temperature did you use to cook it?"

"Cook it?"

In her instructions, she'd neglected to add that the cheesecake, with its four eggs, needed an hour in the oven at 325.

Though the show was off and running — for a long time, we hoped — Bart continued to attend every night and come backstage with extensive notes. A director's job ends on opening night; if he returns and has a critique, he speaks to the stage manager, who relays his messages to the actors. But Bart, it was now evident, felt his job had just begun. His notes after the show, delivered directly to me in the dressing room I shared with George, grew openly hostile.

"You're cheapening everything, pushing too hard for laughs," he said, his pretty face twisted into a sneer.

"Maybe you haven't noticed, Bart," I said, trying to keep my tone light, "but this is in fact a comedy."

"Imagine what kind of grotesque farce it would be if I'd let you do it the way you wanted," he said.

Matt was caught in the middle, trying diplomatically to calm down whoever was most upset. He certainly did not blindly take my side, and I understood why; I had a lot to learn as an actress and did sincerely want to improve. But at the same time, I wasn't sure what I was doing wrong; everything was going so well.

A few weeks into our run, Bart stormed into the dressing room after a show and told me my performance had been so over-the-top, it had made him physically ill. "You looked like a clown in a Shriner's circus!" he hissed.

Enough. I turned to our sweetly ineffectual stage manager. "Louise," I said, trying to still my shaking hands while continuing to wipe off my makeup, "please tell the director that from now on, he should give his notes to you, and you can give them to me."

George stood up, his face red, and threw his coffee mug — his special mug, given to him by the famous British actress — across the room, where it shattered against the wall.

"Louise," he shouted, "find me another space. I refuse to stay in this dressing room a minute longer."

Poor quivering Louise moved George's makeup and good luck trinkets to a corner of the business office and set up a makeshift dressing table for him there.

So began a surreal and horrible experience: performing seven shows a week in a light-weight comedy, two shows every punishing Saturday, with a fellow actor who refused offstage to speak to or even to look at me. Three acts, just me and my former good friend George, he playing a vicious prude — my character Deedee actually called him a "pansy jerk," a line I could really get my heart into now — and I a pathetically misguided yet affectionate flake who couldn't see the truth about the guy she loved, even when he was yelling at her. I had to pretend, seven shows a week, to fall in love with a man who despised me, whose eyes, even in what passed for our love scenes, were icy with scorn and whose mouth, when we had to kiss, was so hard, my lips felt bruised.

This was a travesty, the opposite of everything I'd ever wanted to do in the theatre. Matt couldn't help me, caught as he was between his girlfriend and his investment — not of money, but of time, effort, and hope. He begged me to find a way to make it work.

Repeating the "cruel and ugly child entrusted to my care" mantra was no longer enough. I found a *Life* magazine with an inspiring story about the recent Nobel Peace Prize winner Mother Teresa, in which she described the infinite compassion needed to live on this earth. A few years before, when she visited Vancouver during Habitat Forum, I'd gone to hear this minuscule nun speak and, though I was high on cocaine at the time, I'd never forgotten her message. "Gif more," she'd said in her Slavic accent. "Gif until it hurts, and zen gif more." Recalling her words took me back to L'Arche, where giving more was the main requirement. Each night before going on stage, I re-read the article about her, drew from the bottom of my soul, and struggled to give until it hurt, to keep it all alive.

George and I were professional enough that audiences seemed not to discern the cold war being played out in front of them. But despite their laughter, despite Mother Teresa and my own ambition and my great concern for Matt's, I reached the point when I could not do it anymore. The run had lasted eight weeks when I told my fiancé, weeping, that I couldn't bear the soul-destroying nightly sham. Though hugely disappointed, he understood.

The last seven performances with my furious, freezing co-star were the hardest test of stamina and fortitude I'd ever endured, trying to the last minute to create, at the least, a passably pleasurable experience for the audience, delivering three acts worth of lines I disliked to a man I had come to loathe. During the final curtain call, while the smiling audience clapped away, I had to fight not to sob with relief.

Packing up my stuff for the last time, I looked at the ludicrous, sweat-stained costumes hanging nearby, the messy fishing tackle box of makeup I'd brought through the years to every show, the sticks of greasepaint to smear on so I'd look natural under the lights. My job as an actor, since playing mouthy Jane dangling her doll twenty years ago, was to put on another face, wear someone else's clothes, speak someone else's words. To become the composite human creation visualized by the playwright and the director and animated by me.

But the person I wanted to become was myself. I wanted to figure out who I was and be her and live her life. The Montreal director had said I was too intelligent to be an actress, but he was wrong. *It's not that I'm too smart*, I thought, looking at my naked face, pale and greasy with cold cream under the harsh lights of the dressing room mirror. To stick with it and thrive, an actor must need the adrenaline and applause, the fraught intimacy with the audience, the many challenges of the profession itself the way living creatures need air and water. At L'Arche there'd been none of those things, and yet I'd been more fulfilled than ever before. I knew I was good at entertaining, timing, intuiting the mood of spectators and drawing them in — talents instilled in me at birth. But I no longer wanted to use those talents for the job of turning into other people.

I remembered what had shone for me in Vermeer's work, the depth of his compassion for his fellow man, his quiet curiosity and understanding. Would it be possible to create a feeling like that with a typewriter rather than a paintbrush? One day it'd be good to give that a try.

Matt picked up my makeup box, I the stack of good luck cards and dried flowers from opening night, and we headed down the dingy stairs, passing the deafening, smoky bar on the way out. I didn't even look in the door.

***

Several jobs had been offered for the fall, including the starring role in a giddy new comedy. But I couldn't bear the thought of plunging into another production, not yet, even as the star, or perhaps especially as the star, and though it scared me to do so, I turned them down. A few days after *Wing* closed, there was a letter in our mailbox from UBC. I stood trembling with the piece of paper in my hand, reading it over and over, before rushing to call Matt and tell him I'd been accepted into the Creative Writing MFA Program, to start in September.

Was it time to embark on a new career, as a writer? Just saying the word made me feel faint; I imagined scribbling it on an application form. *Occupation: writer.* No, way too pretentious. When were people who wrote allowed to call themselves writers?

As much as the invitation to start in a new direction, I was grateful for the opportunity, at last, at exactly the right time, to take a break from the stage. I knew it would be hard to make the transition from a noisy profession crowded with colleagues and applauding audiences to one that meant sitting alone in a silent room ripping thought and emotion from the core of my being, weaving sentences and then making them better, clearer, wiser. But I was eager to begin.

Though there was no guarantee of a single cent ever coming from this work, the impending lack of salary didn't concern me for now. My savings and a recent birthday gift from Pop would pay tuition and rent for a bit, and as for clothing and food ... well, I was still a fervent Goodwill shopper, and, as long as I was the one in the kitchen, my hardworking partner didn't mind feeding us both for a while.

This was my chance to sit in E9. Maybe just for a bit.

Maybe forever.

***

On August 1, 1980, my thirtieth birthday, Matthew took me to dinner at Umberto's, one of the best restaurants in Vancouver. I told him about the surprise chili at Gail's on my last birthday, how sure I was he'd soon meet her and Alain. I'd written months ago to my dear friend, of course, about my brand new life. "*You know how Alain is stubborn and bossy, like me?*" I wrote. "*Well, Matthew is giving and generous, like you. He is sweet and gentle and honest and very wise, and he loves me.*"

"*I'm so happy for you!*" she'd replied, adding that she and Alain had indeed made me the godmother of their new baby girl. I wrote back that though I knew nothing about God and even less about being a mother, I was honoured.

At the end of the meal, waiters rushed to our table with a cake, and Matthew presented me with a little box. Recently we'd poked about in a jewelry store, and I'd admired both an opal and a garnet ring, not expensive but delicately pretty. On my twenty-first birthday, I told him, my American grandmother had given me two of her own rings, an opal and a garnet. I'd made the mistake of wearing them to the theatre one special night during *The Club* and leaving them at my place in the dressing room. Because I wore them so rarely, the show had closed before I realized they'd been stolen.

I opened the box. Though we'd sworn ourselves to thrift, he'd bought both.

Eating the birthday cake, I marvelled at my shining hands, the newly sparkling fingers, the wrist with its slim, gold bracelet. *While I was busy saying no,* I thought, *this greatest of blessings might so easily have passed me by.*

After dinner, we climbed into the red truck and drove not to our apartment but over the bridge to West Vancouver. A friend who lived in a rustic gatekeeper's cottage right on the sea had asked if we wanted to housesit for a few days, and I'd managed to persuade Matt — as always, committed to his work to the point of burned-out exhaustion — to spring himself for the weekend so we could take advantage of this isolated, scenic spot. We sat on the rocks in the darkness, skipping stones into the ocean and talking about the future, about his intention to go on producing new Canadian plays, a goal that had my wholehearted support, and my hope that studying writing would lead me down a fresh creative path. For my three majors, I'd chosen poetry, playwriting, and my favourite, non-fiction. "Why not fiction?" Matthew asked, sending a flat rock spinning across the turbulent surface. "Fiction sells."

"Why invent plots and characters," I replied with heat, inspecting small stones for my collection, "when real life is so bloody interesting?"

Another possibility had opened up: a group of activist friends and I had just met to discuss founding a theatre company that would produce plays on topical issues: Vancouver's housing crisis, sexism, racism, plays that mattered. When our Headlines Theatre got underway, I'd still be involved in the performing arts but as a producer, director, or playwright. I could use my mind, not my face and body, my voice on the page not my voice on the stage, to earn a living. That was ideal.

Perfect happiness. Perfect.

In our friend's big comfortable bed that night, the sea muttering against the rocks outside the window, Matthew and I made love without birth control. Yes, he and I had been a couple only half a year, but we were both so sure. Or at least, I was sure enough for us both.

In the saltwater darkness, his body was my body, his soul my soul. And I knew. The instant she happened, I knew.

I knew why I'd been put on this earth.

POSTSCRIPT

Since its founding in 1964, L'Arche has grown from one community in northern France to a hugely successful international organization comprising 147 communities in 35 countries on 5 continents. Its founder died in 2019, aged 90.

That year, L'Arche launched an independent investigation and in February of 2020 released a shocking revelation: during his decades at L'Arche, Jean Vanier had coerced at least six women into sexual activity in the guise of mystical communion. None of the women were handicapped, but all were vulnerable and trusting; one was a nun. The investigators also reported that he knew about the sexual abuse of many women by his mentor, the priest Père Thomas, and had lied repeatedly, saying he knew nothing.

During his lifetime, the good Vanier did was so admired and unquestioned, he was given many awards, including the two-million-dollar Templeton Award. Humble and soft-spoken, this son of a governor-general of Canada was considered a quasi-saint. There was talk he would be canonized.

And then the world learned of the hidden side of this man, and his legions of acolytes were shattered and angry. I too was appalled. And yet, for the immense gifts it gave me, I remain deeply grateful to L'Arche and thus to Vanier. The fact that the man had two faces, one of them deceitful, even borderline criminal, does not take away from the wondrous good his communities have done and will continue to do worldwide.

This book celebrates the spectacular humanitarian gift a complex, deeply flawed man gave to the world.

***

Headlines Theatre, started in 1980 by a group of Vancouver theatre professionals to create dramatic plays about topical issues, continued its work for almost forty years, until disbanding in 2018.

***

Bart and George went on to make successful careers in one Canadian theatre after another, with muttered complaints about abusive behavior ignored, decade after decade, by boards of directors. After the pair's retirement from a large regional playhouse, the new artistic director, on hearing reports of bullying and harassment, investigated and issued a public apology. Subsequently, Bart was one of very few people ever expelled from Canadian Actors' Equity. No specific public allegations were ever made.

***

Dr. J. Gordin Kaplan, from 1981 until his too-early death from cancer in 1988, served as Vice-President Research at the University of Alberta. He was most proud of founding the organization WISEST — Women in Scholarship, Engineering, Science, and Technology — to encourage girls to consider, and assist women to break into, these male-dominated fields. He was also proud of his subscription to *Ms.* magazine.

During her twenty-four years of widowhood, Sylvia Kaplan, beautiful until her last days, continued to send her siren song to men. After a lifetime of worrying about the fatal frailty of her heart, she died on Christmas Day 2012, aged 89.

They are much missed.

***

Gail is still my best friend, despite the fact that she went on to have not one but two more daughters. I go regularly to France to visit her and Alain, and as ever, we eat, talk, argue, shop, drink, talk. Eat. Their faith, though battered, is as strong as ever.

***

Matt and I had a daughter and got married. His ambition and supercharged work ethic led us to move across the country and then from city to city, from one big theatre job to another even bigger. For me, that meant leaving behind work contacts, friends, and school. I finished the MFA long distance, mailing my thesis, the biography of my great-grandfather the Jewish Shakespeare, the day before giving birth to our second child, a son.

On New Year's Day 1986, after six years together, I woke up with a shock to our reality: he was a workaholic, and I was once again lost, unable to communicate what I needed since I had no idea myself. Five years after that, we separated and divorced. I raised the children in an old house in downtown Toronto. He supported us financially and flew in from New York, as often as possible, on weekends.

I eventually became not just a writer but a teacher of creative writing — memoir, personal essay — in Continuing Studies at two Toronto universities. Teaching provides the welcome obligation to use my acting skills; a class is a show, and it's my job to keep the audience of students engaged, laughing, informed. For more than twenty-five years, I've done my best to help student writers unearth their most important stories and tell them well.

My daughter is a social justice warrior who has taken as her life's work to change the world for the better. From childhood, this sensible old soul made clear she didn't want to hear any of my secrets and would divulge none of her own. My very funny son has the showman gene, skillfully deployed in the restaurant business. For both my generous, open children, hospitality involving quantities of good food matters a great deal.

Matthew and I still hold each other dear. He made a hugely successful career in the States and remarried. I have remained happily single in the same cherished house; when Matt comes to visit us, he stays in the spare room. Our son and daughter live two blocks apart on the other side of town, she with her partner and their two boys. The joyful day I became a grandmother, at the age of sixty-two, I stopped dyeing my hair brown. My older grandson, who sometimes so resembles my father as a boy that he takes my breath away, says he likes my shiny silver hair. So do I.

Periodically, I think about that vital epiphany, when I stood leaning on the door in Gail's house and experienced the most important insight of my life. And I touch the delicate gold bracelet that is always on my wrist.

As a friend of mine once said, sometimes life encourages us to be smarter than we know we are.

With Mireille and Jean-Claude on a visit to the Moulin in 2017.

ACKNOWLEDGEMENTS

During its six-year journey into the world, this book was blessed with four superb editors. My dear friend Rosemary Shipton, one of the best nonfiction editors in the country, read a clumsy, meandering first draft and, then and later, offered nothing but supportive, carefully worded suggestions. Colin Thomas shaped the manuscript with a fierce eye and a sharp sense of humour. Christopher Cameron, a fine writer and thoughtful editor, made everything richer and deeper, as did Laura Cameron, a meticulous reader who happens to be his daughter.

Thanks to those who read some or all of various drafts and let me know their honest thoughts, good and bad — mostly, I'm happy to say, pretty good: Lani Ashenhurst, Curtis Barlow, Kathy Belicki, Barbara Berson, Marilyn Biderman, Gretchen Bingham, Suzette Couture, Tara Cullis, Rita Davies, Peg Evans, Isabel Huggan, Valerie Hussey, Judy McFarlane, Carol McPhee, MJ McPhee, Nick Rice, Kathryn Shaw, Tracy Siklos, Sam Stanley-Paul, Allan Stratton, Elke Town, Jennifer Venner, Stella Walker, Dame Harriet Walter.

Cheers to Kate Henderson and the invaluable Sally Keefe-Cohen and the equally invaluable Jason Allen for expert advice on and help with legal, contractual, and technical issues.

A toast to the practical souls who make my impractical life possible, even liveable: John Greeniaus and John Sinclair.

I'm thankful for the friends whose loyal long-term support has meant a great deal: Edgar Dobie, Bruce Kellett, Chris Loranger, Ken Maclennan, and the inimitable Wayson Choy.

Merci to the publisher who said yes: Greg Ioannou of Iguana Books, and to his trusty sidekicks Heather Bury, Olivia Thompson-Powell, and especially Meghan Behse for her gorgeous design and efficiency.

Enormous gratitude to Lynn and Denis Blin and family, Michele Denis-Duphil and Daniel Denis, Magali de Terris, and the men of Le Moulin de L'Auro

And finally — to those I write for and live for:

Anna

Sam

Thomas

Eli

and Ben

my love.

www.ingramcontent.com/pod-product-compliance
Lightning Source LLC
Chambersburg PA
CBHW020328170426
43200CB00006B/310